MORE PRAISE FOR *SHO-TIME*

"OK, I'll admit it. I'm obsessed with Shohei Ohtani. I missed out on watching that Babe Ruth guy, but I feel lucky to have watched this guy. I even thought I knew a lot about him until I opened my copy of Jeff Fletcher's brilliant new book. *Sho-Time* taught me so much I didn't know about the most unique baseball player of our lifetimes. From the moment I read that phrase '10-tool player,' I was hooked!"

　　　　　　　　　　　　　　　　　—Jayson Stark, *The Athletic*

"This is one the best baseball books ever published relevant to Japan-US relations. Jeff Fletcher is the most experienced of the Angels beat writers and usually the first one to ask Shohei Ohtani questions after the game. I admire the way he has exchanged information with Japanese writers for four years. This book is the fruit of his efforts. I always follow Jeff's work in order to find new information relevant to Ohtani or Major League Baseball."

　　　　　　　　　　　　　　　　　—Hideki Okuda, *Sports Nippon*

"I thought I knew everything about Shohei Ohtani because I had seen all of his games and interviewed him for the first time in Tempe in 2018, but I didn't quite know the extent of everything he did to redesign himself on the physical and mental side until after I read *Sho-Time* by Jeff Fletcher. I really appreciated learning about Ohtani's dedication to be the best, starting from his days in Japan. I realized how much it took for him to get to this point, to have the best year in baseball history."

　　　　　　　　　　　　　　—Mark Gubicza, Angels television analyst

SHO-TIME

SHO-TIME

THE INSIDE STORY OF

SHOHEI OHTANI

AND THE GREATEST BASEBALL SEASON EVER PLAYED

JEFF FLETCHER

DIVERSION
BOOKS

Diversion Books
A division of Diversion Publishing Corp.
www.diversionbooks.com

First Diversion Books edition, July 2022
First Diversion Books Trade Paperback edition, August 2023
Hardcover ISBN: 9781635767971
Paperback ISBN: 9781635769234
eBook ISBN: 9781635767766

Printed in The United States of America
3 5 7 9 10 8 6 4 2

Library of Congress cataloging-in-publication data is available on file

Interior design by Neuwirth & Associates, Inc.
Cover Design by Michel Vrana
Front cover and interior photos: Associated Press

For Marvin Fletcher.
Thank you for being a great dad and introducing me to baseball.

CONTENTS

FOREWORD
by Joe Maddon

At the end of the 2021 season, we were playing Oakland. Shohei was pitching and it was a really hot afternoon. I signaled to our catcher to walk Matt Olson, the A's first baseman. When Shohei got the sign, he looked at me with a grin and started wagging his finger back and forth. He didn't want to do that. He didn't *need* to do that. I understood and smiled back. Later in the game Olson came up and the count went to 2-and-0. I did it again, and again he gave me the same treatment. He knew what he wanted to do with Olson. He felt very confident in getting him out. He didn't need any interference. Olson's numbers against him? They're horrible. He struggles against Shohei and Shohei knows that. I got finger-wagged, but with a smile. Although I overruled him and walked Olson both times, I appreciated Shohei's confidence.

Shohei is unique, obviously, someone we have never seen before. What he does and how he does it so easily is just different. But such a big part of who he is was evident that afternoon: the joy he derives from the game itself and the competition. He does not like to lose. At the same time, he is humble, polite, and kind. There is an old-school component to him. He may listen to a hitting coach talk about another pitcher. He may listen to a scouting report about how to pitch to hitters, but when it comes down to it, this guy is pretty much out there with a brush in his hand and he's painting all the way. He knows what he wants. He reacts to the situation. You don't have to tell him. He's just better than most everybody else. And he's able to adjust on the fly and react to what is working for him or what he sees is necessary to beat his opponent in that game.

My first year with the Angels was 2020, which was of course the pandemic year. I didn't know much about Shohei. I was really following everyone else's cues there. It was eyes and ears open, mouth shut. But going into 2021, I knew that I needed to talk to Perry Minasian, our new general manager, about what kind of leash we were going to put on him. We decided that there would be no leash. I give Perry a lot of credit for not trying to restrict him. Taking the shackles off of him was a big part of his success. Much of that success occurred because nobody got in the way of it.

What really surprised me was Shohei's durability as a pitcher. I thought he would answer the bell offensively, but I didn't know what it would look like if we pushed him to the number of innings we did. He handled it extremely well and could have pitched more. As we move forward, we have to be aware that this guy wants to be out there all the time, because when he's out there he believes he is going to impact the game in a way to help us win.

When he's pitching, he wants to be able to hit because he badly wants to contribute to the win. When he's hitting, he wants to steal bases and do other things to help us win games. When he hits a routine groundball to second base and knows he's got a shot at beating it out, he switches to another gear and here we go. It's pretty spectacular. He's like a big wide receiver. Big, lanky, strong, and fast. Really fast.

Again, his joy for the game cannot be overstated. With all of the success he's had, he still has that joy. That's where I draw the parallels with Cal Ripken Jr. It's not a physical comparison. It's what I perceive to be a pure joy for the game and the competition. From a distance, I always thought that was Cal's greatest asset. He loved to play and he loved to compete. I believe Shohei is the same way. Shohei also reminds me of Cal in his competitive nature. Shohei doesn't want to lose. He is always competing and I think that is what drove Cal. Shohei is the same. We have a little bumper pool table near his locker and sometimes when I'm leaving the ballpark an hour after the game, he's still there playing. That's Shohei: always competing and having fun doing it.

PREFACE

When we described Shohei Ohtani's 2021 performance as "the greatest baseball season ever played" in the subtitle of this book, we weren't counting on him doing it again the next year. In 2022, Ohtani was a better pitcher and almost as good a hitter. It took a historic season from New York Yankees slugger Aaron Judge to keep Ohtani from a second straight MVP award. Months later, Ohtani was the MVP of the 2023 World Baseball Classic, leading Team Japan to the title. His final pitch was a beautiful sweeper that struck out Mike Trout, his teammate on the Angels and the captain of Team USA. It delivered baseball fans on both sides of the globe the kind of spotlight moment they craved to see from Ohtani. His 2022 season and the WBC are chronicled in Chapter 16, which was added in this 2023 edition. The first 15 chapters, which were written between the 2021 and 2022 seasons, examine Ohtani's baseball journey, from his youth in Japan through the MVP season that made him forever a part of baseball history.

—JEFF FLETCHER

PROLOGUE

Three years after "The Babe Ruth of Japan" made his debut in the major leagues, the baseball world was focused on Angel Stadium on April 4, 2021, to see if he had finally returned. Shohei Ohtani had come from Japan to join the Los Angeles Angels for the 2018 season, and he amazed fans and fellow players with his ability to hit and pitch at a high level, something no major leaguer had done since Ruth a hundred years earlier. At that point Ohtani was just twenty-three years old and seemed to be destined for greatness. Unfortunately, a fantastic ten-week start to his career would be followed by two surgeries and a series of on-field disappointments, leaving serious doubts in the minds of even his most fervent supporters that he would ever meet that potential.

When the ESPN Sunday Night Baseball crew put the Angels and Chicago White Sox on the sport's ultimate regular season stage for its first broadcast of 2021, announcers Matt Vasgersian and Alex Rodriguez spent the segment leading into the first pitch talking about Ohtani. "We're in store for a good one," Vasgersian said. "It's The Shohei Show."

Ohtani, now twenty-six, was the Angels' starting pitcher and number two in their batting order.

Although the Angels would not manipulate their lineup to accommodate ESPN—at least, they wouldn't admit to it—the network's executives were no doubt thrilled that Manager Joe Maddon had scheduled Ohtani's first start of the season for their broadcast. That Ohtani was going to hit *and* pitch in the same game for the first time in his big league career made the game even more enticing to the network and its viewers. "Expectations are always sky high whenever Ohtani participates on one side of the scorecard, let alone on both in the same night," Vasgersian said.

This was the start of the forty-ninth season in which the American League used the designated hitter. A pitcher hitting in an AL game was rare. In fact, a starting pitcher had been in the lineup only six previous times in nearly a half-century of games with the DH. One of those was a mistake. In 2009, Maddon—then managing the Tampa Bay Rays—handed umpires an incorrect lineup card with two third basemen and no DH, so pitcher Andy Sonnanstine had to hit for himself. San Francisco Giants righthander Madison Bumgarner, widely considered the best-hitting pitcher of his generation, got to hit in a 2016 interleague game, as the Giants passed on using the DH at Oakland. Otherwise, you have to go back to 1976, when lefthander Ken Brett pitched and hit in two games for the Kansas City Royals. Texas Rangers righthander Ferguson Jenkins (in 1974) and Oakland A's lefthander Ken Holtzman (in 1975) also started one AL game apiece hitting for themselves.

Ohtani's presence in the Angels lineup was clearly not an accident or a one-off, though. Ohtani was batting right in front of superstar Mike Trout because Maddon believed that his starting pitcher was also one of his best hitters.

That, of course, was exactly how Shohei Ohtani had been billed when he came from Japan in December 2017. Stories of his exploits across the globe had reached mythic levels, with tales of 100-mph fastballs and home runs that soared into the farthest reaches of ballparks. By then everyone had seen that YouTube clip of him hitting a ball through the roof of the Tokyo Dome. And Ohtani actually lived up to the hype for a couple months with the Angels in 2018, but it disappeared just as quickly. Ohtani tore an elbow ligament and underwent Tommy John surgery, a reconstructive operation that typically costs pitchers twelve to eighteen months. When he finally completed his rehab and returned to the mound—delayed further by the global pandemic that pushed the start of the 2020 season from April to

July—he faced just sixteen batters in two outings that were, honestly, difficult to watch. He seemed lost on the mound, and it was easy to question whether his two-way career was over. Another injury kept him from taking the mound again that season.

Ohtani hadn't been the hitter he was supposed to be either. His numbers declined from 2018 to 2019 and they cratered in the pandemic-shortened 2020 season, to the point that he was benched. He had been bothered in 2019 by a congenital knee condition that would eventually require a second trip to the operating room in two years.

To put it bluntly, Ohtani had been a disappointment in the two years leading up to the 2021 season. Although Spring Training was sprinkled with reasons to be optimistic, the week prior to that start against the White Sox had provided more fuel for the skeptics. Six days earlier, Ohtani had taken the mound at Dodger Stadium for his final exhibition outing, and he gave up seven runs in 2⅓ innings, walking five Dodgers batters. He said afterward that he was bothered by a blister that affected his control. As the DH, Ohtani had 3 hits in 13 at-bats in his first three games of the regular season. He did have a homer, but he had also struck out six times, at times with the same flailing swing that had marked his embarrassing season at the plate in 2020.

It was against that backdrop that Ohtani jogged to the mound in front of a national TV audience and a coronavirus-limited crowd of 12,396 at Angel Stadium. Which Ohtani was going to show up? Would "The Babe Ruth of Japan" finally be back, or was this the start of another year of unmet expectations?

Ohtani's first pitch to White Sox leadoff hitter Tim Anderson, the 2019 batting champion, was a 98.2-mph fastball, barely missing the bottom of the strike zone. Ohtani would pump four straight fastballs, each at least 96 mph, and then get Anderson to ground out on a slider. Against No. 2 hitter Adam Eaton, Ohtani started with a curve but then went to his fastball. When he got two strikes on Eaton, Ohtani fired a pitch at 100.6 mph over the inner half and Eaton fouled it off.

Ohtani then threw his signature splitter and Eaton struck out, his bat missing the pitch by a couple feet. Ohtani threw two more pitches at 100 mph or harder to reigning MVP Jose Abreu, eventually walking him, before he escaped the inning by getting Yoan Moncada on a groundout.

Ohtani strutted off the mound as observers nodded their heads in cautious optimism. His exceptional velocity, which was missing in his short-lived comeback in 2020, had returned. He'd thrown all four of his pitches for strikes. He had worked through the top of the order of one of the best teams in the American League, posting a scoreless inning. It was only one inning, but it was a good one.

A few minutes later in the bottom of the first, Ohtani was at the plate against Dylan Cease, a six-foot-two righthander who had emerged as a reliable member of the White Sox rotation in the previous year. Cease stood on the mound with a repertoire that included a fastball in the upper nineties, a slider, a curve, and a changeup. His first pitch to Ohtani was a 97 mph chest-high fastball, perhaps too high to even be called a strike. Ohtani lifted his right heel off the ground and then planted it in the dirt, a quick trigger mechanism to set in motion a swing that ripped the barrel of his bat squarely into the pitch. The ball rocketed off his bat at 115.2 mph and it sailed 450 feet, landing about ten rows into the seats beyond the fence in right-center field.

Within a span of a few minutes, Ohtani provided dramatic evidence, with high-tech detail on national television, that 2021 could be different.

Radar equipment tracks everything that happens on the field in Major League Baseball, which makes it easier to quantify accomplishments that a decade or two earlier would have been simply described with flowery language like "a booming home run," or "an electric fastball."

In that first inning, Ohtani had thrown three pitches at 100 mph or harder. Only 57 of the 909 pitchers (6.3 percent) who appeared in the majors in 2021 would throw even a single pitch at 100 mph. He also hit a ball 115 mph. Only 51 of the 1,049 hitters (4.9 percent) who came to the plate would hit a ball that hard in 2021. Needless to say, Shohei Ohtani was the only player whose name was on both lists, and he accomplished each feat within a span of a few minutes in the first inning of his first start of the season.

After the game was over—the Angels won on a walk-off homer by first baseman Jared Walsh, and Ohtani didn't get the victory—Ohtani said it was a satisfying beginning to his season, but he stopped well short of declaring that he'd accomplished anything.

"I'm glad I got this game under my belt," Ohtani said through his interpreter. "It will lead to more confidence. . . . It's just one game. I'm going to take it one game at a time. I'm not out to prove the doubters wrong or anything."

His manager was more bold.

"What he did tonight was pretty special and you're going to see a lot more of that," Joe Maddon said. "It was fun to watch. I think everybody was entertained. That's what he signed up to do and you're going to see more of it."

Ohtani proceeded to have a remarkable season, good enough to win the American League Most Valuable Player Award, along with the Commissioner's Historic Achievement Award and the MLB Players Association's Player of the Year Award.

On the mound, Ohtani finished with a 9–2 record and a 3.18 ERA in 23 starts, striking out 157 batters in 130⅓ innings. At the plate, Ohtani belted 46 homers, the third-highest total in the majors. He hit .257 (league average was .245) with a .372 on-base percentage and a .592 slugging percentage. His OPS (On Base Plus Slugging Percentage) of .965 ranked fifth in the majors and second in the American League.

Ohtani's combined excellence at the plate and on the mound made him the Major League leader in Wins Above Replacement (WAR), a statistic that quantifies a player's total value to his team including all facets of his production. FanGraphs and Baseball-Reference, the sport's two dominant statistical sites, have slightly different formulas for WAR, but Ohtani led in both. FanGraphs credited him with 8.1 WAR, beating out Milwaukee Brewers pitcher Corbin Burnes (7.6). According to Baseball-Reference, Ohtani accumulated 9.1 WAR, which was well ahead of Philadelphia Phillies pitcher Zack Wheeler (7.7). All of that is a statistical way of saying that Ohtani was the best player in the majors in 2021.

Along the way, Ohtani became the first player ever selected to the All-Star Game as both a pitcher and a hitter. In fact, Major League Baseball twisted its rules for the All-Star Game—just an exhibition, after all—to allow Ohtani to start the game as a pitcher and still stay in the game as a designated hitter after he was done on the mound.

Few questioned MLB's willingness to accommodate Ohtani, because by that point in the season it was obvious that he had become one of the sport's most amazing spectacles.

"I think it's probably a once-in-a-lifetime player we're seeing right now," Los Angeles Dodgers third baseman Justin Turner said the day before the All-Star Game. "A generational player that people are going to talk about for a long time."

Dodgers first baseman Max Muncy, also an All-Star, said: "This guy is hitting balls farther than anyone in the league, throwing it harder than anyone in the league, running faster than anyone in the league. He's a freak of nature."

St. Louis Cardinals third baseman Nolan Arenado was just as awed by Ohtani. "There's nobody doing what he's doing. He's an incredible talent. . . . He's doing stuff that I haven't seen in our lifetime. Not since Babe Ruth."

Of course, Ohtani himself had done it for a couple months in 2018, but Arenado and others could be excused for failing to remember that. In the three years since, Ohtani had hit a series of low points that cast doubt on his ability to do what he did in 2021. Ohtani was finally able to reach his potential because he avoided injury, which allowed him to take his offseason preparation to a new level in the winter of 2020–21.

And when Spring Training began, the Angels finally decided that all of the well-intentioned restrictions they had placed on Ohtani's workload in order to keep him healthy and improve his performance had failed. Instead, they went into 2021 with the idea that they'd simply let Ohtani play. No more mandatory days off before and after he pitched. No more separating his pitching and hitting days.

Early in the experiment, after that first start against the White Sox, Maddon made a comment he would repeat often in 2021. He believed that Ohtani would flourish with fewer restrictions.

"It's all interconnected," Maddon said. "Everything we do is interconnected. He is a very introspective, bright young man who loves to play baseball. Let's stay out of his way. Let him play baseball and see what happens."

What happened was historic.

SHO-TIME

CHAPTER 1

A *Yakyu Shonen*

About three hundred miles north of Tokyo, or three hours by train, sits the city of Ōshū. With a population of about 120,000 spread among the rice fields and hot springs of Iwate Prefecture, Ōshū marks its history with the remnants of Isawa Castle, erected after battle a thousand years ago. Ōshū marks its present with the cattle industry. In the future, though, it may be best known as the birthplace of Shohei Ohtani, a baseball player who became a star in Japan and a history-maker on the other side of the globe.

Toru Ohtani had been a semi-professional baseball player, working at the local Mitsubishi factory and then playing in the industrial league. His wife, Kayoko, was an Olympic-caliber badminton player. The athletic couple had a son and a daughter before welcoming their third child, Shohei, on July 5, 1994. Toru said that he raised Shohei and his other children with a gentle hand. "I wasn't particularly tough in his upbringing," he explained. "It was very ordinary, really just ordinary." Shohei was the more adventurous of his sons, often fearlessly pushing his limits at the playground, for example. "He was a child who would try anything," Toru said. "If you didn't take care to watch him, it was dangerous."

Not surprisingly, both of Toru's sons played baseball, but he did not push them. Toru was not one of those fathers who tried to get his sons to go beyond where his athletic ability had taken him. In fact, Toru would come to regret that he did not spend enough time cultivating the baseball skills of his older son, Ryuta. When Ryuta was young, Toru was working long hours at the factory, and that took a toll on the time he could give his son. By the time Shohei was old enough to play baseball, around age eight, Toru had decided to become more involved, and he coached his younger son. He taught him techniques for hitting and throwing, and he taught him a respect for the game. Years later, after Ohtani made his major league debut with his father in the stands, he said the foremost lesson he learned from his father was to play the game hard.

Considered a *yakyu shonen*, or a child who lives for baseball, the young Ohtani would often watch games on television when he wasn't playing. He especially loved watching the Yomiuri Giants. "I watched baseball players and they looked so cool," Ohtani said. "I was always anxiously waiting for the weekend so I could play." Hideki Matsui, the Giants' famous slugger, was a favorite. Ohtani also became a fan of Yu Darvish, one of Japan's best pitchers. Both players would take their talents from Nippon Professional Baseball to Major League Baseball, blazing a trail Ohtani would follow years later. Ohtani also idolized Ichiro Suzuki, who had already left Japan for instant stardom in the majors by the time Ohtani was seven.

Ohtani developed as a lefthanded batter and righthanded thrower, a somewhat uncommon combination that would serve him well many years later, allowing him to balance the stress on his muscles as he hit and pitched at the highest level. When he was young, though, his lefthanded swing meant that he was mostly powering balls over fences in right field. That became an issue when he played at a field alongside the Isawa River. Ohtani hit so many home runs over the right field fence that the team was actually losing too many balls in the river, which became a costly problem. As the story goes, Ohtani then developed a skill for hitting the ball to the opposite field, to left field. That also would serve him well years later.

In those early years, before high school, Ohtani mostly stuck to the local scene around Ōshū. Unlike many talented young players, both in Japan and the United States, Ohtani did not travel for many tournaments when he was young. He said he simply didn't think he was good enough for those teams. "I assumed there must be many players better than me," Ohtani recalled years later.

Perhaps because Iwate Prefecture is much colder than other parts of Japan, the region was not known for its baseball talent. "There's a lot of snow," said lefthander Yusei Kikuchi, another Iwate product who moved from NPB to the majors. "You can't run. You can't throw." The region's production of talent began to change, though, when Hiroshi Sasaki, a former college catcher, began building up the program at Hanamaki Higashi High School, about thirty minutes from Ōshū. Ohtani followed the team closely while he was in middle school, and when he was ready for high school, he went to Hanamaki Higashi and joined a program that he learned was about much more than baseball.

Sasaki ran the program with strict rules and philosophies that went beyond pitching and hitting. A self-help book Sasaki read shortly after college had helped form his ideas about how to shape young men through baseball. When players first began in the baseball program at Hanamaki Higashi, they were asked to write down their primary goal in the sport. Around that, they wrote the necessary attributes to achieve that goal. Ohtani's goal was to be a first-round pick in NPB. He listed the eight qualities he felt were necessary to reach that goal, which included both physical and mental characteristics. Later in high school, Ohtani did a similar exercise, but by then his sights had already moved up. By age seventeen, his aim was to skip NPB and go straight to the United States. Other items on his goals list were ordered by age, and they were quite specific. For example, he wanted to sign when he was eighteen, and reach the major leagues when he was twenty. He hoped for his initial salary as a rookie to be

$13 million. He expected to win 16 games in his first year in the starting rotation, at age twenty-one, and win the Cy Young Award when he was twenty-two. At age twenty-four, he hoped to throw a no-hitter and win 25 games. At age twenty-six, he wanted to get married and win the World Series. He even planned for the next generation, hoping he would be thirty-seven when his first son would begin playing baseball. Ohtani also accounted for the end of his career, guessing that his skills would begin to deteriorate at age thirty-eight, prompting a plan for retirement. He had scheduled his final game for age forty. In it, he would throw a no-hitter. He then planned to return to Japan and introduce the American way of baseball to his native country.

Ohtani's detailed plan for baseball greatness was accompanied by his physical blossoming. An MRI exam upon entry into the Hanamaki Higashi baseball program—another standard procedure at Hanamaki Higashi—showed that Ohtani's growth plates were still far apart when he was sixteen years old, which indicated that he had continued growth ahead of him. Initially, Ohtani did not even pitch. He played right field and batted fourth, the team's most powerful hitter. Although he was skinny, he still generated fastballs up to 90 mph when he moved to the mound. That is when Sasaki realized that Ohtani was able to generate velocity with more than mere strength. "He didn't have any muscles and could pitch like that," Sasaki said.

Still Ohtani's pitching mechanics were inconsistent, and he often had trouble with control. Then a hip injury, perhaps the result of a growth spurt, kept him from pitching in his junior year, so his development on the mound stalled. He was still growing quickly, making for the awkward movements of not-fully-fleshed-out teenager. As a hitter, he was more advanced. Takashi Ofuchi, the scout for the Hokkaido Nippon-Ham Fighters who would eventually sign Ohtani, said he was one of the good players, but not elite.

By Ohtani's final year in high school, he had grown to six foot four, and his frame began to fill out. The latter was the result of devouring up to ten bowls of rice a day. Ohtani also read books about nutrition and training, helping him gain forty-five pounds during high school.

At the plate, he continued to be impressive, including one memorable homer against Shintaro Fujinami, another high school star who would go on to play in NPB. On the mound, his fastball reached 99 mph, which is elite at any age, in any country.

While Ohtani was rising to prominence on his team, with his physical stature and on-field performance turning him into something of a local legend, Sasaki was interested in keeping all of his players humble. The players in his program lived in dorms for most of the year, with each player responsible for certain chores around the facilities. The pitchers, including Ohtani, were responsible for keeping the toilets clean. The job was intended to help the pitchers stay grounded away from the field, in contrast to being a focal point on the field. "The pitcher, especially in Shohei's case, is literally and figuratively at the highest point on the field," Sasaki said. "Once they get up there, they are at the pinnacle, so for the rest of the day I tell them, 'You have to do the lowest job.' Shohei never complained."

On the field, Ohtani was indeed the center of attention, not only from the locals and from professional baseball teams in Japan. Word of the six-four kid with the 99-mph fastball had even reached the United States. The Los Angeles Dodgers, Texas Rangers, Boston Red Sox, New York Yankees, and San Francisco Giants all pursued the young Ohtani. This was nothing new to Sasaki, who had gone through a similar experience a few years earlier with pitcher Yusei Kikuchi, whose arrival had helped the Hanamaki Higashi program rise in prominence. Eight Major League teams, and all twelve NPB teams, held meetings with Kikuchi in an effort to recruit him. For years, there had been a gentlemen's agreement with Major League teams that they would not sign Japanese amateur players. That began to erode when pitcher Junichi Tazawa signed with the Red Sox in 2008. When Major League teams were pursuing Kikuchi, Sasaki tried to remain openminded, but he admitted later that he felt Kikuchi might be risking his relationship with Japanese teams if he left for the major leagues. (Kikuchi eventually decided to stay and begin his professional career in Japan.)

Ohtani had been a middle schooler at the time Kikuchi was being courted. When Ohtani arrived at Hanamaki Higashi, he inherited the number 17 that Kikuchi had worn, a number that he would later wear again with the Los Angeles Angels. When Ohtani also followed Kikuchi's path in becoming a target for teams from both sides of the Pacific, Sasaki again was a close advisor. This time, though, Sasaki's feelings had changed. He encouraged Ohtani to go to the US.

In October 2012, eighteen-year-old Ohtani held a press conference in which he announced that he would bypass NPB to begin his professional career in the US. "Great players from every country go there," Ohtani said. "I don't want to lose to those players." Although Ohtani hadn't yet reached an agreement with any Major League team, his announcement was intended to prevent NPB teams from drafting him.

The Fighters, however, were undeterred. The Fighters had a reputation for going against conventional wisdom, using advanced metrics for decisions more than other NPB clubs at the time. A year earlier, the Fighters had used their first-round pick on pitcher Tomoyuki Sugano, even though he had informed teams he would not sign with any club except the Yomiuri Giants, who were managed by his uncle, Tatsunori Hara. Sugano actually sat out the entire season rather than signing with the Fighters, and a year later ended up with the Giants. Despite losing out on their gamble with Sugano, the Fighters felt the upside with Ohtani was high enough to take the chance again. Ohtani had been watched closely by Ofuchi, the Fighters scout, for years. Ofuchi was enamored with his talent as a pitcher and a hitter. "I knew for certain he'd be our number one draft pick and would become a top player when fully developed," Ofuchi recalled years later. So the Fighters drafted Ohtani. But then they had to convince him to sign, rather than heading for the United States.

The process of wooing Ohtani lasted about a month. Led by General Manager Masao Yamada, the Fighters used a variety of means to show Ohtani that they could offer him something better than he could find in the US. In Japan, Ohtani was likely to head directly to the highest level, while in the US he would certainly begin in the minor leagues. The Fighters showed him videos that portrayed the difficult life of a minor leaguer in the US: playing in small towns with sparse accommodations, enduring long bus rides. They even pointed out how difficult it would be to find a Japanese girl to date. The Fighters acknowledged that Ohtani was destined to reach the major leagues, but they believed beginning his career with them would help him get there. They showed Ohtani statistics indicating that players had been more successful when beginning their careers in Japan and then going to the major leagues. As a further inducement, the Fighters offered him jersey number 11, which had been worn by Yu Darvish, one of his role models. All along, Ohtani listened to their recruiting efforts with little indication of his feelings, Ofuchi said. "It was difficult because I felt like I was negotiating with an adult, not a high school student," Ofuchi said. "He's really smart in that sense." Ohtani said later he appreciated the connection he made with the Fighters, which foreshadowed the decision he made five years later when coming to the US.

Aside from the way Yamada and Ofuchi and the rest of the Fighters contingent connected with Ohtani, the organization also had a significant trump card. While Major League teams and even the other NPB teams would have insisted on Ohtani becoming a pitcher full-time, the Fighters were willing to let him be a two-way player. Ohtani said later he hadn't even considered the notion until the Fighters put it on the table. He'd assumed that any professional team would want him to specialize on the mound. The Fighters, again bucking conventional wisdom, had an idea that Ohtani could pull it off.

Ofuchi had believed, just like practically everyone else who worked in professional baseball on either side of the Pacific, that a player could not succeed at the highest level while splitting his time between hitting and pitching. And then he saw Ohtani and began to change his mind.

"If a person has the possibility to do everything, we need to look at that person and his talent and bring his skills along all at the same time. It's like Michelangelo and Einstein. They could do art and science, everything," Ofuchi said. "As a scout, I have to look at the person and his abilities and see if this high school player was capable. Ohtani is the player who changed my way of thinking."

Ofuchi and the Fighters believed that he could succeed in something so difficult that it was hardly ever attempted. The Fighters were willing to let Ohtani try to make history, by hitting and pitching.

Ohtani was convinced. The major leagues would have to wait.

CHAPTER 2

"He Proved It To Me"

While the Hokkaido Nippon-Ham Fighters took a gamble on drafting Shohei Ohtani, five years later it had clearly paid dividends. By the end of the 2017 season he had won an MVP and made five All-Star teams. He was named to the Best Nine, which honors each league's top player at each position, in 2015 and 2016. In 2016 he was actually named at two positions, pitcher and designated hitter. As it became clear he could dominate on the mound and in the batter's box, he earned the nickname "The Babe Ruth of Japan."

Stories of Ohtani's exploits had reached Brandon Laird before he left the United States to continue his baseball career in Japan. A Southern California kid, Laird had played in the minors with future Major League stars like Buster Posey and Andrew McCutchen. His older brother, Gerald, had a thirteen-year major league career. Laird was skeptical about the Ohtani hype before he signed with the Fighters, prior to the 2016 season.

"He can't be that good," Laird recalled a few years later. "I just wanted to see it." In the first intrasquad game that they played, Laird saw Ohtani throwing "effortless" 90-mph fastballs. He saw Ohtani flicking balls over the fence the opposite way in batting practice. And then he watched Ohtani have his best season, living up to his billing. "He proved it to me," Laird said. "At his age, he's one of the best, if not the best player I've ever played with or against." Laird referred to the commonly cited "five tools" of baseball—hitting, hitting for power, running, throwing, and playing defense—when he said of Ohtani, "He's almost like a ten-tool player: a pitcher and a hitter who can do it all."

As Ohtani demonstrated his incredible talent on the field, Laird watched him become a star off the field, too. Taller than most of the players in NPB—or almost anyone in Japan, for that matter—and with boyish good looks, Ohtani grew into a huge celebrity.

Ohtani, however, seemed immune to it all. According to his former teammates and those around him, his celebrity status never interfered with his single-minded pursuit of being a great baseball player. Despite the money and the fame and the reporters following him looking for any scandal, Ohtani did little away from the field other than go back to his dorm room, get his rest, and prepare to play again the next day. "He's pretty secluded from the world," said Anthony Bass, an American pitcher who was Ohtani's teammate with the Fighters in 2016. "What impressed me the most is his ability to separate his superstar status to that of a really good teammate. He's a very down-to-earth person. I could only imagine it's not easy to be in the limelight like that and perform on a consistent basis. He had a lot of pressure on him and he was able to do that."

Pressure comes from expectations, which were high from the moment that Ohtani reversed his plans of taking his immense talent to the United States, instead staying in Japan. As the company that owns the Fighters, Nippon Ham obviously used its baseball players to help promote its food products. The company trotted out an eighteen-year-old Ohtani at an event before he'd even begun his first Spring Training in 2013. Ohtani was shepherded around an exhibition hall shoveling meat products into his mouth while cameras snapped his picture and some 3,000 fans crowded around, trying to get a closer look at the young star. Wearing an ill-fitting gray suit that he'd borrowed from a teammate, Ohtani did his best to appear at ease. Perhaps it was all of those toilets he'd cleaned in high school that kept him grounded. After admitting that he was initially "nervous," Ohtani said he grew more comfortable with the attention as the event continued. "It was a good experience," Ohtani said afterward. "I understand you have to get along with fans as well as sponsors as a professional player."

Certainly, Ohtani would be more comfortable holding a baseball than eating a sausage for cameras, and the start of his first Spring Training would come soon enough. Wearing the number 11 that Yu Darvish had worn with the Fighters, Ohtani began that spring with the *ni-gun* team, Japan's version of the minors, but he was promoted before the season began. The first time he threw a bullpen session, it was an event chronicled by the media and watched by fans. The Fighters were searching for the best way to fit him into their lineup. They even had him try playing shortstop, a position he hadn't played since before he was in high school. When that didn't work, they put him in the outfield.

As Ohtani began his pro career, there was significant skepticism from the NPB community that he could succeed as a two-way player. "Most of the guys were against it," said Masaya Kotani, a baseball writer for *Sports Hochi*, a daily sports newspaper in Japan. "They didn't think he could do it. It was only [Hideki] Kuriyama, the manager, and the Fighters who believed in him. People said it's not going to be that easy."

* * *

A century before Shohei Ohtani challenged conventional wisdom as a two-way player for the Fighters, Babe Ruth had done the same for the Boston Red Sox.

While Ohtani and Ruth succeeded at pitching and hitting at an elite level, their paths were different. Ohtani has been adamant throughout his career on both sides of the Pacific that he wanted to be a two-way player, but Ruth showed little interest in continuing to pitch once he established himself as a premium hitter.

Ruth pitched exclusively for the first few seasons of his career, and then pitched and hit for just two seasons. After that, he finished with sixteen seasons in which he was one of the most dominant hitters in baseball history, all while barely stepping on the mound.

Ruth was nineteen years old when he first reached the Red Sox in 1914, and he became one of their top pitchers in 1915. He pitched in 32 games and pinch-hit in 10 more. Although he came to the plate just 103 times that season, he hit 4 home runs. At that time, homers were so rare that no one else on the Red Sox hit more than 2, including players who had more than 600 plate appearances.

Ruth also hit .315 in 1915 (league average was only .248), inspiring Paul Eaton to write in *Sporting Life* that summer that Ruth was "one of the best natural sluggers ever in the game," and that he "might even be more valuable in some regular position than he is on the slab—a free suggestion for Manager [Bill] Carrigan."

Although the everyday player notion persisted among writers—and certainly in Ruth's mind, according to many who interviewed him— the Red Sox managers in those years never relented by putting Ruth anywhere in the lineup when he wasn't pitching.

Ed Barrow became the Boston manager prior to the 1918 season, and he flatly rejected the idea. "I'd be the laughingstock of baseball if I changed the best lefthander in the game into an outfielder," Barrow said early in the 1918 season. Ruth, after all, had been 67–34 with a 2.07 ERA as a pitcher through the 1917 season.

Ruth wanted to hit, though, and he would soon get the chance, in part because of events beyond the baseball field. So many big league players had gone to fight World War I in 1918 that teams were scrambling to fill out their rosters. (Ruth was eligible to be drafted by the military but was never called to service.) What's more, Boston's regular first baseman, Dick Hoblitzell, was late arriving to their Spring

Training camp in Hot Springs, Arkansas. That prompted Barrow to give Ruth a shot at first base when the Red Sox played their first exhibition game, which was against the Brooklyn Dodgers. Ruth, twenty-four years old at the time, had reported to camp in the best shape of his young career, thanks to a winter spent chopping wood to heat his cottage in Massachusetts, as the legend goes. He wasted no time in showing off his strength.

Ruth belted 2 homers in his Spring Training debut at first base, the second one soaring so far beyond the right field fence that players from both teams applauded the slugger, according to multiple newspaper reports. The ball landed on an alligator farm across the street. In 2011, an engineering crew used old photos to determine the locations of home plate and the ball's landing spot to estimate that the homer traveled 500 feet. Ruth hit 4 homers in just 21 at-bats that spring.

A couple months later, on May 6, 1918, Hoblitzell was slumping and injured, pushing Barrow to make the move he had previously said would make him a "laughingstock." The manager put Ruth at first base for a game against the New York Yankees, the first time in the big leagues Ruth played any position but pitcher in the field. Ruth had 2 hits that day, including a homer. Yankees owner Colonel Jake Ruppert was sitting next to Boston owner Harry Frazee and joked right then that he would give Frazee $150,000 for Ruth, as Frazee told the *Boston Herald and Journal*. Both men laughed. The comment was prophetic, because the following year the Red Sox sold Ruth to the Yankees for $125,000, in one of the most infamous deals in sports history.

Ruth's success at the plate created friction between the player and his manager. While Barrow still wanted to keep Ruth as a pitcher, only sparingly using him as a position player, Ruth objected. At one point Ruth claimed he had a sore wrist and could not pitch. Allan Wood, author of *Babe Ruth and the 1918 Red Sox*, said there's no way to know if Ruth was legitimately hurt, but circumstantial evidence suggests that Ruth simply didn't want to pitch. Ruth would later leave the Red

Sox briefly in July, returning after Frazee agreed to pay him a $1,000 bonus for playing two positions.

Ruth ended up pitching 20 games in 1918 and 17 games in 1919, less than half of the normal workload for a starting pitcher in those days. Meanwhile, he played 72 games at first base or the outfield in 1918 and 116 in 1919. Technically, Ruth was a pitcher and a position player, but it was increasingly clear he was reluctant to return to the mound.

"I don't expect that manager Barrow will ask me to play two or three positions this year, for I would rather play in one position," Ruth said before the 1919 season. "I enjoy being in the game every day, and there is nothing I like better than to get in there and take a hard swing at the ball when some of the boys are on the bases."

Ruth maintained that it wasn't simply that he preferred hitting; he didn't believe it was feasible to handle the physical demands of pitching and hitting.

"I don't think a man can pitch in his regular turn, and play every other game at some other position, and keep that pace year after year," Ruth said in 1918. "I can do it this season all right, and not feel it, for I am young and strong and don't mind the work. But I wouldn't guarantee to do it for many seasons."

In fact, Ruth would not do it for much longer. Once the Yankees acquired Ruth, they used him to pitch just five times over the next 15 seasons. Three of those were in the first two years. The other two were in the final days of the 1930 and 1933 seasons, both against the Red Sox. "That seemed like more of a [public relations] thing," Wood said.

The Yankees likely kept Ruth off the mound because they saw that he was more valuable as a hitter. Modern statisticians use ERA+ and OPS+ to determine how good a player's numbers are, relative to his era, using 100 as average. Over 158 games as a pitcher with the Red Sox from 1914–19, Ruth had an ERA+ of 125, which means he was 25 percent better than the average pitcher. In 1,332 plate appearances with the Red Sox, Ruth's OPS+ was 190. Once with the Yankees, when he was only a hitter, his OPS+ was 209. While there were other pitchers in the same class as Ruth, there were no other hitters like him.

• • •

Unlike Babe Ruth, who established himself as a pitcher for years before spending most of his career as a hitter, Ohtani was used as a two-way player almost immediately by the Fighters. He played right field on Opening Day of his rookie season of 2013, notching 2 hits and an RBI. After that, he would play outfield and hit for the Fighters in their games at night, after spending some mornings doing pitching workouts with the nearby Minor League team. Hitting seemed to be going well enough: a .307 average through his first 39 at-bats.

The Fighters were finally ready to put him on the mound in an NPB game on May 23. After promoting the appearance days in advance, the Fighters actually gave certificates to fans, so they would have a memento from what they assumed would be a historic game. Ohtani gave up 2 runs and 6 hits against the Tokyo Yakult Swallows in a game that ended in a tie. Although his performance was unspectacular, he'd made history simply by taking the mound. The last player to pitch and hit in the first season after being drafted out of high school had been Kikuo Tokunaga, who had done so in 1951.

Ohtani ended the season going 3–0 with a 4.23 ERA in 61⅔ innings on the mound over 13 games. At the plate, he hit .238 with 3 homers and 20 RBI in 189 at-bats. Injuries affected his season significantly: He missed a few weeks with a sprained ankle suffered in mid April. Later in the season, while he was doing some running in the outfield during batting practice, a batted ball hit him in the face, fracturing his cheekbone.

Despite the injuries and rather pedestrian numbers, fans still voted him into the All-Star Game. When it came time for Rookie of the Year voting, Ohtani finished second, collecting 4 of 233 votes, with the award going to Takahiro Norimoto, a pitcher who had gone 15–8 with a 3.34 ERA for the Tohoku Rakuten Golden Eagles.

By Ohtani's second season, he had made enough progress that he played full-time with the Fighters, with no more morning trips to the *ni-gun* team. Still, the Fighters needed to devise a way to best use his pitching and hitting skills without burning him out or getting him hurt. In his rookie season, he'd played 54 of his 77 games in the outfield, with the rest coming at designated hitter or as a pinch-hitter. In his sophomore season, he played just 8 of his 87 games in the outfield. Playing the outfield "was too much workload for his body," said *Sports Hochi*'s Kotani. "Whatever the team wants him to do, he'll do it. It's not like he has a will to insist on playing outfield. That's not his thing." The Fighters also made sure to give him the days before and after he pitched off. He would eventually settle into a routine of pitching every Sunday, which was convenient because NPB teams have Mondays off.

Once again, Ohtani was named to the All-Star team, and in that game he wowed fans by firing a fastball at 101 mph. During the 2014 season, Ohtani left no doubt that he could play both ways successfully. He hit .274 with 10 home runs in 212 at-bats, and also went 11–4 with a 2.61 ERA in 155⅓ innings. No player in NPB history had ever hit 10 homers and won 10 games in the same season. No one had done it in the major leagues since Babe Ruth in 1918. As you'd expect, "The Babe Ruth of Japan" was drawing more and more attention from Major League teams. Scouts crossed the Pacific to watch Ohtani, who was still just twenty years old by the end of the 2014 season.

In the off-season, Ohtani got to show his stuff against actual Major League competition. He was picked for an NPB All-Star team that faced off against a lineup of Major League All-Stars in November. Ohtani appeared in relief in one of the games, and he started another game. In his start, he pitched 4 innings and struck out seven. Although the major leaguers scored 2 unearned runs against him, he did not factor in the decision, won by the major leaguers.

Ohtani nonetheless left an impression. Los Angeles Angels pitcher Matt Shoemaker, who would become Ohtani's teammate years later, was one of the big leaguers who made that trip, and actually pitched against Ohtani. "What I remember is a twenty-year-old kid throwing 100," Shoemaker said. "That's what everyone was talking about." Shoemaker said he also remembered the way the crowd reacted to every pitch, cheering if his pitches cracked 161 km/hr, and groaning if they were just short. Although there isn't any magic line separating 160 from 161 km/hr, fans were versed in the conversion, and appreciated the jump from 99 to 100 mph.

In 2015, Ohtani's two-way game went in two different directions. As a pitcher, he continued to blossom. Ohtani went 15–5 with a 2.24 ERA in 160⅔ innings over 22 games. He gave up just 100 hits and he struck out 196. These were dominant numbers, all in a season in which he turned twenty-one. He again made the All-Star Game as the starting pitcher. At the end of the season, he was named as the pitcher on the Best Nine team. His hitting, on the other hand, declined. In his first season hitting exclusively as the designated hitter, Ohtani batted .202 with 5 homers in 109 at-bats.

In the winter of 2015–16, the Fighters invited Yu Darvish—former Fighters pitcher and teenage Ohtani idol—to work with some of their players, including Ohtani. Darvish had left for the major leagues in 2012, which was Ohtani's last year of high school. An instant success in the majors, Darvish made the All-Star team in each of his first three years with the Texas Rangers. But that winter, the Rangers hurler was working his way back from Tommy John surgery, the reconstructive elbow surgery that requires twelve to eighteen months of rehab. During that time, Darvish worked with Ohtani and helped teach him about nutrition and fitness. Ohtani added twenty pounds of muscle that offseason. He also began training differently, focusing less on bulk and more on explosiveness. He eliminated sugar from his diet and began eating brown rice instead of white rice. "I've learned a lot about the kinds of food I eat and the timing of when I eat," Ohtani said later, about a year into his new Darvish-inspired routine. "It's challenging, but it's very important. Every year I learn more interesting things. I've put on weight and I feel more power in everything I do."

Ohtani's new workout and nutrition regimen showed results immediately, when the Fighters traveled to Arizona for Spring Training in February 2016. The rare journey onto American soil for an NPB team gave Major League scouts a convenient opportunity to get a close look at Ohtani. Ohtani began blasting balls in batting practice, which immediately showed Matt Winters, an American who worked as an international scout for the Fighters, that Ohtani had improved. "He's looked much better than he did a year ago," Winters said. "His approach looks better. He took two extra BPs that were something else. [Scouts'] jaws were dropping. There were about fifty people, scouts and general managers, here the other day for his game and after his second at-bat, when he was done, they began leaving in packs of five. By the end of the game there were about three left. It's no secret why they're here."

When the 2016 regular season came around, Ohtani had his best year with the Fighters. As a pitcher, he was just as dominant as he had been the year before. Despite missing two months on the mound with a blister issue, he went 10–4 with a 1.86 ERA. Ohtani pitched 140 innings, in which he gave up only 89 hits and he struck out 174. The difference, however, was his bat. Ohtani lifted his average more than 100 points, to .322. He belted 22 home runs in 323 at-bats. He was so dangerous at the plate that opponents often simply pitched around him, walking him 54 times. (In his first three years, he'd had a total of only 41 walks in 557 plate appearances.) The Fighters began occasionally forfeiting the use of the designated hitter so Ohtani could also hit on the days he was pitching.

Ohtani helped lift the Fighters to the Nippon Series championship. Along the way, he threw a one-hit shutout with 15 strikeouts in a critical late season victory over the Saitama Seibu Lions.

Relief pitcher Chris Martin, who was with the Fighters in 2016 before returning to the US and becoming a productive reliever for the

Rangers and Atlanta Braves, was taken by the way Ohtani seemed to be able to sail through games without much effort most of the time, but could crank it up when the game demanded it. "I think once he got into a groove it was really impressive and fun to watch," Martin said. "I think he would try to work on other things, then he'd get in a little trouble. You could see when he'd give it his whole effort, it wasn't even fair. It was pretty fun to watch."

American infielder Brandon Laird, who had joined the Fighters in 2016, also remembered Ohtani's flair for big moments. "He came in and closed one game to go to the [Nippon] Series," Laird said. "He was pumped. He was throwing 165 [102 mph]. His breaking balls were just nasty. When he wants to turn it on, you'll know."

Ohtani's hitting exploits were also the stuff of legend, including monster home runs to all fields. In November 2016, Ohtani was playing an exhibition game with Japan's World Baseball Classic team. Facing a team from the Netherlands, Ohtani hit a ball that disappeared through the roof of the Tokyo Dome. Although ground rules resulted in Ohtani getting just a double, reports estimated that the ball would have traveled some 525 feet had it gone unobstructed. Video of the shot went viral on YouTube.

Ohtani's success on the field only accelerated his fame off the field. He was hugely popular because of his baseball talent and the uniqueness of being a two-way player. Truth to be told, his looks also made him a favorite of young women. Ohtani exploded as a celebrity in 2016. "He's on every billboard, every train, commercials," Laird said after returning to the United States one winter. "He's a superstar over there. He goes outside when we're on the road, they are all over him. You see Ohtani walking around the city, and they are following him for miles, taking pictures. I've seen young girls crying. They are so emotional that they saw Ohtani."

Ohtani, meanwhile, was still trying to live the life of an anonymous young *yakyu shonen*, whose only care is baseball. Although he was making more than $2 million a year, not including endorsements,

Ohtani lived off an allowance of $1,000 a month, distributed by his mother. Ohtani still lived in the team's dormitory, like a college student. If he wanted to leave, he would need permission from Kuriyama, the manager, or another team official. Young players in NPB live like this, but the bigger stars and older players generally get their own, more luxurious, accommodations.

Ohtani wanted to keep things as simple as possible, so he spent almost all of his time at the ballpark or at the dormitory. The Japanese media followed him intensely, looking for any scandals or further insight as to who he was beyond the field, and they came up with nothing. "If he was up to anything, people would find out," Jason Coskrey from the *Japan Times* said. "There's been no scandals, no controversy. He's just as normal a kid as you can possibly be—humble, mild-mannered, down to earth, even-keeled."

While Ohtani was living a quiet life off the field, his career was booming, and Major League scouts had fully taken notice. After the 2016 season, one high-ranking Major League official declared Ohtani "the best baseball player in the world." Kazushi Nagatsuka, a veteran Japanese baseball writer, said: "I would say he's easily the best player I've ever seen. Every time you watch Ohtani, he makes you think he might do something you have never seen. You can't compare him to Darvish, Ichiro [Suzuki], [Hideo] Nomo—whoever. It's not fair to compare him to these guys. Because Ohtani does stuff nobody else does."

Of course, all of this would spark even more discussion about Ohtani's inevitable move to the major leagues. Normally, players are contractually bound to remain in Japan for nine years. The Fighters, however, had said they would agree to let Ohtani go early if he asked. The process involved the Fighters receiving a $20 million posting fee from a Major League team in exchange for allowing Ohtani out of his NPB commitment.

Although his stock could not have been higher after his sensational season in 2016, Ohtani decided to stay in Japan for one more year. "I didn't feel ready to go to the MLB—not yet," he said, recalling his decision later that winter. "Last year we won, but I didn't feel like a winner. I didn't feel ready. It's hard to explain. There are no achievements I want to have before I go. It's a feeling. When the time comes, I'll know I'm ready.

A week after winning the 2016 MVP award, Ohtani agreed to a $2.37 million salary to come back to the Fighters in 2017. At the time, he told the team that he might want to leave for the United States as soon as the 2018 season. "There are no clear criteria [as to when to move]. I could have that desire to move [over the course of] next year and we just talked about how things will go in those moments. First I will give 100 percent for the Fighters next year to be Japan's best again. I'll put my soul into it."

While Ohtani had decided that he would wait at least one more year to become a full-time major leaguer, it was expected that he'd get a chance to compete against big leaguers sooner than that. The World Baseball Classic, an international tournament operated by Major League Baseball, was set to be played in March 2017. The event, played every four years, has showcased many of the best players in the world, as major leaguers temporarily put aside their team affiliations in exchange for the colors of their countries. Ohtani had vivid memories of watching on television as Ichiro Suzuki helped lead Japan to the championship in the inaugural WBC in 2006. Pitchers Kenta Maeda and Masahiro Tanaka, who had gone on to the majors since, both played for Japan's WBC team in 2013.

Ohtani had been training over the winter—again with Darvish—in hopes of playing in the 2017 WBC. But he had been bothered by a nagging ankle injury suffered when he stepped on first base awkwardly during the Japan Series in October. Finally, just weeks before the WBC opened, Ohtani was taken off the Japan roster, much to the disappointment of Ohtani and fans all over the world who had hoped to see him play on an international stage. "I feel sorry for not being able to play in the WBC," Ohtani said after the decision. "Originally I thought I was going to get better and I was trying to get ready. But I couldn't."

Instead, Ohtani focused on getting ready for the Fighters season, but the injury still affected him when the NPB season began. He could not be the two-way star that he had been in the past. Ohtani was limited to hitting at the start of the season, and even then he was instructed not to run full speed. Then he injured a left thigh muscle trying to beat out an infield hit in early April, and couldn't play for the Fighters again until June. He didn't pitch until July.

Unable to get into a groove, Ohtani slumped through midseason before finally picking up his game late in the summer. "I don't really think I've been especially good, I'm just trying to get better with every game," Ohtani said after an August contest.

There were new adjustments to make. Pitchers were treating him differently. According to many who watched him, throughout much of Ohtani's career the pitchers in Japan did not pitch him inside. He was such a star, and there is such a culture of respect for your opponents in Japan, that pitchers did not want to risk hitting him with a pitch and injuring him. Ohtani had been so successful driving pitches on the outside corner over the left field fence—a skill he'd honed when trying to keep balls out of the river beyond the right field fence as a boy—that the pitchers had no choice but to adjust. "He was driving the ball to left center out of the park with no issue, then people started to throw him hard inside," recalled Ohtani's American teammate Anthony Bass. "His hands were so fast. He started to realize they were trying to beat him inside, and he was turning and hitting balls into the right field bleachers. He makes adjustments really quickly."

Those types of adjustments were encouraging to many of the big league scouts who had been crossing the globe to watch Ohtani. Although there was skepticism that he could hit major league pitching, which is much better than pitching in Japan, there was also a belief in the industry that he would be able to make whatever changes were necessary, an idea that would be tested months later.

As the season continued, there was rampant speculation that Ohtani had already decided he would go to the majors for 2018.

Ohtani insisted he had not yet made up his mind. "I just want to do my best through the end of the season," he said when asked at one point late in the season.

With his playing time limited by the injuries early in the year, Ohtani ended up pitching in just 5 games, with a 3–2 record and 3.20 ERA in 25⅓ innings. However, he hit .332 with eight homers in 202 at-bats over 65 games.

To Ohtani and to the Major League scouts, many of whom had been watching him since high school, it was enough.

CHAPTER

3

An Unprecedented
Recruiting Battle

After Shohei Ohtani had spent five years proving what he could do in Nippon Professional Baseball, the inevitable occurred. Just as he had suggested a year earlier, Ohtani told the Fighters in November 2017 that he wanted to be released from his contract to pursue a career in the major leagues.

Ohtani and the Fighters management met for about a half hour on November 10, discussing the future. From the Fighters' perspective, the decision did not seem that difficult. They had wooed Ohtani away from the major leagues when he was eighteen, promising he could still get there, with their help. Certainly, the Fighters understood that after what he'd done on the field in five years Ohtani was ready to go. Speaking at a press conference in a Tokyo hotel, Fighters manager Hideki Kuriyama said: "Everyone in our ballclub accepts his thoughts."

While there was little doubt that Ohtani was ready for the major leagues in strict baseball terms, there were financial implications that clouded the issue. Just about a year earlier, Major League Baseball had changed its rules for international signings, raising the age at which an international player could sign without restrictions from twenty-three to twenty-five. Ohtani, who was twenty-three after the 2017 season, might have been able to sign a contract guaranteeing him $200 million if he waited two years. He'd have to settle for a bonus of less than $5 million if he went as a twenty-three-year-old.

"Personally, I don't care about money," Ohtani had said months prior to finally making his decision. "But this is not only my problem. . . . It's going to be a tough decision for me—I'm going to be the first guy under the new system and new rules to go over there. This is going to be for everybody who plays baseball in Japan. I can't make a decision personally."

When it came down to that November 2017 meeting with the Fighters management, though, Ohtani opted to put aside concerns of finances or the precedent for future players. Ohtani always had high goals for himself on the field, wanting to be the best player in the world. He knew that the only way to reach those goals was to push himself at the highest level, and he'd already done all he could do in Japan.

Besides that, Ohtani had endorsements that helped supplement his income in Japan, and that figured to increase with a move to the majors. According to Harlan Werner, a Los Angeles–based agent who specializes in getting endorsements for athletes, Ohtani had a chance to earn significant money in addition to his baseball income, because of his celebrity status. "This is a very, very special and unique situation," Werner said, adding that Ohtani had the chance to be the first baseball player to earn $10 million a year in addition to his salary. "Maybe even the first $20 million-a-year baseball player. The key is if he lives up to the hype."

Ohtani was eager to prove that he could live up to hype. His goal was always to become one of the best players in the world, and going to the majors was a necessary step toward that end. "I am not a complete player yet, and I want to go to an environment where I can continue to get better," Ohtani said during his press conference, a day after the Fighters had announced they would let him go. "I felt the same way when I graduated from high school. And it is my strongest reason for wanting to go now."

Ohtani was ready, but the path he would take to go from Japan to the majors was not quite clear. In addition to the age-based finances, there had been other recent changes in the process, which had been evolving for more than fifty years.

Masanori Murakami was the first Japanese player to play in the major leagues, in 1964. The Nankai Hawks loaned Murakami, a twenty-year-old lefthander, to the San Francisco Giants. It was an unprecedented move in order to allow him to develop against better competition. Murakami flourished in the United States, despite speaking no English and having no interpreter. He initially played in the Giants' Minor League system, but he was promoted to pitch nine games in relief with the Giants, with a 1.80 ERA. It was enough that the Giants wanted to keep him the next season, but the Hawks also wanted him back. The two leagues negotiated for months before finally agreeing that Murakami could pitch for the Giants in 1965, but then he'd return to Japan.

After that, the two leagues reached an agreement that they would not raid each other's players. If an NPB team agreed to sell a contract, a player could cross over. Free agents could switch leagues, too. While many Americans went to Japan—in search of more money than they could make as lower-level Major League players—no players from Japan came to the major leagues for thirty years after Murakami. NPB rules did not allow a player freedom to go to another league until after he'd accumulated nine years of service in Japan. Most players would be past their prime after nine years, and less desirable to Major League teams.

Righthander Hideo Nomo found a loophole to that rule in 1994. He formally retired as an NPB player after his fifth season, at age twenty-six. That allowed him the freedom to sign with a Major League team, and the Los Angeles Dodgers inked him to a deal the following February. Nomo won the Rookie of the Year Award in 1995 and went on to have a twelve-year career, including an All-Star appearance and two no-hitters. Two years later, in January 1997, the San Diego Padres purchased the contract of righthander Hideki Irabu from the Chiba Lotte Marines. Irabu, however, had no interest in playing for the Padres. He said he'd only play for the more successful and prestigious New York Yankees. The Padres eventually traded Irabu's rights to the Yankees, who signed him to a $12.8-million, four-year contract. Around the same time, infielder Alfonso Soriano, a native of the Dominican Republic, also sought to get out of his contract with the Hiroshima Toyo Carp by retiring, using the Nomo loophole. Soriano's NPB team objected, saying they had changed the rules since Nomo left. MLB Commissioner Bud Selig said that MLB had not recognized any new language in the NPB rules, and the clubs in the United States were free to sign Soriano. He also signed with the Yankees.

After the three controversial cases, the two leagues came up with what they believed was a more equitable process to allow players from Japan to come to the majors: the posting system. If any NPB player wanted to go to the major leagues before he had played for the necessary nine years, his club could post him and allow Major League teams to bid for his rights. The highest bid—a posting fee—would serve as a transfer fee to be paid to the NPB team. The big league team would then have a window of a few weeks to work out a separate deal with the player himself. If the MLB team could not reach an agreement with the player, the posting fee would be returned.

The first prominent player to come to the majors via the new posting system was outfielder Ichiro Suzuki. The Seattle Mariners paid the Orix BlueWave a posting fee of $13.125 million for the rights to Ichiro, who was most commonly known by his first name. The Mariners then signed Ichiro to a three-year, $14-million deal. Ichiro won the Rookie of the Year and the MVP awards in 2001, the start of a career that would see him amass more than 3,000 hits in the majors.

Over the years, dozens of players would leave Japan for the majors this way, and the posting fees increased. The Boston Red Sox paid

$51.1 million for righthander Daisuke Matsuzaka in 2006, and the Texas Rangers paid $51.7 million for Yu Darvish in 2011. As a reaction to those rising fees, MLB negotiated a new agreement in 2012. Instead of having Major League teams bid, the NPB teams would set a posting fee for each particular player, up to a maximum of $20 million. Any team that was willing to pay that fee would have the right to negotiate with the player. The team that reached an agreement with the player would then pay the fee to the NPB club.

In 2017, when Ohtani announced he wanted to leave NPB, the posting agreement was about to expire. About three weeks after Ohtani announced that he would be coming to the majors, the two organizations agreed to a new posting system. Under the new rules, the posting fee would be based on the amount of money the player received. That system would not go into effect until the winter of 2018, so Ohtani could still be had with the $20 million posting fee going to the Fighters. That would be the most significant part of the investment any Major League team would make in Ohtani. The other element of the transaction, the money paid to Ohtani himself, was strictly limited because Ohtani was only twenty-three.

When touted players like Matsuzaka and Darvish had come to the majors, the posting fee and the amount of the contract for the player were both unlimited, which meant that the Major League teams with lesser revenue streams had trouble competing with big spenders like the Yankees and Red Sox. But in 2017, the new collective bargaining agreement changed the classification of international players. Previously, any player who played in a foreign league and was twenty-three or older was classified as a professional, and therefore not subject to any limits. Those players could sign for as much money as the open market dictated. In the new CBA, though, that age was raised to twenty-five. Any player who was younger was treated as if he was an amateur. So Ohtani, a twenty-three-year-old who had been a star for five years in NPB, was suddenly classified the same as a sixteen-year-old amateur from the Dominican Republic.

Further suppressing the money that players like Ohtani could earn, the spending limits on international amateurs went from a soft cap to a hard one. Each team had an allotment, based on the previous year's standings, of how much it could spend on signing bonuses for international amateurs. Previously, teams were allowed to go over that limit, but they would be subject to penalties: a tax on the overage, and a limit of $300,000 for any one player over the next two international signing periods. Starting in 2017, teams could not exceed their limit.

That confluence of changes, along with Ohtani's immense and unique talent, made him the most fiercely pursued player to come on the international market in the history of baseball. The maximum posting fee was $20 million, affordable to any team for a player of this caliber. Also, the maximum bonus Ohtani could receive was limited to about $3.5 million, depending on which team signed him. What's more, once Ohtani signed, he would be treated just like any rookie, making near the Major League minimum salary for three years and not eligible for free agency for six years. The result was that Ohtani was a star-level talent who could be acquired for a mere fraction of what he'd be worth on the open market. It meant every team, no matter its finances, could afford Ohtani. The battle for his services was about to begin.

* * *

Even before the Fighters had formally agreed to let him go, Ohtani had found the group that would help him navigate the transfer. Ohtani hired agent Nez Balelo of Creative Artists Agency, one of the most prominent firms handling athletes and entertainers. Balelo was a former minor leaguer who became an agent in 2003, subsequently rising to prominence in the industry. He had represented Major League stars like Ryan Braun, Buster Posey, Adam Jones, and Andre Ethier. Balelo also represented Japanese players like Nori Aoki and Junichi

Tazawa, the pitcher who almost a decade earlier had spurned NPB to sign with the Boston Red Sox.

Balelo began laying the groundwork for Ohtani's move before he left Japan, and before he was formally posted. Balelo sent all thirty Major League clubs a memo with a questionnaire, of sorts, to help Ohtani pare down his list. With teams unable to simply win Ohtani's services by offering the most money, Balelo wanted the teams to distinguish themselves in other ways. According to the Associated Press, which obtained a copy of the memo, each club was asked "to evaluate Ohtani's talent as a pitcher and as a hitter; to explain its player development, medical training, and player performance philosophies and facilities; to describe its Minor League and Spring Training facilities; to detail resources for Ohtani's cultural assimilation into the team's city; to demonstrate a vision for how Ohtani could integrate into the team's organization; and to tell Ohtani why the team is a desirable place to play." The presentations were expected to be in English and Japanese. The request came right around Thanksgiving, saddling clubs with a vital piece of homework to do while most Americans were gorging on turkey, visiting with family, and shopping.

Billy Eppler was ready. The Los Angeles Angels general manager had been through this before, most recently when he was the Yankees assistant general manager and the team signed Masahiro Tanaka. Eppler also was quite familiar with Ohtani and Japanese baseball. He made scouting trips to Japan annually, including three visits specifically to see Ohtani. He remembered the trips vividly. "You remember 'wow factors' and 'wow events,'" Eppler said. "He had a 'wow factor.'" Most of the baseball world had dismissed the Angels as serious contenders for Ohtani's services because teams like the Yankees, Mariners, or Dodgers seemed to be more prestigious or have a more significant history with Japanese players. Undeterred and sufficiently sold on Ohtani's talent, Eppler committed a full recruiting effort. When Balelo asked for the presentations, it was "all hands on deck," in the Angels front office to produce the materials as quickly as possible.

A few of Eppler's front office members had been traveling to visit family for Thanksgiving, and Eppler asked them to come back to the office in Anaheim for an intense weekend of work. "It was 3:00 or 4:00 in the morning and we were still working," Eppler said. "I would imagine that was true of a lot of clubs." Eppler and his staffers were sending documents back and forth at all hours, revising and tweaking and editing. Yoichi Terada, the Angels massage therapist, had to translate everything into Japanese. They also put together a thirteen-minute video that they planned to show Ohtani if they got the chance to have a face-to-face meeting. Eppler guessed that he got about 3½ hours sleep over the entire holiday weekend, with the finished product finally sent to CAA on Monday morning, November 27. Although Eppler said they were told they had a week to submit the presentations, he believed that "sooner would be better, would be advantageous."

All told, twenty-seven of the thirty teams in the majors produced presentations to try to woo Ohtani. One of the exceptions was the Atlanta Braves, who were out of the running because they had just been hit with significant penalties for violating baseball's international spending rules. Braves general manager John Coppolella was banned for life from Major League Baseball, and the Braves also lost twelve Minor League players they had signed in violation of the rules. Those penalties cast a shadow over the Ohtani negotiations: any team that tried to circumvent the rules to sweeten the financial offer to Ohtani would do so knowing that the penalties would be severe.

While it was clear that money was a small part of the equation, there was nonetheless some wiggle room for teams to position themselves to make the best possible financial offer. All teams began the international signing period with a predetermined amount of money they were allowed to spend on signing bonuses. This international bonus pool space ranged from $5.75 million to $4.75 million per team, with the teams that had the worst records in the previous year getting the largest pools. The international signing period starts every year on July 2, so by late November many teams had already spent most of their money. There were also twelve teams that, regardless of the total amount of their pool, were limited to $300,000 for any single player, a penalty that carried over from the previous system. By the time Ohtani got to the market, no team could offer him more than the $3.535 million the Texas Rangers had left in their bonus pool. The Yankees also had more than $3 million. The Angels had just about $100,000, one of the smallest totals in the majors. It was another reason that few gave the Angels much chance of landing Ohtani as the posting process began.

However, the rules also allowed the teams to trade for each other's pool space. No actual cash would change hands in these deals. One team would simply transfer its spending allowance to another team, in exchange for something else. The Braves had $1.21 million of pool space, but they weren't allowed to use it because of previous violations. Essentially, their allowance was useless to them. The Braves also had veteran reliever Jim Johnson, who had a disappointing season in 2017 and was still under contract for 2018, guaranteed another $4.5 million. On November 30, days after the Angels had completed their presentation for Ohtani, they swung a deal with the Braves. The Angels got all of the Braves' pool space, and in return they took Johnson and his contract off the Braves' hands. (The Angels also sent the Braves a lightly regarded Minor League pitcher, Justin Kelly.) The significance of the deal was to officially put the Angels' hat in the ring for Ohtani. "The money acquired in this deal was with an eye toward Shohei Ohtani and the pursuit of him as a player for us," Eppler said the day of the deal. It was the first time Eppler said publicly they were trying to sign Ohtani.

Although the Angels still had only about one-third of the money that the Rangers or Yankees could offer, they had vaulted above most of the other teams in the majors, including all of the teams operating with the $300,000 limit. "It makes us stand out a little bit more in the crowd and puts us in the upper tier of clubs and the bonus they could pay," Eppler said.

The Angels had invested a low-level prospect and $4.5 million to get to the table. They had created their written presentation for Ohtani and made a video they hoped to show him. They just had to wait for Ohtani.

On November 29, two days after the Angels completed their presentation, Ohtani arrived at Los Angeles International airport, greeted by about a dozen members of the Japanese media. *Sports Nippon* had broken the news that Ohtani was on the way, so their Los Angeles-based baseball writer, Hideki Okuda, was among the reporters who spent a few hours camped out at the airport waiting for him. It was nothing new to Okuda, who had participated in a similar vigil when Masahiro Tanaka came from Japan to LAX. That day, Okuda and the other Japanese writers never found Tanaka. This time, though, Okuda spotted a limo waiting at the international terminal. The license plate included "O11." Ohtani had worn number 11 with the Fighters. Okuda had a hunch that the limo was there for Ohtani, and he was right. Ohtani emerged with a small entourage. Reporters snapped photos, but Ohtani did not answer any questions. He was whisked away. Although reporters would spend the next week trying to catch Ohtani—at the CAA offices and even at the medical offices where they expected him to go for his physical—they never found him, Okuda said.

Ohtani, Balelo, and the other CAA staffers had plenty of material to go over during that week, with twenty-seven teams having submitted presentations. It would be impractical to try to have face-to-face meetings with all of them, so they had to narrow the list to a manageable number. Also, they had to wait until Friday, December 1, for the posting agreement to be officially ratified by Major League owners, allowing Ohtani to be posted. That would start a twenty-one-day window for him to select a Major League team.

Meanwhile, because Ohtani and Balelo were saying little about the criteria they were using to pick a team, speculation ran rampant in the baseball media about Ohtani's wish list for his new club. Some suspected that he would want to be on the West Coast, because of its proximity to Japan. There was a belief that he wanted to go to a team that had no other Japanese stars, perhaps because he wanted to blaze his own trail or perhaps because he didn't want to cut into the spotlight of another current player. Everyone assumed he wanted to be a two-way player, but that would obviously work differently if he were with an American League or National League team. Ohtani had stopped playing the outfield after his second season in Japan, with his hitting limited to the DH role. If he played in the NL, with no DH, he would have to play a position if he was going to hit on days he wasn't pitching. Would he be willing to do that? Could he play outfield? Could he play first base, a position he had never played in Japan? There was even a theory that a National League team might make Ohtani a full-time outfielder but have him pitch as a closer. The financial situation also sparked discussion. How could a team that had only $300,000 to offer compete with a team that had more than $3 million? Mostly, the experts assumed that money didn't matter to Ohtani. If it did, he would have waited until he was twenty-five to come to the majors.

It didn't take long for the picture to become clearer. On Sunday, December 3, just forty-eight hours after Ohtani had officially been posted and less than a week after he'd touched down at LAX, teams learned if they had made the initial cut. The first public word of the selection of finalists came from Brian Cashman, the general manager of the New York Yankees. He was at a Christmas event when he told reporters that he'd gotten word that his team had been eliminated. That news sent shock waves around the baseball world. The Yankees were considered one of the favorites to sign Ohtani, and they had not even made it past the first level of the process. Cashman said his understanding was that Ohtani preferred to be on the West Coast, in a smaller market. The Yankees were neither, obviously. That sparked baseball writers across the country to check in with the teams they covered to find out if they had gotten word from the Ohtani camp. One by one, reports throughout the day surfaced of teams that had been included or excluded from the next phase of the process.

Within twenty-four hours, a list of seven teams had emerged: the Angels, Los Angeles Dodgers, San Diego Padres, San Francisco Giants, Seattle Mariners, Texas Rangers, and Chicago Cubs. That prompted a whole new round of analysis of Ohtani's preferences. As expected, money was clearly not a driving force. Teams like the Yankees, with over $3 million to spend, were out, while four of the teams with the $300,000 limit were in (the Dodgers, Giants, Cubs, and Padres). Five of the six West Coast teams made the cut, all except the Oakland A's. But the Cubs and Rangers were also on the list. Avoiding a team with either a current or former Japanese player couldn't have been that critical of a consideration, because Ohtani included the Mariners, Ichiro's team, and the Dodgers, who had Kenta Maeda in their rotation. The list also included NL teams, so Ohtani must have been at least somewhat open to playing a position, or else becoming a full-time pitcher. About the only common element for all seven teams was that they had Spring Training in Arizona, as opposed to Florida. Ohtani had trained twice in Arizona with the Fighters, so he was familiar with the area.

While the baseball world continued to speculate on Ohtani's preferences, his camp at CAA was arranging meetings at a speedy pace. Eppler said he got word on that Sunday that the Angels would have their two-hour meeting the next day. Although Eppler didn't know the schedule at the time, Ohtani would meet with three teams on Monday, three on Tuesday, and the last one on Wednesday. The quick turnaround meant another all-nighter for Eppler and his staff. They knew their time was limited, and they knew the conversation would be slowed by translations. Eppler said they planned to spend about fifteen minutes showing Ohtani the video. For most of the rest of the meeting, they would go over what they'd provided in their written presentation, but with the chance to elaborate and get feedback from Ohtani. They did "dress rehearsals," at their Angel Stadium offices, making sure they had the message exactly as they wanted, and preparing for any questions Ohtani might ask.

The other six teams no doubt went through a similar frantic preparation. Several of them also hurried in players to help sway Ohtani. Dodgers ace Clayton Kershaw came from Texas on his wedding anniversary, while third baseman Justin Turner interrupted preparation for his own wedding to participate. The Cubs brought in Kyle Hendricks, an Ivy League–educated pitcher who they felt could connect with the inquisitive Ohtani. They also showed Ohtani the virtual reality technology they used to prepare for games, figuring it would appeal to him.

By most accounts, the bulk of the meetings involved the teams selling themselves to Ohtani, with Ohtani and his side mostly listening. However, at least two teams came away from the meetings with a feeling that Ohtani had a clear preference for the American League, because he was more comfortable as a DH than trying to play the outfield or first base. "It's a lot easier to do what he's doing as a DH versus playing the outfield, which he admitted to us he had not done much of," San Francisco Giants manager Bruce Bochy said months later. Kershaw was more blunt when reflecting a few months afterward, saying the meeting was a "gigantic waste of time." Kershaw added: "It really just seemed like it was predetermined that he wanted to DH. I'm kind of mad at his agent for making us waste all that time and effort. Fifteen teams should have been out of it, from the beginning." Balelo denied that Ohtani had eliminated the NL teams before holding meetings with them. Dodgers president of baseball operations Andrew Friedman said he went into the meeting understanding their predicament. "The burden was on us to try to sell the National League," Friedman said. "We appreciated that it was an uphill battle, but it was well worth the effort."

The Angels had no such issues. Eppler knew they had a few elements in their favor: the American League, a city with a large Japanese population, and the chance to play with the best player in the world. The Angels would have loved to have Mike Trout, their twenty-six-year-old superstar, sitting at the table when they met with Ohtani. However, Trout was back in New Jersey, preparing to get married at the end of the week. Instead, the Angels connected Trout via FaceTime, and he spent a few minutes selling Ohtani on how much he enjoyed playing for the Angels. Otherwise, Eppler did most of the talking during their meeting, which he said lasted only about ninety minutes. Owner Arte Moreno opened the proceedings and Manager Mike Scioscia cracked a few self-deprecating jokes, which Eppler said got Ohtani to laugh. Eppler said he and his staff walked out of the meeting cautiously optimistic.

The next day, the Mariners met with Ohtani. The Mariners seemed like another of the strongest suitors among the final seven because they were in the AL, played in a city with a large Japanese population, and had a history with Ichiro. The Mariners also had the second-most money to offer among the final seven, at $1.55 million as the meetings began. The day after the Mariners met with Ohtani, they and the Angels engaged in a duel of deals with the Minnesota Twins, with each club getting an additional $1 million worth of pool space from the Twins. It jumped the Angels to $2.315 million and the Mariners to $2.55 million. A day after that, the Mariners raised the bet once more, in a trade with the Miami Marlins. The Mariners got speedy second baseman Dee Gordon and another $1 million in pool space, giving them a total slightly above the Rangers' $3.535 million. The Mariners already had an All-Star second baseman, Robinson Cano, and they sent two of their top prospects to the Marlins for Gordon, who was owed $38 million over the rest of his contract. There was an assumption that the deal only made sense for the Mariners if they did it because that $1 million in pool space would get them Ohtani. (The Mariners conceded the Ohtani chase was part of the rationale, but they also wanted Gordon to play center field.)

While the baseball world was buzzing about the Mariners seemingly paving the way to land Ohtani, few knew that Ohtani was on his way to Anaheim, literally. Just as the Mariners were finishing the Gordon trade, Balelo had called Eppler and told him that Ohtani wanted to make the trek from the CAA offices in Los Angeles down the freeway to Anaheim to get a look at Angel Stadium. Thrilled as the Angels were to get another opportunity to sell themselves to Ohtani, there was a problem: the NFL's Philadelphia Eagles were using Angel Stadium. The Eagles had played in Seattle the previous weekend, and instead of crossing the country twice before a game against the Los Angeles Rams, they stayed on the West Coast and borrowed the Angels' stadium for practice. Eppler was trying to keep Ohtani's visit under wraps, and he couldn't do that with an entire football team—along with their support staff and media—hanging around. "A six-foot-four Japanese guy is going to stand out," Eppler said later. "Everyone knows he's in LA. We aren't hiding this one. We coordinated a way to get him in the stadium unseen." Once the Eagles had left, around 5:30 p.m., Ohtani got a tour of the ballpark, which was in midwinter disarray, with construction of new scoreboards and other upgrades going on around the temporary football field. While the Angels had done much of the talking during the meeting days earlier at CAA, this time Ohtani asked more questions, Eppler said. They spent a couple hours together, and then parted ways for the night. After the meeting, Balelo called Eppler to tell him what to expect. Balelo said that he had no idea when Ohtani would make his decision. Ohtani still had two weeks left before the deadline, and Balelo said he might even go back to Japan before deciding.

The next morning was Friday, just four days after the Angels had their first face-to-face meeting with Ohtani and eleven days after they had submitted their written presentation. Eppler headed into the office with no expectations. In the car, he got a call from Balelo, who wanted to make sure that he had warned Eppler that whenever Ohtani made his decision, it was going to be announced quickly. The losing teams would probably find out from the media before hearing from

Balelo. Eppler assured Balelo that he was okay with however they had to do it. A little later, after Eppler had arrived at the office, his phone rang again. It was Balelo. Eppler said he was puzzled to hear from him again so soon, but he popped into one of his assistants' offices and closed the door to take the call.

"There's something I forgot to tell you in our last conversation," Balelo said, as Eppler recalled.

"What's that?"

"It's that Shohei Ohtani wants to be an Angel."

"What?!"

"Congratulations. You got him. You reeled him in."

Speechless for a moment, Eppler stepped backward to sit down, but the chair slid along the hardwood floor away from him, and Eppler ended up crashing to the ground. As he stumbled to his feet, Balelo got his attention through the phone: "Billy! Billy! You have to call Arte." Balelo wanted Eppler to call Arte Moreno, the Angels owner, immediately, because they were going to send out a statement to the media any minute, and the news would spread quickly.

An email from CAA went out to selected members of the national and Los Angeles media, which prompted the news to immediately hit Twitter. That sparked a roar within the Angels offices, even before Eppler had opened the door to give the news directly. Across the country, a handful of Angels players cheered and celebrated the news as they were going to the rehearsal for Trout's wedding.

Once the world learned that Ohtani had picked the Angels, the next question was why. In the days, weeks, and months to come, the answer to that would remain somewhat vague. Balelo's initial statement said Ohtani had made his selection because "he felt a strong connection with the Angels and believes they can best help him reach his goals in Major League Baseball." Balelo added: "While there has been much speculation about what would drive Shohei's decision, what mattered to him most wasn't market size, time zone, or league but that he felt a true bond with the Angels. He sees this as the best environment to develop and reach the next level and attain his career goals."

The next day, the Angels hosted a press conference outside Angel Stadium, attended by hundreds of fans and dozens of media members from all over Southern California and Japan. Ohtani sat on the dais, on live television, and he gave a little more information about what led him to the decision. "It's hard to explain," he said. "With the Angels, I just felt something click. . . . When you break it all down, there were so many factors. I just felt that I wanted to play for the Angels. It's something I cannot describe in words."

The last time Ohtani had faced this type of decision was in 2012, when he had to choose between signing with the Fighters or pursuing a career in the majors as an eighteen-year-old. At the time, he also described a "feeling" that he got from the Fighters. He connected with them, and believed they had his best interests at heart. That decision proved to be a good one, because he flourished in five years in NPB, improving his value to Major League teams.

Although few gave the Angels a chance to win the Ohtani sweepstakes when it began, in retrospect it shouldn't have been such a surprise. The American League was clearly a better fit for Ohtani, and the Angels offered a West Coast city with a major Japanese population.

Also, there was the Eppler factor.

Eppler, at the time a forty-two-year-old who had been working in baseball since he was making $5,000 a year as a part-time scout at age twenty-four, had risen through the sport's ranks in large part because of a willingness to listen to anyone and blend ideas from different groups. As modern baseball front offices have evolved, the majority of executives either played the game professionally or got advanced degrees in economics or statistics or business. Eppler had done neither. His playing career ended in college because of a shoulder injury, and then he began working as a financial analyst for a real estate company. His love for baseball encouraged him to start at the bottom, making a meager salary scouting while delivering flowers and living with his mother. Rising steadily for sixteen years, Eppler reached the pinnacle by getting one of thirty general manager jobs in October 2015, when the Angels hired him. Weeks after he was hired, he'd already made an impression. "Billy is super energetic," said former Angels director of baseball operations Justin Hollander. "A really positive person. Extremely inclusive. The group in the front office is in his office all the time. . . . He is a very easy person to like and get along with."

That was the Eppler—personable, energetic, inclusive, open-minded—who wooed Ohtani to the Angels. After the news of Ohtani's choice, one agent told baseball writer Ken Rosenthal: "Eppler made this happen. One hundred percent all him. He has been on Ohtani since he was in high school and I will bet he absolutely crushed the presentation. This is a credit to him."

Eppler has since said he's flattered by such comments, but he believes it was the Angels, not him, that sold Ohtani. "He felt there was a family-like atmosphere here," Eppler said, "and it was something he wanted to be a part of for a lot of years to come."

CHAPTER

4

Blessed and Cursed

Until December 9, 2017, Shohei Ohtani had been almost a mythical figure as far as American baseball fans were concerned. They had seen some highlights, perhaps that YouTube clip of him hitting a ball through the roof at the Tokyo Dome. They may have seen one of a few interviews he had done with United States media. More likely, they had seen nothing. Because he was still far from wearing a big league uniform, he was far from the consciousness of most fans. On a sunny Saturday afternoon in Anaheim, though, Shohei Ohtani became a major leaguer. At a press conference set outside Angel Stadium, between the enormous iconic Angels caps that mark the home plate entrance, Ohtani pulled on a bright red Angels jersey, with the number 17 he had worn in high school. He smiled for the attending fans and the television audience on both sides of the Pacific. Then he said, in perfect English: "Hi, my name is Shohei Ohtani." The crowd roared. Ohtani then continued in Japanese, with an interpreter. "This is the first time I've talked in front of such a big crowd that I actually kind of forgot what I was going to say," he said. "You guys are making me nervous." Ohtani, who didn't give much of his personality in interviews, proceeded to crack a few jokes during his introduction to the US fans and media. When asked why he had picked number 17, he said: "I actually wanted 27, but somebody else was wearing that number." That someone else was Mike Trout, the Angels superstar outfielder. When he was asked if he was more excited to win his first game or hit his first home run, Ohtani said he hoped he could do both in the same game.

That comment, of course, brought to the surface what made Ohtani unique. Plenty of other players had come from Japan with star-level resumes, but none of them brought the possibilities—and questions—that Ohtani did. The most obvious question was whether the Angels actually planned to allow him to pursue his dream of pitching and hitting in the majors. "We definitely plan on him being a two-way player, no doubt about that," Manager Mike Scioscia told the crowd, which roared in approval. "As far as what his usage will be, you can script everything out now, but in the first pitch of the season, everything changes."

The theory of having a two-way player was one thing, but putting it into practice was another. There were reasons that it had been a century since any player had attempted to combine the roles in a substantial way. The physical demands and time requirements of both pitching and hitting are significant. Juggling Ohtani's roles would be complicated, and the Angels weren't ready to fully divulge how they planned to do it. That was partly because, up until that day, Ohtani had not been a part of the project. "When we sat down with Shohei we presented a plan," Eppler said after the press conference. "I don't want to say that plan gets completely ripped up, but I bet a large portion of that plan now gets modified because it was from a one-party perspective. Now we have two parties. The most important party has joined it."

Eppler did concede a few guidelines that would shape Ohtani's usage. He said the Angels were open to using a rotation of six starting pitchers, instead of the traditional five. That would help them introduce a pitcher who was used to pitching once every seven days in Japan, as well as perhaps be a benefit to the Angels' other pitchers, who had been ravaged by injuries in recent years. As far as getting Ohtani at-bats, Eppler said the Angels had no plans to have Ohtani play outfield or first base or anywhere in the field. He was going to be a designated hitter. That meant that Albert Pujols, a thirty-eight-year-old future Hall of Famer who had been limited to DH duty for much of the previous two years, would have to spend significant time at first base. Pujols was in the midst of his first winter in three years without undergoing surgery, so the Angels were optimistic that he could handle the extra work of playing in the field. Plenty of other questions remained: *How often could Ohtani be the DH? Could he hit on days he pitched? What about the day after? Would he be used to pinch-run? Would he be on an innings limit?* The Angels deferred them all, in many cases because they hadn't had time to figure it all out yet. "Our job, and we've got a lot of work ahead of us, is to see exactly how you get a multidimensional two-way athlete like Shohei to bring his talent on the field," Scioscia said, "and bring his talent on the field often enough where he leads us to that championship."

• • •

A championship is any team's goal, but one with slightly more urgency for the Angels, a franchise that was in neutral, with an increasing feeling of pressure, at the time they added Shohei Ohtani. An expansion team that played its first season in 1961, the Angels scuffled along without reaching the playoffs until 1979. They seemingly always played second fiddle to the more successful Los Angeles Dodgers. In search of an identity, they changed their name from the Los Angeles Angels to the California Angels to the Anaheim Angels and back to the Los Angeles Angels. For much of that time, failure was the defining characteristic, even at their high points.

In the Angels' second trip to the postseason, in 1982, they won the first two games of a best-of-five series against the Milwaukee Brewers.

One win away from an American League pennant, the Angels lost the next three. In 1986, they were up three games to one against the Boston Red Sox, with a 5–2 lead heading to the ninth inning of Game 5. They were just three outs away from the pennant. But they gave up 4 runs in the ninth and lost the game in extra innings. They lost the next two games to lose the series. After that, they missed the playoffs for fifteen consecutive seasons. That included the disastrous 1999 season, when the team was so dysfunctional that exasperated Manager Terry Collins quit with a month to go in the season, coming to tears in a press conference. It was perhaps the lowest point in the franchise's history.

Out of the ashes of that mess, though, the Angels made the franchise-altering decision to hire Mike Scioscia as their manager. Scioscia grew up near Philadelphia and had reached the big leagues as the Los Angeles Dodgers' catcher at twenty-one years old in 1980. From there, he developed into one of the game's best backstops, known mostly for his ability to block the plate and handle a pitching staff. Scioscia helped the Dodgers to World Series titles in 1981 and 1988, in the latter season working with righthander Orel Hershiser on one of baseball's greatest streaks: 59 straight scoreless innings. Scioscia's playing days ended with a torn rotator cuff suffered during Spring Training in 1993 with the San Diego Padres, so he began a coaching career that many assumed would eventually lead to the manager's office. He spent a few years working with Dodgers minor leaguers, including managing at Triple-A. Believed to be the heir apparent to Hall of Fame manager Tommy Lasorda, Scioscia was passed over when the Dodgers instead hired former shortstop Bill Russell as manager.

The snub by the Dodgers proved to be the Angels' gain. The Angels hired Scioscia after the 1999 season, and he led the franchise to its most successful period. In Scioscia's third season, the Angels celebrated their first World Series title, beating the San Francisco Giants in a dramatic seven-game series in 2002. Scioscia had led the Angels to the playoffs five times in the next seven years. The run earned him a ten-year contract extension, shocking in an era when most managers had a shelf life of four or five seasons. Scioscia was beloved by the fans and his players throughout a decade of excellence.

After the Angels' appearance in the American League Championship Series in 2009, though, the shine began to fade from the Scioscia era. They reached the playoffs just once, in 2014, and they were swept by the Kansas City Royals. In 2016 and 2017, they endured their first consecutive losing seasons in Scioscia's tenure. Scioscia was accused of being reluctant to adjust to the times, with decisions increasingly being made by front office executives who leaned more on math than on instincts developed on the field. Although Scioscia bristled at the suggestion that he was closed-minded to guidance from his superiors, General Manager Jerry Dipoto abruptly resigned in the middle of the 2015 season because he didn't see eye to eye with Scisocia. The fan base was getting antsy for a return to prominence, particularly because the lean years coincided with the presence of a player who quickly demonstrated he was a generational talent.

The Angels had plucked Mike Trout out of Millville, New Jersey, with the twenty-fifth pick in the 2009 draft. Trout was available that far into the draft because there were questions about whether a kid from the East Coast really measured up against players from California, Florida or Texas, where the weather allowed for year-round development of their baseball skills. The Angels had a connection to Trout's family, though. Angels scout Greg Morhardt had briefly played in the minors with Trout's father, Jeff. Whenever Morhardt came to see the younger Trout play, he became further convinced that he was going to be a star. Morhardt and scouting director Eddie Bane filed glowing reports on Trout, all of which quickly proved to be accurate.

With blazing speed and exceptional power, Trout arrived in the majors for good in 2012 at age twenty. He quickly became a star, unanimously winning the Rookie of the Year Award. Many believed Trout also should have won the MVP Award in his rookie year, but Detroit Tigers slugger Miguel Cabrera won the Triple Crown—leading the league in batting average, home runs and RBI—that season, which earned him the award. Trout had another outstanding season in 2013, and again he lost to Cabrera for the MVP. Two second-place finishes in the MVP voting in his first two years were enough to earn Trout a six-year, $145-million deal from the Angels days before the start of the 2014 season. Trout responded to that contract by winning the MVP in 2014, leading the Angels to baseball's best record in the regular season. He finished second in the MVP voting again in 2015, before winning the award for the second time in 2016. Trout was so good in 2016 that he won the award despite the fact that the Angels finished in fourth, with a 74–88 record.

It was becoming a theme for the Angels and Trout. Although Trout was putting up historic numbers, it wasn't translating to success for the franchise. Their only playoff appearance with Trout—in 2014—had ended in a disappointing three-game sweep. The Angels narrowly missed the playoffs in 2015, but had losing records in 2016 and 2017.

Meanwhile, Albert Pujols, the team's other star, was in decline. Although he was still adding items to his Hall of Fame resume, including reaching the 600-home-run milestone in 2017, he had become a shadow of his former self. The Angels also suffered a run of pitching injuries that spoiled any chances of getting to the postseason. Garrett Richards, their most talented starting pitcher, took the mound for just 12 games in 2016 and 2017, missing most of both seasons with two separate arm injuries.

To much of the baseball world, it seemed that the Angels were "wasting Mike Trout." Trout, who turned twenty-six during the 2017 season, was in the prime of his career, and he was generally considered the best player in the world. He also had just three years left on his contract. The Angels didn't seem to be making any progress toward winning a championship while he was in their uniform. Angels fans worried that the team would have no chance of re-signing Trout beyond the end of his contract, in 2020, if management didn't show some sort of commitment to winning.

As the Angels seemed to be sitting on the sidelines each winter when the biggest names in baseball were changing teams, they were no doubt still reeling from a disastrous contract they'd given Josh Hamilton in December 2012. A number one pick who was out of baseball for years because of drug problems, Hamilton had turned his life around and became an MVP with the Texas Rangers. The Angels then inked him to a five-year, $125-million deal. Hamilton had two disappointing, injury-marred seasons with the Angels. He then had a drug relapse, and never played for the Angels again. They traded him away, eating almost the entire contract. Owner Arte Moreno, frustrated that he was still paying about $25 million a year to a player who wasn't on the Angels, did not spend enough over the next few years to satisfy most Angels fans.

The Angels needed another big hitter to support Trout in the lineup. They needed an ace at the top of the pitching staff.

When twenty-three-year-old Shohei Ohtani pulled on an Angels jersey in December 2017, it allowed fans to dream that maybe they'd found both in one player.

* * *

At Shohei Ohtani's introductory press conference on that sunny afternoon in front of Angel Stadium, Manager Mike Scioscia went to the podium, stood at the microphone and, in one statement, praised Ohtani and issued a challenge to his bosses, owner Arte Moreno and General Manager Billy Eppler.

"His ability both on the mound and in the batter's box is something that doesn't come along, really never comes along," Scioscia said as he motioned to Ohtani, sitting to his left. "Our excitement is very, very high. As we move forward, Billy and Arte aren't done this winter to make our team the well rounded team we can be."

A day after the hoopla that was the Ohtani press conference, Eppler and the rest of his top assistants in the baseball operations department would be off to Lake Buena Vista, Florida—near Orlando—for the Winter Meetings. The annual December gathering of everyone who is anyone in baseball is no longer the prime time for trades and free agent signings that it used to be. With most business now taking place by phone, or even text, it's not necessary for the executives to be in the same building to get deals done. However, the Winter Meetings are still the most active time for the media to focus on the teams and their needs, with reporters all over Walt Disney World's Swan and Dolphin resorts, digging for any stories or rumors they can find.

The Angels were suddenly a popular topic of conversation. The Ohtani signing had quieted some of the "wasting Mike Trout" talk. Now, everyone wanted to know how the Angels were going to address their other needs, so they wouldn't be "wasting Shohei Ohtani," too. Eppler was in the middle of a week in which he would fill two more glaring holes—signing free agent Zack Cozart to be their third baseman and trading for Ian Kinsler to be their second baseman—when the conversation took a new direction.

"Recent physical shows Angels' Shohei Ohtani has a damaged elbow ligament," blared a headline on Yahoo! Sports around 8:00 p.m. on December 12, the second day of the four-day Winter Meetings. Ohtani had undergone a physical in late November, before he was posted, and the medical report was distributed to all Major League teams. A copy of that report was leaked to baseball writer Jeff Passan, who wrote the story, reporting that Ohtani had a grade 1 sprain of his ulnar collateral ligament (UCL), an injury that had required him to get a platelet-rich plasma injection in October. The report suggested that this injury put Ohtani at increased risk for a more serious UCL tear that could require Tommy John surgery. For a couple hours, the Winter Meetings were buzzing. *Had the Angels made a mistake? Were the dreams of Ohtani throwing 102-mph fastballs in an Angels uniform dashed already?*

The Angels immediately shifted into damage control, as Eppler tried to douse the fire on a story they believed to be sensationalized and misleading. Eppler said the Angels had seen the medical report, as had every other team in the majors, and they had also seen the results of another MRI exam from December 7, the day before Ohtani signed with the Angels. "Shohei underwent a thorough physical with MRI scans to both his elbow and his shoulder," Eppler said in a statement. "Those are scans we conduct whenever we sign a pitcher. Based on the readings of those MRIs, there are not signs of acute trauma in the elbow. It looks consistent with players his age. We are pleased with the results of the physical and we are very happy to have the player."

A day later, Stan Conte, a former Major League athletic trainer who was running an injury analytics program, said his interpretation of the Ohtani report was that it was no call for alarm. A grade 1 sprain simply means the ligament is stretched, but not torn. He said there was no need for surgery with that type of condition, which is fairly common among pitchers.

All the fuss over Ohtani's elbow, however, brought into sharper focus the task the Angels faced in managing him. Major League pitchers had been getting injured in increasing numbers for years, and the Angels were about to add one who was unique. Not only did he have the ability to throw 102 mph—and high velocity is one of the characteristics that often leads to injury—but he was going to be hitting, too. In addition, Ohtani was going to be transitioning from Japan, where he pitched once a week, to the United States, where starting pitchers usually work every five days.

By now, it was becoming increasingly clear one of the ways the Angels were going to integrate Ohtani into their team was to not even attempt to have him pitch every fifth day. Eppler had suggested, even before signing Ohtani, that a six-man rotation might be best, to preserve the health of all their pitchers. Now, it seemed like a certainty they would go that direction.

"We're tasked with doing what we feel is best for the long-term health of our players," Eppler said. "That's really important to me. You're striking a chord of my DNA. I'm not putting players at risk. If there's a methodology that can help players out, we're going to present it to them. I feel I have a moral responsibility to do that."

But the science wasn't quite so clear, according to Conte. "Intuitively, you would think five days of rest would be better [than four], but that's not necessarily true," he said. "Nothing has been proven on a six-man rotation. I sure don't think having extra rest is necessarily going to hurt. With all these pitchers going down with injuries, it is time to try some different ideas. A six-man rotation is one. I don't know what else you can do. You have to think a little out of the box if you are trying to keep starting pitchers healthy."

In order to keep Ohtani healthy, the Angels needed to know as much as possible about his history, so Eppler took a trip to Japan. He brought special assistant Eric Chavez, a former big league third baseman. He also brought two members of the training and fitness staff: director of sports science and performance and head physical therapist Bernard Li and massage therapist Yoichi Terada.

The idea was to have a few days of detailed meetings with the people who knew Ohtani and his routine the best, the Hokkaido Nippon-Ham Fighters' front office and training staff. The Angels wanted to know all that the Fighters could share about the type of training Ohtani did, the ways they kept him fresh enough to do both roles. Fighters manager Hideki Kuriyama said later that he had warned Eppler that Ohtani was not the kind of player to ever speak up when he felt fatigued or sore, so it would be the Angels' responsibility to monitor him and manage his workload.

With Spring Training just weeks away, it was clear to the Angels that Ohtani would need to be treated carefully. They would need to slow him down, even when he said he was feeling good and wanted more. At all times, the thinking went, the Angels would need to err on the side of caution.

CHAPTER

5

"You Have To Give It Time"

The first sign that Spring Training was going to be different in 2018 was when an Angels public relations staffer had to trek out to the cactuses beyond the outfield fence of one of the club's Tempe, Arizona, practice fields to shoo away the camera-toting Japanese media members. They were there—along with a handful of fans—to try to see and record what they could of the informal workouts taking place before camp officially opened to the media. It was Shohei Ohtani's first Spring Training in the major leagues, and he was among the players who had arrived before the official reporting day. Video of Ohtani's first days in an Angels uniform would be valuable to any media organization across the Pacific. The Angels expected the crush, but they nonetheless tried—often in vain—to shield Ohtani as much as possible. They knew the adjustment to life in the major leagues was going to be difficult for the twenty-three-year-old Ohtani, and they preferred that he not have to go through it with the added pressure of the world watching every single step and misstep.

There would be plenty of the latter during that first Spring Training. Ohtani had difficulty adjusting to the baseballs used in the major leagues. He was not throwing with his full velocity, perhaps just lacking the regular-season adrenaline here in Spring Training with just a smattering of people in the stands. Ohtani was not even accustomed to the way Major League teams took batting practice, in much shorter sessions than the lengthy workouts in Japan. He struggled against teams full of hitters and pitchers who he had never faced. And, of course, he was figuring it all out while living in a new country, and trying to learn a new language.

The results were disappointing and concerning to many, although not to the Angels. At every opportunity, after each time that Ohtani had a bad day at the plate or on the mound, General Manager Billy Eppler or Manager Mike Scioscia would reassure reporters, and by extension the fans, that there was nothing to worry about. This was just Spring Training, they said, and they had five years' worth of Ohtani's performance in Japan to tell them all they needed to know about his talent and potential.

By the time the season started in late March, Ohtani proved the Angels were right. His performance was exceptional, providing further evidence of the baseball truism that Spring Training doesn't mean anything. Although perhaps fans and all of those Japanese reporters shooting video from the cactus would have been better served to just ignore what happened in Arizona, it did begin to paint a picture of who Shohei Ohtani is. It was the first, and most dramatic, illustration of his ability to adjust and improve on the fly, an ability that would help him rise to stardom after reaching a career crossroads a couple years later.

Back in February 2018, though, all we knew was that we were watching something different in Shohei Ohtani.

Although Ohtani was now sharing a clubhouse with Mike Trout, the consensus best player in the major leagues, and with Albert Pujols, who was in the latter years of a Hall of Fame career, Ohtani was the only player whose arrival in camp warranted the use of a ballroom at an adjacent hotel for his first press conference of the spring. About two hundred reporters from both sides of the globe would attend, asking

Ohtani about everything from how he felt about his swings in batting practice to what he planned for Valentine's Day.

Ohtani would continue to have press conferences throughout the spring at a tent erected in a parking lot beyond the right field fence at Tempe Diablo Stadium. Dozens of Japanese and American reporters filed into the tent every couple days and peppered Ohtani with questions about everything he'd done on the field, from batting practice to simply playing catch.

Ohtani's presence prompted an addition to the Angels public relations staff. Grace McNamee, who was born in Southern California but had spent a few years of her youth in Japan, was hired by the Angels to serve as a bilingual liaison between the club and the Japanese media. It was the reprisal of a role she had filled with the Los Angeles Dodgers when Hideo Nomo was a star there in the mid-1990s. That spring of 2018, and in the years since, McNamee would often be seen huddling the media together to tell them how many throws Ohtani had made in the bullpen or when he'd next be holding a press conference. When Ohtani was too busy, or simply unwilling, to talk to the media, McNamee would ask him a few questions about the topic of the day and distribute his responses to the media, in English and Japanese.

When Ohtani spoke directly to the United States media, he did so with the help of Ippei Mizuhara, his full-time interpreter. Mizuhara had been born in Japan but grew up in Diamond Bar, California, about a twenty-five-minute drive from Angel Stadium. As a boy, he watched Nomo-mania and he fell in love with baseball. He eventually found his way back to Japan and a job working as an interpreter for the English-speaking players on the Hokkaido Nippon-Ham Fighters, Ohtani's team. Mizuhara's connection to Ohtani and to Southern California made him a natural choice as Ohtani's interpreter. He would become a vital part of the Ohtani story because his job was much more than helping Ohtani conduct interviews. As the Angels tried to figure out how to use Ohtani's unique talent in the majors, Mizuhara was the one who needed to accurately relay to coaches, trainers, and club officials how Ohtani was feeling. Mizuhara would be the one to help Ohtani understand the scouting reports, and to help Ohtani and the catchers come up with a game plan on the mound. At times Mizuhara would be the one to play catch with Ohtani, because his routine left him to work out at a time when all of the other pitchers were doing something else. Mizuhara even worked as Ohtani's catcher sometimes during offseason bullpen sessions. Mizuhara became an always-visible fixture around Spring Training, following Ohtani around the field and toting a backpack full of whatever Ohtani might need for the day.

Although Ohtani was the only player with an interpreter and a corps of media following him around all day, he nonetheless tried his best to blend in with his new teammates. Ohtani played golf with a few of his teammates and he shot some basketballs. He also went to see the NHL's Phoenix Coyotes with fellow starting pitcher Andrew Heaney. Early on Ohtani assimilated through video games, specifically playing Clash Royale, a game in which players assemble troops to attack a virtual tower. Relief pitcher Blake Parker, an avid player, developed a rivalry with Ohtani, complete with bilingual trash talking. "You always learn the bad stuff first," said Parker, referring to the fact that he and Ohtani had each learned a few choice phrases in the other's language. "He just wants to be one of the guys," Parker said. "That's how I feel. He wants to fit in. He wants to have fun. He wants to stay loose. He's obviously a competitor on the field, but he likes to joke around and have fun." Members of the Japanese media corps who had covered Ohtani with the Fighters suggested that he seemed to be more relaxed, and more playful, in his new environment than he had been in Japan. "I don't know how everyone else feels, but I feel I am fitting in well," Ohtani said early in camp. "I have no problems off the field. Everything is fine."

The most visible one-of-the-guys moment for Ohtani came during an early exhibition game, when he stepped to the plate as the ball-park public address system blared a bouncy Japanese pop song that would be more fitting for a thirteen-year-old girl than a Major League baseball player. "Fashion Monster," by Kyary Pamyu Pamyu, was selected by Ohtani's teammates as a way to poke fun at him for the skinny jeans he often wore to the ballpark. Angels players exploded in laughter in the dugout and Ohtani smiled as he heard the tune, showing the expression he often flashed around the clubhouse.

"He's always smiling," pitcher Garrett Richards said. "He always looks like he's in a happy mood." Outfielder Kole Calhoun figured that Ohtani's good mood wasn't simply because of his new friends and video game rivals. "If I was him, I'd be happy, too. He can throw 100 and hit a ball 500 feet," Calhoun said.

Ohtani impressed his teammates with his on-field exploits during busy workdays, which saw him bounce from one field to the next at the Angels' Spring Training complex. He typically worked out with the pitchers first, either throwing or working on fielding drills, and then he would take batting practice with the position players. There was no blueprint for how Ohtani's daily routine would look. "It's uncharted waters, really," Angels hitting coach Eric Hinske said. "The last guy to do it was Babe Ruth, right?" In the early days of camp, it was clear that the Angels preferred for Ohtani to focus on pitching first, and squeeze batting practice in where he could. The Angels didn't have Ohtani take any swings on the days that he was doing his most intense pitching workouts, like throwing a bullpen session or facing hitters in live batting practice. Pitching had been the Angels' weakness over the previous few years, so they wanted to focus on Ohtani's development on the mound. Besides, many scouts who had seen Ohtani in recent years in Japan figured that was his better role.

"He's going to get the most looks as a pitcher," Manager Mike Scioscia said. "If he can pitch to his capabilities, that will influence your team more than what he would do hitting, but he's going to be important on the offensive end also."

His initial work on the mound revealed an issue, though. The baseballs used in Japan and in the major leagues are not the same. The Japanese ball is slightly smaller—the difference in circumference is less than a centimeter—and significantly different to the touch. Balls used in Japan and South Korea are produced by Mizuno and have a tacky surface, which allows pitchers to have a solid grip on the ball. Major League Baseball uses balls manufactured by Rawlings that have a smoother, slicker surface, requiring additional substances to be applied for pitchers to get a proper grip. The rosin bag, which sits on the back of the mound at every game, has been deemed by many pitchers to be insufficient for the job, so they have taken to applying various concoctions of sunscreen, sweat, pine tar, or other products so they can properly spin and control the baseball. The applications would become a focus of Major League Baseball by 2021, when the sport began to crack down on the use of such substances, checking pitchers for any sticky goop they may have brought to the mound hidden on their caps, gloves, or belts. But back in the spring of 2018, the issue of gripping the baseball was a new one for Ohtani.

The first time he pitched to hitters in Spring Training, his breaking balls were erratic, which was a combination of the slick baseballs and the dry air of the Arizona desert. "He's going to experience that all of Spring Training because of the weather here," veteran catcher Martín Maldonado said. "You see a lot of guys with really good command of the curveball and they can't command it here. The same with sinker-ballers because the weather here is so dry. It doesn't break the way it should break during the season." When Ohtani spoke in the media tent that day, he introduced reporters to what would become a familiar theme that spring. Essentially, he said not to worry about what went wrong, because he would figure it out. "There were good parts and bad parts," Ohtani said, "but I was happy to get through 30 pitches. There are adjustments I'll need to make the next time I'm on the mound."

The adjustments would soon come into focus not only for the dozens of journalists who lined the fence of an Angels practice field, but also for the world to see. On February 24, Ohtani pitched in a Cactus League game for the first time, facing the Milwaukee Brewers. The game, like almost all Angels Spring Training games, was televised back to Southern California, but this one was also shown in Japan. It was certainly one of the most eagerly anticipated exhibition games in Angels history, and accordingly it drew a crowd of 6,019, an exceptional figure for the Angels that early in the spring.

Spectators saw Ohtani face just seven hitters in a Brewers lineup that was largely devoid of established big leaguers. He recorded four outs, two of them strikeouts. One of the strikeouts came at the expense of outfielder Brett Phillips, who flailed at Ohtani's splitter. "His splitter is really good," Phillips said. "He definitely has a chance to be really good. I got to see it all." Ohtani's fastball popped at 97 mph. The Brewers scored two runs, an unearned run in the first and a homer by journeyman outfielder Keon Broxton in the second. "Fastball down the middle . . . big league hitters are going to take advantage of that," Maldonado said. "That won't be the last homer that he's going to give up." Although it was a decidedly mediocre performance, nothing that happens this early in the spring sends up any red flags. "I like what I saw," Maldonado added. "I think he's going to progress in his next start." Scioscia, a baseball lifer who had seen plenty of rough spring starts, was encouraged. "I think that he did enough to where we certainly learned some things," Scioscia said. "He and Martín worked some things out. I think it'll be a step forward for him next time. He threw all his pitches. Some were what we expect him to be, and some he just lost his release point on. It's a step forward for sure." Ohtani seemed just as unconcerned as Maldonado and Scioscia when he addressed a packed media tent after finishing his outing. "Besides the results, I had a lot of fun," Ohtani said. "I think it went well. . . . Every year it's hard to get into a rhythm at this point. It felt just like any other year. I think I'll be able to adjust."

His next outing was in a B Game, also against the Brewers. In Spring Training B Games teams have more control over the environment than they would in a normal Cactus League game with paying customers and a television audience. Pitchers can work without worrying about a long inning because the teams simply agree to end an inning if the pitcher has thrown too many pitches, regardless of how many outs he's recorded. The Angels ended Ohtani's second inning at 20 pitches. Overall he made it through 52 pitches to 12 batters, striking out eight of them.

Ohtani's next start was an exhibition against the Tijuana Toros of the Mexican League, and he was lit up for six runs by a group of players who were nowhere near Major League quality. "I felt like I made a lot of good pitches and quite a few bad ones," Ohtani said. "The good thing I got out of this outing was pitching with runners on base, out of the stretch."

At that point, Ohtani had allowed 10 runs in parts of 6 innings. His 16 strikeouts were encouraging, though. And Ohtani was about to leave the sheltered world of back-field games for another outing against a Major League team in a regulation Cactus League game. On March 16, Ohtani took the mound against the Colorado Rockies before a sellout crowd of 9,616 at Tempe Diablo Stadium. He gave up 7 runs and recorded only 4 outs in a contest for which he'd been scheduled to pitch into the fifth inning. After a clean first, Ohtani allowed seven straight hitters to reach base in the second inning, including home runs by All-Star third baseman Nolan Arenado and veteran Ian Desmond.

Questions about Ohtani's readiness as a big league pitcher were certainly reaching their crescendo after the Rockies game. Ohtani was asked flat-out if he felt prepared for the major leagues and he answered vaguely. "I don't think about it much right now," Ohtani said. "I am trying to worry about what I can do each day, each game. What will happen as a result of that, that's up to the manager and the front office to decide." Scioscia again chose to look at the positive, including a fastball that reached 98 mph. "You saw some electric stuff that he threw, and then you saw some inconsistency," Scioscia said. "You saw the stuff that's there. His stuff is picking up, which is a good sign. Harnessing it is what we're going to have to work on."

Ohtani was struggling just as much at the plate.

Power was the most notable part of Ohtani's offensive game early in Spring Training, with coaches and other players awed by the towering blasts he hit in batting practice. The Angels typically move from their practice fields to the field inside Tempe Diablo Stadium before their first exhibition game. On the first day of workouts in the stadium, Ohtani belted a drive over the batter's eye in center field, which is 420 feet from home plate and 30 feet high. Only the best power hitters can clear it.

Aside from the spectacle of long drives in batting practice, though, Ohtani looked overmatched when facing big league pitchers. He singled and walked twice in his first Cactus League game, which was certainly encouraging, but then Ohtani went into a rut that saw him collect just 2 hits in his first 20 at-bats. The lefthanded slugger seemed to have particular trouble against lefthanded pitchers and breaking balls. In a simulated game against lefty teammate Tyler Skaggs, Ohtani flailed at a curveball as his helmet popped off his head. Ohtani struggled through one stretch of 14 straight hitless at-bats in Cactus League games, sinking into a 3-for-28 hole.

Ohtani was only halfway through the spring when a well-respected national baseball writer blasted him, writing that scouts didn't believe he was ready for the majors. "The verdict is in on Shohei Ohtani's bat and it's not good," blared the headline atop the story by Jeff Passan of *Yahoo! Sports*. Passan reported that eight scouts had shared serious reservations about Ohtani based on what they'd seen so far in Arizona. The crux of the issue, they said, was that Ohtani had not seen the quality of pitching in Japan that he was seeing in the majors, especially the breaking pitches. "He's basically like a high school hitter because he's never seen a good curveball," one scout told Passan. "He's seen fastballs and changeups. And you're asking a high school hitter to jump to the major leagues?" Said another scout: "You don't learn on the job in the major leagues. You can't."

Passan's story was published on March 9, and Ohtani would continue to struggle at the plate over the next few days. A week later

Ohtani had that nightmarish start when the Colorado Rockies knocked him out in the second inning by scoring 7 runs against him.

By that point it seemed perfectly reasonable—albeit disappointing—for the Angels to determine that Ohtani really wasn't ready for the majors. By signing as a twenty-three-year-old and falling under the rules governing international "amateurs," Ohtani not only saved the Angels some money, but he afforded them some flexibility. In that first Spring Training he was still on a minor-league deal, so the Angels were not obligated to put him in the majors. The Angels also could have reaped some long-term benefit by starting Ohtani in the minor leagues. A player can become a free agent in the first winter after he reaches six years of major league service time. If Ohtani played as little as two weeks in the minors, he would not be able to accrue a full year of service time in 2018, and his potential free agency would be pushed back a year. The most public example of this had occurred a few years earlier, when the Chicago Cubs had kept top prospect Kris Bryant in the minors for the first two weeks of the season. Most suspected it was nothing more than a ploy to manipulate his service time. (Bryant's agent filed a grievance that wasn't resolved until 2020, when an arbitrator determined the Cubs were within their rights to send down Bryant.) While the Cubs were roundly criticized for starting Bryant in the minors when many thought he was ready, no one would have accused the Angels of the same thing because of how poorly Ohtani had performed in the spring. The Japanese reporters began asking their American counterparts what it was like in Salt Lake City, home of the Angels' Triple-A team.

The Angels weren't about to send Ohtani to Salt Lake City, though. Despite all the scouts, reporters, and fans who didn't think Ohtani was ready for the big leagues, the Angels believed there was a mountain of evidence that he was. Most notably there were the five years Ohtani had played in Japan. He was not just some twenty-three-year-old who had been at Double-A. Ohtani had been a star in the second-best league in the world.

General Manager Billy Eppler had watched Ohtani numerous times in Japan when he was an executive with the New York Yankees. He described the "wow factor" he felt when watching Ohtani perform in those games, and he was not about to dismiss that because of a few weeks in Spring Training, where the air is thin and dry and the games don't count. "The track record gives us the confidence to move forward with him as a two-way player," Eppler said on March 17, dousing talk about Ohtani starting in the minor leagues. Beyond the confidence that came from what Ohtani had done in Japan, Eppler said there were tangible factors from his Arizona performance that told the Angels he'd be fine.

"We look at walk rate and strike-throwing and the ability to get hitters to swing and miss," Eppler said. "As we look at those things, those are the foundation of our evaluative methodologies, and those things are in place." As for Ohtani's performance at the plate, Eppler also saw good signs within what was, at that moment, a 2-for-20 stat line. "I know he doesn't have the results he would want to have or people outside would want to see, like batting average," Eppler said. "There have been some at-bats that have been more difficult for him and he's faced some pretty good pitchers. He's struck the ball hard. He doesn't chase pitches outside the strike zone. He does some things we value. I would say he's been better than his slash line."

The Angels also suspected Ohtani would improve with the increased adrenaline of the regular season. Spring Training games don't count, and everyone knows it. Aside from the fact that the ballparks are often half-empty, the players treat the games as glorified workouts. Often, the players who aren't scheduled to play in a particular game will practice in the morning and be on a golf course by the time the game has started in the afternoon. It's not unusual for a player to walk into the clubhouse in the morning with no idea what team he is facing that day. All of this is not to say that players don't work hard during Spring Training; it's just that they are concerned with more than their batting average or earned-run average.

So it was against that backdrop that the Angels were willing to give Ohtani the benefit of the doubt.

"I'll tell you something, once the lights come on, it's a different ballgame," veteran catcher Rene Rivera said after working with Ohtani in that exhibition game against the Tijuana Toros in a virtually empty ballpark. "It's tough to pitch here. There are no fans. . . . The adrenaline is not there. Once the lights come on and they say 'Play ball,' you'll see something different. More velocity, sharper pitches. It's going to be Ohtani. You have to give it time."

CHAPTER 6

"Out of the Gate Better Than Anyone Was Expecting"

By the time Shohei Ohtani had completed his first ten games in the major leagues, it was easy to forget what had happened in Spring Training. He had won both of his starts as a pitcher, including one in which he took a perfect game into the seventh inning. He had hit 3 homers, including one against a two-time Cy Young Award winner. One sports book had quickly installed Ohtani as the favorite for the American League MVP award. All of those skeptics who watched him in Spring Training and declared that he wasn't ready for the big leagues were quieted.

While Ohtani didn't say much about the dramatic turnaround, or how it felt to have proven something to the naysayers, at least one of his teammates took pleasure in seeing Ohtani respond to the critics with his play. "There are a lot of unwanted and unnecessary negative comments about his game," veteran second baseman Ian Kinsler said. "He didn't have a chance to prove himself [in Spring Training]. It's a lot of fun to see something like that from a guy who has a huge spotlight on him and obviously doesn't let it bother him. He's played extremely well the first week of the season. It's real exciting to see."

Even before Ohtani got off to such a sensational start, Angels general manager Billy Eppler explained that it wasn't that difficult of a decision to put their faith in Ohtani. Hours before the Angels played their first game of the season, Eppler stood in the visitors dugout at the Oakland Coliseum and said he put much more stock in Ohtani's five years in Japan than six weeks in Arizona. "Our evaluations, historical evaluations plus the track record in a league which we deem as close to the major leagues as you can get, point us in the direction of saying 'Give this guy the opportunity to let his ability and his tools show,'" Eppler said. "So that's what we're going to do."

The more difficult decision, as it turned out, was not whether to give Ohtani a chance in the major leagues, but how much to use him. Any top-level starting pitcher simply works every fifth day. Any top offensive player is in the lineup just about every day, allowing for a day off here and there. But there was no major league blueprint for how much to use someone to fill both roles. The Angels started out by roughly following the way Ohtani was used in Japan, but it would become a subject of debate that continued throughout the first years of his career—from concerns about resting him too much in his rookie year all the way to his breakout 2021 season, when at one point the Angels were criticized for using him too much.

Back in April 2018, though, Ohtani himself was the first to suggest that the Angels may have been too conservative. The Angels used Ohtani in just seven of the first thirteen games, five times as a DH and twice as a pitcher. "It's the beginning of the season so I think they are being pretty careful with me right now," Ohtani said. "Once the season gets tougher and the schedule gets tougher throughout the summer, hopefully I can make them want to play me more. I would like to play more. If not, that's what it is. I have to follow what they have to say."

Before the Angels could consider really pushing Ohtani, various issues would require the team to maintain the conservative schedule, or even reduce it. Ohtani came out of an April start because of a blister on his finger. He missed another start when he hurt his ankle after stepping awkwardly on first base trying to beat out a groundball. In late May, the Angels skipped another scheduled start at Yankee Stadium—earning jeers from the New York tabloids—because they wanted to ease his workload. Although careful not to signal that there was anything significantly wrong with Ohtani's arm, they were certainly mindful that Ohtani already had a grade 1 strain of his ulnar collateral ligament, a point that had been made in the screaming headlines back in December.

Just a couple weeks after that skipped assignment in New York, the feel-good story of Ohtani would come to a crashing halt because of that UCL.

* * *

In between the panic over his ugly Spring Training and the disappointment of a potentially career-altering injury in June, though, Shohei Ohtani spent ten weeks showing the baseball world something that no one had seen in nearly a century. Not since Babe Ruth.

Ohtani was in the Angels lineup as their designated hitter for the March 27 Opening Day game against the Oakland A's, batting eighth. He stroked a single into right field on the first pitch he saw from righthander Kendall Graveman. "That's probably an at-bat I'm not going to forget for the rest of my life," Ohtani said. Three days later, on a Sunday afternoon, Ohtani took the mound to start the final game of the four-game series. He became the first player to start as a pitcher and a non-pitcher within the first ten games of a season since Joe Bush of the Boston Red Sox and Clarence Mitchell of Brooklyn Dodgers in 1920. Ohtani picked up a victory, tossing 6 innings and allowing 3 runs, all on one swing from All-Star third baseman Matt Chapman. At one point Ohtani retired 14 of 15 hitters. His splitter, which he hadn't been able to use effectively in Arizona, was devastating. "For all pitchers," Manager Mike Scioscia said, "they like to get out of Arizona. No doubt about that."

Ohtani's fastball reached 99.6 mph.

"I thought he had really good stuff, he showed really good command today and was able to move the ball in and out, up and down and we had a hard time getting consistent contact off him," Chapman said.

Ohtani stood in an interview room in front of a pack of reporters and described his first big league start: "Obviously I'm very happy. I'm satisfied with my outing. I'm more happy the team got the victory."

The Angels then headed home for their first series of the year at Angel Stadium, and Ohtani began to show that his bat was also ready for the big leagues. Less than a month after an anonymous scout had been quoted comparing Ohtani to a high school hitter, the Angels rookie shredded that narrative. Ohtani blasted his first homer against Cleveland Indians righthander Josh Tomlin. After the three-run bomb cleared the right field fence in the first inning, Ohtani returned to the Angels dugout and was greeted with . . . nothing. Per big league tradition, Ohtani's teammates responded to his first homer with the silent treatment. Ohtani got the joke, smiled, and began giving high fives to imaginary teammates as he walked through the dugout. The rest of the Angels soon relented and began to celebrate with him. The next night Ohtani homered again, this time against righthander Corey Kluber, who was coming off his second American League Cy Young Award season. Ohtani homered yet again in the next game on Friday night.

That Sunday, Ohtani returned to the mound, pitching at home for the first time. Ohtani-mania had built quickly. A sellout crowd of 44,742 filled Angel Stadium to see Ohtani pitch, and he did not disappoint. Facing the same team he'd seen a week earlier in Oakland, Ohtani took a perfect game into the seventh inning before shortstop Marcus Semien punched a clean single into left field. The crowd groaned but then roared for Ohtani in recognition of the performance. A few minutes later, after Ohtani allowed another man to reach base, the crowd came to life again when he struck out Oakland first baseman Matt Olson to end the inning, stranding the two runners. Ohtani pumped his fist as he walked from the mound, the most emotion he'd shown since first putting on an Angels uniform.

Ohtani had struck out 12, walked 1, and given up 1 hit in 7 scoreless innings, making an impression in both dugouts and, honestly, all over the baseball world. This was the exclamation point on a week in which Ohtani officially buried the idea that he wasn't ready for the majors.

Ohtani was named American League Player of the Week after his first week. He was also named American League Rookie of the Month for April. He hit .341 with 4 homers. On the mound—not as sharp after his first two starts, in part because of a blister issue—he was 2–1 with a 4.43 ERA.

That finger blister? It was one of the world's most watched skin conditions, with daily articles in the Japanese media.

●　●　●

Grace McNamee was accustomed to being peppered by questions about blisters. Japanese reporters had been obsessed with every bit of minutia surrounding Los Angeles Dodgers righthander Hideo Nomo twenty-three years earlier, when McNamee started working in baseball. She was fresh out of college when the Dodgers hired her to help handle the Japanese media covering Nomo, who had signed before the 1995 season.

The Dodgers learned about Nomo's media entourage on his first day of Spring Training in Vero Beach, Florida. About fifty journalists were awaiting his arrival. Seeing this, Nomo and his interpreter drove slowly in a loop as the reporters followed them on foot. "They drove around in circles, and the media ran after them until they finally just tuckered out," recalled former Dodgers media relations director Derrick Hall. "We watched this go on for about thirty minutes and thought, 'Oh my goodness, the following this guy has.'"

Nomo was something of a pioneer. No Japanese player had been in the majors since pitcher Masanori Murakami played with the San Francisco Giants in the 1960s, which was such a different era for the media that it may as well have been the 1860s. When Nomo arrived there was no playbook for a team on how to handle a crush of reporters who came from Japan to cover one player. In the years to come, a similar media contingent would follow all of the Japanese stars, from Ichiro Suzuki to Hideki Matsui to Yu Darvish to Shohei Ohtani. It all began with Nomo. "We kind of created a lot of the guidelines for the other teams," McNamee said.

McNamee had left the Dodgers after the 1998 season, putting her baseball career aside to work in marketing for a film company and to raise a family. Two decades later, she found herself back on a baseball field. McNamee's experience with Nomo, and the fact that she already lived nearby in Orange County, made her a natural choice to help the Angels navigate the new world they entered the day Ohtani donned an Angels jersey. Aside from the fact that the reporters were requesting credentials by email instead of by fax, little had changed from the days of Nomo to the days of Ohtani, McNamee said.

In 2018, the Angels issued eighty credentials to Japanese reporters, including television crews, for Ohtani's first Spring Training. There were around three hundred media members at his first formal press conference, held at a hotel adjacent to the ballpark. During the regular season, there were typically around fifty members of the Japanese media, more on the days that he pitched. Although the travel restrictions from the pandemic and the Olympics in Japan in 2021 shrunk the numbers somewhat, by the end of 2021 there were again about fifty members of the Japanese media covering Ohtani on a daily basis.

While there were many who came and went throughout the season, three beat writers chronicled Ohtani nearly every day through his first four seasons in the majors. Yuichi Matsushita and Tomohiko Yasuoka represent Japan's two biggest wire services, *Kyodo News* and *Jiji Press*. Nobuhiro Saito works for *Nikkan Sports News*, which is one of the three major national sports newspapers in Japan. The routine is grueling for the three Japanese beat writers, who filed multiple stories from just about every game. (Their American counterparts typically cover 60 to 75 percent of the games, with backup writers filling in on the rest.) Japan's other major daily sports newspapers—*Sports Nippon* and *Sankei Sports*—also had reporters covering Ohtani regularly, although they were not present at every Angels game.

The job is challenging. Write about one player, a player often unavailable for interviews. When Ohtani first arrived in 2018, he spoke to the media a few times a week. That spring, he would first conduct interviews with the United States media, accompanied by interpreter Ippei Mizuhara, and then with the Japanese media. Usually the sessions took place in the media tent constructed in a parking lot next to Tempe Diablo Stadium. During the season, Ohtani would speak in an interview room at Angel Stadium or perhaps in the hallway outside the clubhouse when the Angels were on the road. He would almost always be standing in front of a background including the logo of whatever Japanese company was the current sponsor. Ohtani rarely spoke in front of his locker, the way other players do, because the Angels were trying to keep the media horde from crowding in the clubhouse. In subsequent seasons, though, the interviews became less frequent. Initially the decrease was because Ohtani was rehabbing injuries. Later, the pandemic limited all interviews to Zoom sessions.

"It's pretty difficult without much opportunity to talk to him," Yasuoka said after the 2021 season. "We have to talk to coaches and opponents." Even when Ohtani would speak, it would only be to groups of reporters. Just about all other players make themselves available for one-on-one interviews, at least with the beat writers who follow the team all the time. Ohtani kept a strict routine in which he would only talk in group interviews. "We all have the same quotes," Matsushita said. "That's the most frustrating part for me."

Los Angeles Times columnist Dylan Hernandez, who speaks Japanese because his mother is Japanese, has been chronicling Ohtani on both sides of the globe. He said Ohtani has never done many interviews, not even in Japan. "The Fighters did everything to protect him, and that included media stuff," Hernandez said. "My understanding is when he was in Japan, his media obligations were less than anybody who had ever come before."

When he did speak, Ohtani also developed a reputation for spitting out bland, businesslike comments to the media in their group settings. At one point the reporters called him "Robot" because of the emotionless interviews. According to his teammates and those who are around him in more casual moments, this is not his true personality. McNamee said Ohtani has an "infectious" laugh and smile, and he is "an all-around great guy." Matsushita got a small taste of the real Ohtani when he covered him with the Fighters. "If you have a chance to interview him one-on-one, he is a very interesting person," Matsushita said. Ohtani certainly could share more of his personality, but there is no indication that he has any desire to do so. "He's just kind of closed off," Hernandez said. "I shouldn't say he doesn't care how people view him, because I don't think that's true, but I think he's happy with this image that's out there. People don't know much about him. *Judge me on my performance.*"

Further complicating the reporters' jobs, the Angels at times have shielded Ohtani from the cameras. When Ohtani was throwing his first bullpen session at Angel Stadium in 2018, reporters climbed the faux rocks in center field to get pictures and video, but the Angels shooed them away. Later that season, when Ohtani was rehabbing from his elbow injury, he pitched a simulated game at Tempe Diablo Stadium on an August off-day before a series against the Arizona Diamondbacks. Japanese reporters were initially invited, but were later told it would be closed to the media. They watched from the parking lot of the hotel that sits next to the ballpark.

While the relationship between the Japanese media and the Angels is strained at times, mostly there seems to be an understanding that each does its best to accommodate the other side. "We have to remember there's an entire country following his every move," former Angels vice president in charge of communications Tim Mead said in 2018. "We have a responsibility to help facilitate that, and we recognize that—and Shohei recognizes that." Although there are problems, most notably dealing with more reporters than can fit comfortably in the clubhouse or press box, Mead said the Angels remembered the significance of what they were seeing. "This is going to be challenging, but it's also going to be exciting," he said. "We're looking at it as we're just going to have a larger media contingent. Our following has just grown."

McNamee said one of the ways she tries to defuse the media crush surrounding Ohtani is to encourage reporters to write stories about other Angels players. "Even though they're here just to focus on that one player, I try to make it so that I can introduce the team and other players to audiences in Japan," McNamee said.

The Japanese reporters also talk to other players and coaches about Ohtani. McNamee facilitates interviews with Angels hitting coaches or pitching coaches or even bullpen catchers. In Spring Training, an unknown minor leaguer might find himself surrounded by Japanese reporters if he had just hit against Ohtani on a practice field.

The thirst for all manner of detail about Ohtani would cause reporters to meticulously count the number of home runs he hit in batting practice or the number of throws he made while playing catch in the outfield. When Ohtani would do interviews, the American writers would often ask more general questions about his performance, but the Japanese writers would drill down on why Ohtani had thrown 10 split-finger fastballs one game after throwing 15 in the previous games, or why he was using a different bat.

"They're more about the details of the game," Hernandez said of the Japanese media. "They're tracking every pitch. I'm sure there are some American reporters that watch the game at that level of detail, but for the most part, we write about the person."

When the Japanese reporters can't question Ohtani, they often resort to interviewing American reporters to learn their assessment of Ohtani or their predictions for how many homers he will hit, how many games he will win, or what awards he will receive.

Beyond the writers, there are a handful of Japanese television networks that have cameras constantly trained on Ohtani. NHK, which is Japan's government-owned television network, has a crew at every single Angels game, there to record Ohtani whenever he steps on the field. NHK also broadcasts games back to Japan, focusing on the teams with Japanese players. Although they show games featuring pitchers Yu Darvish and Yusei Kikuchi, Ohtani is the main draw. It helps that he's a two-way player, so he plays far more often than the other Japanese pitchers.

The interest in Ohtani boomed when he first appeared in the big leagues in 2018. After a dip during his incomplete seasons in 2019 and 2020, the attention was back in full force for his magical fourth season.

"Ohtani is special," Matsushita said in 2021. "He is special right now. He is the only one. The talk shows in Japan are not talking about politics, but Ohtani."

* * *

In 2018, Japanese reporters and fans no doubt had circled the Angels' early May series against the Mariners in Seattle on their calendars. It was supposed to be the first matchup between Ohtani and Ichiro Suzuki, who at that point was the most accomplished Japanese player ever to play in the majors. Ichiro had more than 3,000 MLB hits to go with 1,278 for the Orix Blue Wave in Japan. Ichiro had been one of Ohtani's heroes when he was growing up in Japan. Although the two had met for occasional dinners, arranged by a mutual acquaintance, this was to be the first time they had played against each other. That dream was spoiled a few days before the Angels arrived in Seattle, though. Ichiro, who was forty-four at the time, was removed from the Mariners active roster because they had other, more productive players they wanted to play. Ichiro would spend the rest of the season in a non-playing role with Seattle. (He would return for two more games, when the Mariners opened the 2019 season in Japan, and then officially retire.) Ohtani nonetheless had the chance to chat with Ichiro in the outfield before the first game of the series.

Once the game began, Ichiro saw Ohtani collect a single and a double, although the Mariners fans took much more pleasure out of the time Ohtani struck out. Ohtani had spurned the Mariners back in December, and the fans let Ohtani know they remembered. "I'm not really used to being booed," Ohtani said. "It was kind of weird, awkward. In the first at-bat I was trying to do too much maybe." A couple days later Ohtani had the chance to hurt the Mariners from the mound, when he gave up just 2 runs in 6 innings in an Angels victory. The ballpark had an electric atmosphere that day because Ohtani was sharing the mound with Mariners ace Félix Hernández. Ohtani came out on top, which not only made a statement about him as a pitcher, but also showed he was fully healthy after his previous start had been scratched because he tweaked his ankle running the bases. Coincidentally, this watershed game fell on May 6, 2018, exactly a hundred years from the date when Babe Ruth officially became a two-way player, starting his first regular season game at a position other than pitcher.

Ohtani's status as something of a modern Babe Ruth reached a new peak a week later. In a May 13 start against the Minnesota Twins, Ohtani gave up 1 run in 6⅓ innings, striking out 11. It came just a couple days after Ohtani had opened the series with a double and a homer, prompting Twins first baseman Logan Morrison to make the most dramatic evaluation of Ohtani to date.

"He was really good," Morrison said. "He's only twenty-three years old and is going to get better. I think he's doing something that nobody probably has ever done and it might be a long time before you see it again. There's another guy in that clubhouse who is a really good player, but to me, with what he does on the mound and with the bat, he's probably the best player in the world."

Morrison's suggestion that Ohtani had already surpassed teammate Mike Trout, at that point a two-time MVP, rocked social media and served to only elevate the Ohtani hype.

A few weeks earlier, San Francisco Giants pitcher Madison Bumgarner had spoken with admiration about what Ohtani had accomplished. Bumgarner is generally regarded as the best hitting pitcher in the majors, so he had a special perspective on what Ohtani had achieved as a two-way player.

"I didn't think it would work," Bumgarner said. "And I don't know if it will still work. Nobody knows. We just have to see how it goes for an extended amount of time. But he's definitely gotten out of the gate better than anybody was expecting, especially after [Spring Training]."

Much of Ohtani's improvement after Spring Training was due precisely to what the Angels had been telling everyone in Arizona. Ohtani had to get used to the baseballs and the mound, both of which are slightly different in the majors than Japan. He had to get out of the dry, thin air of Arizona to get his pitches to work better. He needed the adrenaline of regular season games in ballparks full of fans.

One significant change, with his hitting, was not predictable. It demonstrated Ohtani's exceptional ability to adjust, which is one of the major reasons that he would continue to pull himself up from his low points to have his 2021 breakthrough.

Ohtani came from Japan with a leg kick in his swing. Throughout Spring Training, Ohtani's timing seemed to be off as he struggled to handle big league pitching. The Angels had left Arizona to play their traditional final three exhibitions against the crosstown Los Angeles Dodgers before Opening Day. One afternoon at Dodger Stadium, Angels hitting coach Eric Hinske suggested to Ohtani that he had enough power without the leg kick, so he should try to swing without it. Ohtani did it, and immediately began crushing balls deep into the seats at Dodger Stadium. Ohtani told Hinske: "I'm in." The leg kick was gone, just like that.

Ohtani was seemingly able to incorporate a significant change to his swing at the flip of a switch, which further awed teammates who are in a constant struggle to maintain the right mechanics. "Guys will move their hands a quarter inch or a half an inch and feel completely uncomfortable," veteran second baseman Ian Kinsler said. "It's been awesome to see." Kinsler said it was even more incredible because Ohtani takes time away from hitting so he can work on pitching. Most hitters, Kinsler said, need to take batting practice just about every day to be effective at the plate. At that time, Ohtani was taking time away from the cage every week to be a pitcher.

Ohtani's new swing, minus the leg kick, was just as effective as Hinske had suggested it would be. The extra momentum from the leg kick was not necessary, Hinske said, because Ohtani was blessed with exceptional power, which comes from a combination of strength and flexibility. Bat speed is generated by the torque as the body rotates.

"Everybody's hips move differently, some are looser," Hinske said. "He's able to hit into his front side really well, and snap into that straight front side and it creates a lot of torque."

If a hitter's hands stay back, while his hips begin to rotate forward, it creates more force when the body pulls the hands through the zone. Furthermore, some players are able to strike the ball in such a way as to impart more backspin, which adds more lift to make the ball go ever farther.

"When it all syncs up mechanically, he hits the ball farther than I think we've ever seen, especially in batting practice," Hinske said. "It's off the charts. It's what scouts call 'light tower power.'"

When Ohtani pounded a baseball over the batter's eye at Tempe Diablo Stadium his teammates laughed and shook their heads in amazement. The show would continue into the season. Some of the homers he hit in games were impressive, but the balls he hit in batting practice were sometimes jaw-dropping.

Early in the season, at the Texas Rangers' Globe Life Park in Arlington, Ohtani belted a ball off a roof above a row of offices over a hill beyond the center field fence. Angels assistant hitting coach Paul Sorrento said he'd never seen anyone but Mike Trout hit a ball there. Asked how Ohtani generates such power, Sorrento simply pointed a finger at the sky, suggesting it was God-given ability.

A few weeks later, the Angels were at Coors Field in Denver. Because of the high altitude and thin air, it's the most hitter-friendly venue in the major leagues. Ohtani did not start either of the two games there because it's a National League park, so the Angels couldn't use the designated hitter. He did, however, take batting practice. He blasted one ball after another into the far reaches of the park in right field. One shot in particular had the locals in awe. He hit a ball to the top of a row of seats in the third deck, in right center. It was so far that Ryan Spilborghs, a former player working on the Rockies TV broadcast, was dispatched up to the area where the ball hit during the next day's game. "Everybody was really impressed with that," Angels shortstop Andrelton Simmons said. "We were hoping he'd hit it out of the stadium, but that will suffice."

Less than two weeks later, Ohtani's batting practice exploits would reach a new milestone back at Angel Stadium. The fence in straight-away right field is 348 feet from home plate, and 18 feet tall. Beyond it are 41 rows of seats. Above that is a 9,500-square-foot, state-of-the-art video board that was installed in the winter before the 2018 season. It was unthinkable that a baseball would ever hit it, until Ohtani hit a drive in batting practice on May 18 that struck the scoreboard, about 20 feet above the bottom of the screen. It took the Angels a day to come up with a distance estimate for the curious media. They said it traveled 513 feet.

* * *

Ohtani's tape-measure homers and electric performances on the mound throughout April and May of his rookie season put to rest the questions about his talent or his ability to succeed at the big league level. The narrative instead shifted to the way the Angels were using him.

There is more than a century's worth of trial and error to help teams and players learn how to best condition themselves to get through the rigors of a season as a pitcher or a hitter. But not both.

When the Angels signed Ohtani, they said they had a plan, but the details of that plan emerged gradually throughout Spring Training and into the season. It was a plan they had devised with the input of Ohtani and the management and trainers who had worked with him in Japan, along with the Angels performance staff.

The Angels had also been warned by Fighters manager Hideki Kuriyama that Ohtani would never tell them he needed a break, so it would be up to them to slow him down. Once the season began, it was clear that the main guidelines they'd use for Ohtani would be that he wouldn't pitch on less than six days' rest, and he wouldn't hit the day before or the day after he pitched. The Angels also would not have Ohtani pitch and hit on the same day, which he had done occasionally in Japan. Aside from the workload that would place on Ohtani, it would create a strategic issue. The Angels would forfeit the use of the DH if Ohtani began the game as a pitcher and hitter, which meant that any relievers who followed Ohtani to the mound would also need to go in the batting order.

In late May, the Angels further put the brakes on Ohtani. Four days before Ohtani was expected to pitch against the New York Yankees in the Bronx, the Angels announced that he would skip that start because of "workload management." This was no routine start that he was missing, though. Ohtani had been scheduled to pitch against Masahiro Tanaka, the first time he'd share the mound with one of Japan's other stars. It was a highly anticipated event for the dozens of media members following each player and for millions of baseball fans back in Japan. Although they would not pitch against each other, it did mean that Ohtani would hit against Tanaka. "I'm not so disappointed because I have a pretty good chance of facing him as a hitter, so either way I'll get to face him," Ohtani said. "Down the road, I'll probably have a chance to face him as a pitcher also, so I just need to think about my next game and not think too far ahead." Ohtani ended up going hitless in 9 at-bats against the Yankees, including 2 strikeouts and a walk in three matchups against Tanaka.

The decision to have Ohtani skip his start against the Yankees did not sit well with fans in Japan or Yankees fans in New York, many of whom suspected that the Angels were trying to shield Ohtani from pitching against what was, at the time, the most productive lineup in the majors. *The New York Daily News*—the same paper that had called Ohtani a "chicken" in a headline after the news that he wouldn't sign with the Yankees—took the opportunity to poke at him again. This time the headline read: 'Say It Ain't Sho! What Are You Afraid Of? Ohtani Won't Take Mound vs. Murderer's Row 2.0.' Ippei Mizuhara, Ohtani's interpreter, dutifully placed a copy of the paper on Ohtani's clubhouse chair. Ohtani said later that he didn't need to see that, but he seemed to also be amused. When Ohtani was introduced and each time he came to bat during that series, the fans showered him with boos. They'd likely have booed him anyway, but skipping the series on the mound made him more of a target.

The Angels, as you'd expect, said the change in Ohtani's schedule was all about Ohtani, and not about the Yankees. In describing how they came to the decision a couple days before the Angels got to New York, General Manager Billy Eppler reaffirmed a point he'd made over and over: the Angels were going to err on the side of caution with a player doing something virtually unprecedented. "I have the utmost respect for what pitchers endure," Eppler said. "They are the most tired people when the game is over. When you make 90, 95, 100, 105, 110, 115, 120 explosions, that is a lot in my opinion. Then you add on cage work and BP work and games and so on and so forth, there is a lot on this particular individual's plate. We're just trying to be mindful of that. We understand where we are in the calendar. Simple as that."

Ohtani had thrown 103 and 110 pitches in his previous two starts, his highest totals in the young season.

The extra time off amounted to three days, with Ohtani returning to the mound on May 30 against the Tigers in Detroit. It had been ten days since his previous outing. In the first inning, Ohtani threw a 91-mph fastball, which immediately sent up red flags. "I haven't thrown a 91-mph fastball since high school, so I knew something was wrong," Ohtani said. In retrospect it may have been a clue to the diagnosis that would come less than two weeks later. But at the time Ohtani had a more innocent explanation for the reduced velocity. It was humid that night in Detroit, and Ohtani said he worked up such a sweat during his pregame warmups that he thought his arm was ready before it actually was. Ohtani settled into the game and his velocity returned to more normal levels, but his night still ended early. The Angels pulled him after 5 innings because he had sat through a forty-one-minute rain delay. Typically, any time a delay gets to around forty-five minutes, the pitcher who was last in the game is not asked to return. It's a normal measure to prevent a pitcher from getting hurt by heating up after his arm had cooled down for too long. The Angels were again trying to be cautious with Ohtani.

A week later, on June 6, Ohtani took the mound at Angel Stadium against the Kansas City Royals. In the first inning he came out throwing his fastball at 99 mph. He hit that number again in the second inning. In the third, though, his fastballs were 93–96 mph. By the fourth, his velocity had dropped slightly again, including one fastball at 92.6 mph. Ohtani also walked two hitters in the inning and threw a pitch so wild that catcher Martín Maldonado couldn't stop it. "When he started missing with his fastball all the way across the strike zone, I knew something was going on," Maldonado said.

Ohtani had shown Manager Mike Scioscia the beginnings of a blister on his finger when he returned to the dugout after the fourth inning. The blister issue had taken him out of a start back in April, and Ohtani had said at the time it was something he'd battled occasionally in Japan. He returned to make his next start on time, though, and had not reported any issues since then.

The Angels sent Ohtani to warm up for the fifth, but Scioscia didn't like the way he looked and dispatched athletic trainer Eric Munson to the mound to check on him. Without much discussion, they decided to remove Ohtani from the game. There was no immediate report on what was wrong with Ohtani, but after the game Scioscia told reporters that Ohtani had a blister, and they wanted to pull him before it got any worse. Ohtani, who had spoken to the media after each of his previous starts, was conspicuously unavailable that night.

The blister, it turned out, would be the least of his problems.

It would be nearly thirty-four months—and two surgeries—before the baseball world would again see the version of Ohtani who had electrified the sport up until that point.

CHAPTER

7

A Discouraging Diagnosis

Two days after Angels manager Mike Scioscia said that he had pulled Shohei Ohtani from a game because of a blister, the team announced a diagnosis that shook baseball fans on both sides of the globe. Ohtani had a damaged ulnar collateral ligament. The Angels explained that Ohtani did, in fact, come out of the game because of a blister, but afterward he complained of some stiffness in his elbow. They sent him for tests the following day, and that's when they received the disappointing diagnosis. A day after that, the team announced that Ohtani had a grade 2 sprain of his UCL, but he did not require surgery.

A medical degree was not necessary to understand the significance of that particular ligament. Anyone who has followed baseball over the past thirty years, and especially over the past ten, would know about that part of a pitcher's anatomy. The UCL runs along the inside of the elbow. It is rarely stressed by normal activities, but pitching is far from a normal activity, and injuries are common. That's why when reports surfaced in December 2017 that Ohtani came from Japan with a grade 1 sprain of his UCL, the Angels responded with a shrug. Anyone who has pitched at a high level is going to have some degree of damage to his UCL. A grade 1 injury means the ligament is merely stretched, so surgical intervention is not necessary. At grade 3, the ligament is torn, so surgery is the only option. The diagnosis that Ohtani and the Angels received in June 2018, though, was a grade 2 sprain. That middle ground covered a wide spectrum of injuries that could lead to a variety of treatments. By the time the Angels announced the injury, Ohtani had already received platelet-rich plasma (PRP) and stem-cell injections. He was to be reevaluated in three weeks.

The more drastic course of action would have been Tommy John surgery, a reconstructive procedure created in 1974. Dr. Frank Jobe revolutionized treatment of otherwise career-ending UCL injuries when he performed the experimental surgery on Tommy John, a Los Angeles Dodgers lefthander who was facing the end of his career if the procedure didn't work. Jobe removed a little-used tendon from John's wrist and looped it through holes drilled in the bones in the elbow. The repurposed tissue would give the elbow the structural integrity it had lost when the ligament failed. John, who was thirty-one at the time of the operation, returned to the mound two years later, and would pitch another fourteen seasons in the majors and win another 164 games. The procedure was so successful that it came to bear the name of its first patient. Eventually it became a common remedy for pitchers, even some who were still in high school. Long-time Oakland A's general manager Billy Beane once quipped: "There are two kinds of pitchers: those who *have had* Tommy John surgery and those who are *going to have* Tommy John surgery." By 2021, more than 30 percent of the pitchers in the majors had undergone the procedure, according to figures tracked by noted Tommy John surgery researcher Jon Roegele.

Shohei Ohtani would eventually be included in that statistic, but in June 2018, neither Ohtani nor the Angels were willing to concede that outcome.

First, as Angels general manager Billy Eppler insisted repeatedly over the next few months, none of the doctors who examined Ohtani or his test results at that time had recommended surgery, so the option wasn't really even on the table. Apparently, Ohtani's ligament was still in good enough condition that doctors believed it was worth trying to treat it without surgery.

Ohtani would say later that he felt stiffness rather than pain in his elbow, encouraging him to choose a non-invasive treatment. "My mind was ready to go back out there," Ohtani said months after the diagnosis.

The calendar gave the Angels further reason to try a non-surgical treatment. The rehab from Tommy John surgery lasts from twelve to eighteen months, but pitchers rarely make it back sooner than fourteen or fifteen months. If Ohtani had the procedure in June 2018, he was not likely to return to the Angels rotation for any meaningful number of innings in 2019. More likely, he wouldn't pitch at all until 2020. If he took the chance of an alternate treatment, only to need the surgery later in 2018, he would still be back in 2020. There was little risk in waiting. The upside was that if the treatment worked, Ohtani could avoid surgery entirely.

Also—and this is where the calculation was different with Ohtani than any other pitcher—for most of the time that Ohtani was rehabbing his elbow as a pitcher, the Angels could get value from him as a hitter. Because Ohtani is a righthanded pitcher and a lefthanded hitter, the damaged UCL in his right elbow had barely any impact on his hitting. In fact, Eppler said that the Angels could have just ignored the injury and turned Ohtani into a full-time hitter at the time of the initial diagnosis. "If he was only a designated hitter and that's all he was in life, probably [he could have continued playing with the injury], but that's not his circumstance and that's not how we want to utilize the player and realize the impact of the player," Eppler said. Ohtani had come to the Angels to be a two-way player, and for the first ten weeks of his Major League career, he proved that he could do it. The Angels, desperate for pitching, also needed what Ohtani could give them on the mound. They were not about to give up on that.

Their hopes of returning Ohtani to the mound without Tommy John surgery, though, were hanging on a treatment that was a longshot.

Platelet-rich plasma and stem-cell therapies involve concentrated versions of the body's self-healing products. Platelets are the smallest blood cells, and they form clots and help to heal tissue when necessary. Blood normally contains about 6 percent platelets. In PRP therapy, blood is drawn from a patient, spun to concentrate the platelets up to around 94 percent, then reinjected at the site of the injured tissue. Stem cells are the body's raw materials. They can become other types of cells when the body needs them. In stem-cell therapy, tissue is extracted from a patient's bone marrow, because it's rich in stem cells, and injected at the site of the injury. Although the effectiveness of using PRP and stem cells to speed up healing is questionable, the risks are minimal, so it was worth a shot to Ohtani and the Angels.

The Angels had been down this road before with lefthander Andrew Heaney and righthander Garrett Richards. Heaney and Richards each were diagnosed with damaged UCLs and underwent PRP and stem-cell treatments in May 2016. Heaney would end up having Tommy John surgery about two months later. Richards, meanwhile, had avoided Tommy John surgery more than two years after his injections. Although he had missed most of 2017 with a different arm injury, by June 2018 Richards was still pitching without requiring surgery on his UCL.

Ohtani himself had also undergone PRP therapy in Japan in late 2017, when the initial damage to his UCL was discovered. It was enough to get him through Spring Training and the first two months of the 2018 season but not enough to prevent another issue.

There was one shining precedent of the success of PRP, and it was familiar to both Eppler and Ohtani. In 2014, Japanese righthander Masahiro Tanaka was pitching for the New York Yankees when he was diagnosed with a partial tear of his UCL. Eppler was the Yankees assistant general manager at the time. Tanaka was treated with a PRP injection, and he returned to the mound just two months later. By

June 2018, when Ohtani was diagnosed, Tanaka was still going strong without surgery. At the time of Ohtani's injury, Tanaka had made 100 starts with the Yankees over the four years since his PRP injection. In 2015–16, Tanaka won 26 games and posted a 3.26 ERA.

But Tanaka was the exception. The vast majority of Major League pitchers who tried stem-cell therapy or PRP to heal their UCLs would go more along the path of Heaney, eventually needing surgery. Richards would also end up having Tommy John surgery just a month after Ohtani's diagnosis. On the day that the Angels announced that Richards needed Tommy John surgery, Eppler was asked if the club had second thoughts about trying PRP and stem-cell injections with Ohtani. "No, every player is biologically unique," Eppler said. "I lean on the people who went to medical school and did residencies and have far more knowledge on this than I do. There's a reason we employ them."

By that time, Ohtani had already taken about a month off from throwing, but he had returned to the lineup. He hadn't thrown a ball or swung a bat for about three weeks. Then he spent four days taking batting practice, including 20 at-bats against Minor League pitchers in two days of workouts at Angel Stadium. He was the Angels' designated hitter on July 3 in Seattle. Ohtani struck out 3 times and went 0 for 4, likely showing the rust of seeing only two days' worth of live pitching in a month. "It doesn't feel like it's Spring Training all over," Ohtani said. "It doesn't feel like that, but it's a different atmosphere up here facing big league pitchers in a big league stadium. I still might need a little more time to adjust to that."

Over the next two months, Ohtani was a full-time member of the Angels lineup. On August 3 against the Indians in Cleveland, Ohtani had his best game to date as a big league hitter, blasting 2 homers, including a 443-foot shot to right field. He finished with 4 hits, including one to spark the winning rally in the eighth inning. He then stole second to get himself into scoring position, representing the go-ahead run. "That's what Shohei can do," Manager Mike Scioscia said. "He was dynamic in a lot of areas, running the bases and obviously driving the ball. That's a great game." Ohtani hit his tenth homer of the season in that game, making him the first player in Major League history to hit 10 homers and have 50 strikeouts as a pitcher in the same season. Not even Babe Ruth had done that, because Ruth pitched in an era when hitters were much more focused on making contact than their twenty-first century counterparts. He averaged just 3.6 strikeouts per 9 innings through his career. By the time Ruth started playing other positions in 1918, he was pitching about half as often, so he struck out 40 in 166⅓ innings. When Ohtani was shut down as a pitcher in 2018, he had already struck out 61 in 49⅓ innings.

Ohtani's chances of adding to that total later in the season grew with each week, as all indications were that his ligament was healing enough for him to throw again. Ohtani was cleared to throw on July 19, six weeks after his injury was diagnosed. At that point, the target was for Ohtani to be pitching in a game by September. "That's one of my goals for this season, to get back on the mound," Ohtani said. "I just have to keep striving and taking the right steps to be able to accomplish it." Scioscia also gave an optimistic outlook: "We do anticipate him pitching for us this year, if everything in his rehab goes as planned."

By August 6—two months after his injections—Ohtani was standing on the mound in the bullpen at Angel Stadium, going through his pitching motion and snapping a towel instead of throwing a baseball. On August 11 he was on the mound again, but this time throwing to a catcher standing behind the plate. A couple days later, he repeated the exercise, with the catcher squatting. Every few days he increased the number of throws and the intensity. Ohtani soon pitched off the game mound at Angel Stadium with different hitters standing in the box. He threw 15 pitches, took a break, and returned to the mound for 18 more pitches, simulating the work of a two-inning outing.

The Angels had an off day in Phoenix on August 20, just before an interleague series against the Arizona Diamondbacks. Conveniently, the Angels were in the neighborhood of their Spring Training facility in Tempe, so Ohtani went there to throw a 50-pitch simulated game, facing Minor League hitters. The Angels had all of the technology they use to measure velocity and spin rates, and the numbers were encouraging. "We're glad he's able to hit each marker," Eppler said. "In the sim games he's thrown so far, the feedback we've grabbed from a qualitative aspect, the coaches on the ground, the video analysis and the medical data, we've been happy with what we've seen." A week later, Ohtani threw another 50 pitches in another simulated game, and felt he'd done enough. "Personally, I feel like I don't need any more simulated games, but it's not up to me ultimately," Ohtani said. "It's up to the coaching staff and training staff. I'll have to talk to them first."

Throughout all of this, one question loomed over the Angels. Why were they even trying to have Ohtani pitch? By August the Angels were well into another disappointing season, with the playoffs out of reach. Many, including Angels fans, felt it was an unnecessary risk to have Ohtani come back to pitch at the end of a lost season. Why not just give him the rest of the season off, let his elbow continue to heal, and start over in 2019? These were fans, after all, who had watched the team be burned by pitching injuries all too often. Just a month earlier, when Garrett Richards had Tommy John surgery, he became the fifth Angels pitcher to have the surgery in 2018 alone. Righthander Keynan Middleton had emerged as the Angels closer in April, just before having the procedure. Righthanders JC Ramírez and Blake Wood and lefthander John Lamb had also had Tommy John surgery in 2018. Since 2014, the Angels had also seen lefthanders Tyler Skaggs and Andrew Heaney and righthander Nick Tropeano undergo the procedure. Injuries to pitchers had been the single biggest reason why the Angels—a team with superstar Mike Trout on the roster—hadn't reached the playoffs since 2014.

To the Angels, though, there was a greater risk in *not having Ohtani pitch*. Eventually, Ohtani's UCL was going to need to be able to withstand the stress of 100-mph fastballs with all the adrenaline and intensity of a Major League game, and so far nothing that he'd done in bullpen sessions or simulated games had been sufficient to find out if it could. The worst-case scenario was that they would shut down Ohtani as a pitcher for the rest of 2018, only to have him start pitching in Spring Training 2019 and blow out his elbow then. If that happened, not only would they lose Ohtani as a pitcher for all of 2019 and maybe even all of 2020, but they'd also miss his bat for a chunk of that time. If Ohtani was going to need Tommy John surgery, the Angels wanted to know as soon as possible. Ohtani also would benefit from going into the winter knowing what was ahead. Either he'd have the confidence that his elbow could withstand the stress of a regular season game, or he'd know he needed surgery.

"Him finishing the season on the mound is a benefit to the player and the organization," Eppler said. "What it allows the player to do is to have peace of mind. That's an important thing. If you ask players who have been injured in their career, if you polled them, the majority, if not all of them would say, knowing that I can have a regular winter to prepare, knowing I can have a regular winter to do my program without any restrictions, that's important to them." The Angels also wanted to go into their winter roster-building knowing if they could count on Ohtani as a pitcher in 2019.

The Angels agreed to give Ohtani the ultimate test a few days after he'd pitched a second simulated game and proclaimed himself ready. The Angels scheduled Ohtani to start on September 2, the final game of a four-game series against the Astros in Houston. Nearly three months after he was diagnosed with a damaged UCL and injected with stem cells to help heal the ligament, Ohtani would pitch against the first-place Astros in a nationally televised game on ESPN's Sunday Night Baseball.

The eyes of the baseball world would be focused on the mound at Houston's Minute Maid Park, as Ohtani would test the integrity of his UCL with each pitch. Every reading on the radar gun and every look on Ohtani's face throughout the game would be scrutinized.

Ohtani retired six of the first eight hitters, his fastball peaking at 99 mph but mostly hovering between 95 mph and 97 mph. He worked around a walk and a single in the first inning. Ohtani then pitched a perfect second inning, but not without incident. The Astros' Marwin González pounded a ball into the ground and Ohtani instinctively reached back with his bare hand to stab at the one-hopper. It deflected off his ring finger to third baseman Taylor Ward, who threw to first for the out. Manager Mike Scioscia climbed to the top of the dugout steps, but Ohtani motioned to him to indicate he was fine. Ohtani struck out Yuli Gurriel on a splitter and got Martín Maldonado—his former teammate who had been traded to the Astros a month earlier—on a groundout to end the inning.

In the third inning, Ohtani's first fastball registered at 90.2 mph. He continued throwing 91–92 mph. Ohtani issued a walk and gave up a two-run homer to George Springer on a thigh-high slider. Ohtani then got José Altuve on a groundout with his forty-ninth and final pitch of the game. Scioscia pulled him with two outs in the third.

The drop in velocity was noteworthy, but not a certain red flag. Ohtani had only thrown 50 pitches in his simulated games, so coming out of the game at that point wasn't necessarily a sign of a problem. After the game, Ohtani said his elbow felt fine. He said his back was bothering him, and his finger had started to swell from the come-backer. "I have to wait till tomorrow to see how my body reacts," Ohtani said. "As of now, my body feels fine. At this point, my elbow feels fine."

A day later, the Angels were facing the Texas Rangers in Arlington, and Ohtani and Scioscia both said that the pitcher's elbow was still okay. "It is a little sore because I threw yesterday in a live game situation, but it's nothing out of the norm," Ohtani said. "I'll see from here and try to prepare for the next start."

Two days after that, though, Ohtani underwent an MRI exam that revealed his UCL was damaged again. This time, the recommendation was Tommy John surgery, the procedure they had spent the previous three months trying to avoid. Ohtani wasn't surprised. "Somewhere in the back of my mind, I was preparing to get Tommy John," he said. "That's something that was in the back of my mind the whole time." Although the Angels' efforts to avoid surgery failed, Eppler defended the Angels' treatment plan and their decision to have him try to pitch again in 2018. He said the Angels had performed extensive tests on Ohtani throughout the previous three months and "all gave us the confidence the ligament was ready for this next step." Ultimately, they could not avoid the fact that all pitchers, especially those who throw 100 mph, have ticking time bombs in their arms. "If you are going to throw hard for a number of years and stress ligaments, you are going to be at risk," Eppler said. "Is throwing hard good? Yes, it helps you get out hitters. Is throwing hard dangerous? Yes, it stresses ligaments."

Although there didn't appear to be any alternatives to surgery, Ohtani nonetheless had to formally agree to undergo the procedure, and he wasn't ready to do that just yet. While he was thinking about it, he demonstrated his mental strength. On the day that he learned he needed the surgery, he slugged 2 homers against the Rangers. "He just keeps going," Scioscia said. "He loves to play. Although there's obviously disappointment in the news today, he wants to play baseball. He had a great game tonight. You couldn't ask for much more."

Regardless of his future as a pitcher, Ohtani clearly could still be a dangerous hitter, and he ultimately decided to maximize his experience at the plate over the final few weeks of the season, before having surgery. "I feel like I'm progressing as a hitter right now, so I'm trying to gain as many experiences as I can while the games count," Ohtani said.

Ohtani spent the rest of September as a full-time hitter. He finished the season with a .285 average and 22 homers in 326 at-bats. His .925 OPS was sixth-best among American League hitters with at least 300 at-bats. Although he pitched just 2⅔ innings over the second half, he finished the year with a 3.31 ERA over 51⅓ innings. The combined hitting and pitching numbers were enough for Ohtani to win the

American League Rookie of the Year Award, selected by twenty-five of the thirty baseball writers who voted. The two-way performance also put Ohtani in a class only with Babe Ruth, who had been the last Major League player to succeed at such a high level as a pitcher and hitter, ninety-nine years earlier.

Ruth had been a two-way player for just two seasons, though, in 1918 and 1919. He said that the physical demands were too great, and he also preferred to hit. Ohtani had been a two-way player for a part of one season. As he underwent surgery on October 1 to have his elbow reconstructed, no one could be sure when—or if—he'd be able to do it again.

CHAPTER 8

Two Challenging Seasons

The day before Shohei Ohtani had surgery in 2018, the Angels' season ended in dramatic fashion. Weeks earlier a report had surfaced that the Angels were going to part ways with Mike Scioscia after the season, his nineteenth as manager. Scioscia denied it—memorably referring to the report as "poppycock"—but as the season's days dwindled, it became increasingly obvious that the report was true. In the final weekend of the season, the Angels did little to hide it. They gave away Mike Scioscia Bobbleheads and played highlights of his career on the video board between innings.

Moments after Taylor Ward's walk-off homer gave the Angels a victory in the final game, Scioscia sat at the front of an interview room packed with reporters and announced he was stepping down. "There's no doubt it's right for me, and I think it's the right move for the organization," Scioscia said, his voice cracking during the ten minutes he spoke before entertaining a question. "I've had an incredible nineteen years. It's been just awesome."

It was truly the end of an era of Angels baseball. And it was a challenging disruption to Ohtani's Major League journey. The manager who had made Ohtani laugh with self-deprecating jokes during their initial meeting in December 2017 was not going to be there for Ohtani's second season.

The job went to Brad Ausmus, a longtime Major League catcher with an Ivy League education from Dartmouth. Ausmus seemed destined to manage even while he was still playing, so it was no surprise when the Detroit Tigers gave him his first job running a team. Ausmus led the Tigers to the playoffs in his first season at the helm. But he lasted just three more years, including a 98-loss season that cost him his job in 2017. Angels general manager Billy Eppler then hired Ausmus as a special assistant, and he spent much of the 2018 season sitting next to Eppler, watching Ohtani's dramatic introduction to the majors. In October, Eppler picked Ausmus to fill the significant void left by Scioscia, and also to inherit Ohtani.

"How are you going to use Ohtani?" would be an annual, and often complicated, question for every manager who had the responsibility of overseeing the two-way star.

When Ausmus faced the question the day before Spring Training opened in 2019, it wasn't so much about *how* as *when*. Ohtani would not be able to pitch until 2020, so the issue was when he would be able to hit. Ausmus said the Angels were not expecting to have him in the lineup until May, which begged the question of why Ohtani hadn't had surgery as soon as it was recommended on September 5? Ohtani had deferred the procedure for almost a month because he figured those at-bats he had in September would ultimately be beneficial.

"I knew there was a possibility that I might not make it on Opening Day, but I felt like last year when the doctor told me I needed Tommy John, I was swinging the bat really well and seeing the ball really well, so I wanted to get that experience to finish out the season," Ohtani said at the start of Spring Training in 2019. "I think that's ultimately going to help this season. I might miss the first month, but in the long run, I think it's going to help myself and the team."

It didn't work out that way, though. Ohtani didn't get any at-bats in Spring Training. His reps instead came against Angels minor leaguers in late April and early May. He returned to the lineup on May 7.

Ohtani then started the season slowly, and he would finish the same way. His OPS dropped from .925 as a rookie to .848, mostly because his power dropped. Ohtani had hit 22 homers in 326 at-bats in 2018, but in 2019 he hit 18 homers in 384 at-bats.

The difference was easy to isolate, thanks to the technology used to track everything that happens on the field these days. "Launch angle" has become one of baseball's ubiquitous phrases in recent years. In basic terms, more and more hitters realized they could do better than simply trying to hit the ball hard. The best production came from getting the ball in the air, too. A hard line drive or groundball could become a single, but getting the ball up offers the chance for a home run and avoids the possibility of a double play.

In 2018, Ohtani had an average launch angle of 12.3 degrees, but in 2019 that dropped to 6.8 degrees. And 49.6 percent of the balls he put in play were groundballs in 2019, up from 43.6 percent in 2018. His flyball percentage dropped from 24.0 percent in 2018 to 18.0 percent in 2019. The rest were line drives. Ohtani's average exit velocity was nearly identical in the two seasons—92.9 mph in 2018 and 92.8 mph in 2019—but his overall performance suffered.

"He's not hitting the ball in the air the way he did last year," Ausmus said, adding that Ohtani was also not getting the bat on the ball out in front of the plate. "He still has the ability to get hits and extra-base hits, but we haven't seen the lift on the ball like he did last year."

Ohtani put on a show with his tape measure homers in 2018, but in 2019 the power wasn't there nearly as frequently. Ohtani spoke vaguely about the issue. "There's just a little tweak that I need to do to my swing," he said in September. "I would say it's more mechanics than timing. I've been fouling off a ton of pitches that I shouldn't be fouling off, so it probably has to do more with mechanics than timing."

Hitting coach Jeremy Reed suggested that focusing on launch angle was easier said than done. A season earlier, Angels right fielder Kole Calhoun had sunk into the worst slump of his career because he altered his swing to increase his launch angle. Calhoun instead got himself into a mechanical mess that required a swing rebuild during a stint on the injured list.

"When guys start to think about loft and launch angle and some of that stuff, there is a lot involved," Reed said, referring to Ohtani. "Sometimes they can tend to try to do too much."

Reed said it was also easy for Ohtani to try to do too much because he had nothing else to do. Without pitching—or playing a defensive position—all Ohtani had in 2019 was the batting cage. Reed said Ohtani sometimes worked too hard at trying to repair his swing. Reed didn't worry, though. He knew what Ohtani could do because he had seen it in 2018. "If you can do it for a year," Reed said, "it's in there."

Ohtani still had a handful of highlights at the plate in 2019, most notably a June 13 game against the Tampa Bay Rays at Tropicana Field. He blasted a three-run homer over the right field fence in his first at-bat. In the third inning, he doubled into left-center. In the fifth, he hit a line drive down the right field line and sped into third with a triple. When infielder David Fletcher mentioned to Ohtani that he needed a single for the cycle, Ohtani replied: "No. I want another homer." Sure enough, in Ohtani's next trip to the plate, he took a couple rib-jarring swings, before dumping a soft single into center on a two-strike pitch. "He was definitely trying to hit a homer, if you watch the at-bat," Fletcher said. "But I'm glad he got the single."

Ohtani was the first Japanese player to hit for the cycle in the major leagues. It was something he had never done in his five years in Japan. No Angels player had hit for the cycle since Mike Trout, six years earlier.

"Simply very happy that I was able to accomplish this," Ohtani said. "There have been so many other great Japanese players that have come before me. Being the first one to accomplish it [makes me] really happy and it makes for a lot of confidence down the road."

The Angels' starting pitcher who was the beneficiary of Ohtani's milestone game also appreciated the performance.

"He's starting to lock it in," lefthander Tyler Skaggs said. "It's really exciting. He's looking like he's the Ohtani of last year, and that's really special."

* * *

Tyler Skaggs and Shohei Ohtani were locker room neighbors, both at Spring Training in Tempe and at Angel Stadium in Anaheim. They shared the same agent, Nez Balelo. And in 2019, Ohtani was rehabbing from Tommy John surgery, a path that Skaggs had been down a few years earlier.

"Shohei really cared about Tyler," Balelo said. "He loved Tyler. And Tyler loved Shohei. Most, if not all, of that clubhouse loved Tyler."

Skaggs was originally drafted by the Angels in 2009, traded in 2010 and reacquired in 2013. He became a favorite in the clubhouse, liked by everyone from his teammates to reporters to the people who cleaned the ballpark.

Skaggs was blossoming as a big league pitcher when he felt tightness in his forearm on a steamy night in Baltimore in July 2014. It turned out to be a torn UCL, and he ended up as another Tommy John surgery statistic. A second injury slowed his rehab, and he didn't return to the mound until July 2016, nearly two years after surgery. In 2018, while most eyes on the Angels were focused on Ohtani's dramatic entry to the majors, Skaggs was pitching better than ever. He had a 2.57 ERA at the 2018 All-Star break. He was snubbed as an All-Star, and then saw his numbers decline in the second half, after he tried to pitch through a groin injury.

As 2019 began, with Ohtani and Skaggs sitting just a few feet apart in the clubhouse in Tempe, Skaggs said he was committed to pitching the way he did at the start of 2018, not the finish. "I don't want to talk much about last year, but it left a salty taste in my mouth and I'm out to show everybody that's not who I am," he said. "I'm excited to regain what I captured in the first half of last season and maintain that."

Skaggs believed he had started his return to form, coincidentally, in the game in which Ohtani hit for the cycle. Skaggs said he felt like he was in a rhythm against the Rays that night, but he was thrown off by a thirty-six-minute delay for a lighting failure in the ballpark. In his next start, in Toronto, Skaggs gave up 1 run in 7⅓ innings. It was a vintage performance for Skaggs, who threw his hardest pitch of the season to get a strikeout to finish the seventh. Skaggs had seen the bullpen in action, suggesting he'd get pulled from the mound, and it fired him up. He returned to the dugout and told Manager Brad Ausmus: "This is my game. Hang up the phone."

Less than two weeks later, the Angels took a trip to play the Texas Rangers and Houston Astros. To commemorate their week in Texas, the players boarded the charter flight on June 30 in cowboy garb. Skaggs was wearing black boots, black jeans, a black shirt, and a black cowboy hat.

That night was the last time his teammates would see him alive.

Police found his body on the bed in his hotel room the next day. Weeks later the coroner announced that Skaggs had opioids in his system. News of the twenty-seven-year-old's death shocked the Angels and the baseball world. The game that night against the Rangers was postponed. When the Angels returned to the ballpark the next day, they did so with Skaggs's number 45 in a patch on their uniforms. Players from around the majors who knew Skaggs also honored him by wearing number 45 on their caps or scratching the number into the dirt on the mound.

"Tyler was a close teammate of mine since joining the Angels last year," Ohtani said in a statement. "Words cannot express how deeply saddened I am by his sudden passing. My sincerest condolences go out to his family."

The Angels managed to win the first two games after the tragedy, and three of the six games on the trip. They beat future Hall of Famer Justin Verlander on July 5 in Houston. The Angels hit 3 homers against Verlander, with Ohtani hitting a bomb on his twenty-fifth birthday.

The Angels returned home after the All-Star break, playing their first game at Angel Stadium without Skaggs on July 12. Every player wore number 45 and "Skaggs" on his back. Skaggs's mother, Debbie, threw out the first pitch. There was a forty-five-second moment of silence before the game, and a tribute video.

The Angels then turned the night from *memorable* to *unforgettable*.

Righthanders Taylor Cole and Félix Peña, a pair of journeymen pitchers, combined to pitch a no-hitter against the Seattle Mariners. Cole worked the first 2 innings and Peña pitched the final 7 of the 13–0 victory. When it was over, the players all draped their number 45 jerseys on the mound. Peña laid his jersey at the top of the mound, on the pitching rubber where Skaggs had worked just a couple weeks earlier.

"I know he's here today," Cole said. "He's looking over us. He's definitely a part of this. That goes without question."

The Angels played their best baseball of the season for a couple weeks. They won back-to-back dramatic games against the Dodgers at Dodger Stadium to improve to 54–49 on July 24, climbing within striking distance of a playoff spot.

Then it all came to a crashing halt, perhaps as the emotions of losing a teammate became too much to handle. The Angels dropped 12 of their next 14 games, including a maddening 16-inning loss to the Baltimore Orioles, who were on their way to a 108-loss season.

With the cloud of tragedy and another losing season hanging over the Angels, Ohtani also went into a slump in the second half. He hit just 4 homers in his last 53 games. He batted .269 with a .767 OPS in that span, and the problem was more serious than an inability to get the ball in the air.

On September 12, the Angels announced that Ohtani would miss the final 15 games of the season to have surgery to repair a congenital knee condition that had been bothering him since Spring Training. Ohtani had been born with a bipartite patella. His left kneecap had never fused together into one bone, as it normally does. Instead, it was split into two parts. Although Ohtani had been living with the condition without a problem, he began to feel some discomfort in the spring of 2019. There was no public mention of it throughout that season, but after the condition was revealed, those around Ohtani suggested it was probably one of the reasons that he hadn't hit as well in 2019 as in 2018.

By September 2019, Ohtani was also deep into his throwing program, nearly one year removed from Tommy John surgery. The Angels believed Ohtani might alter his delivery, leaving him susceptible to another injury, if he tried to throw when his knee was hurting. The Angels determined it was best for Ohtani to have the knee surgery immediately and suspend his throwing program for a couple months.

The news was another tough blow toward the end of a season in which the Angels lost 90 games, their worst season since 1999. The nightmarish campaign cost Brad Ausmus his job after just one year as manager.

The franchise, and Ohtani, were both headed in the wrong direction.

* * *

Joe Maddon represented a link to the Angels' glory days, and he'd since become a celebrity in Chicago by leading the Cubs to a World Series title in 2016, ending their infamous 108-year drought.

As soon as word began to filter out of Chicago that the Cubs and Maddon would likely be splitting when his contract ended after the

2019 season, there was a widespread suspicion that Angels owner Arte Moreno had his eyes on Maddon.

The Angels had signed Maddon as an undrafted free agent out of Lafayette College in central Pennsylvania in 1975. His Minor League playing career didn't amount to much, but Maddon then began a career doing a little of everything in the Angels farm system, from coaching to player development. He scouted amateurs, too, years later often repeating the story of how he convinced iconic Angels outfielder Tim Salmon to sign his first pro contract. Maddon eventually became a part of the Major League coaching staff, including a couple stints as an interim manager. He was the bench coach under Mike Scioscia in 2002, when the franchise finally crawled out from under the playoff failures of 1982 and 1986 by winning the World Series.

The Tampa Bay Devil Rays gave Maddon his first shot as a full-time manager in 2006. The expansion Devil Rays had finished last in eight of their first nine seasons, losing 91 games in their best season and 106 games in their worst.

Maddon was the perfect bridge between the players and the front office. He was a folksy old-time manager with a gift for communicating with players and keeping things loose. He once brought a penguin to the clubhouse to break up the monotony of the season. Maddon blended that personal touch with a cutting edge approach that welcomed the type of analytics the Rays used to try to milk every victory they could out of the limited dollars the small-market team had to spend. Maddon and the Rays employed more aggressive infield shifts than any other team in the majors.

The Devil Rays lost 101 games in Maddon's first season, but in his third, they won 97 games and made the 2008 World Series, losing to the Philadelphia Phillies. The Rays went to the playoffs in three of the next five years under Maddon.

Before the 2015 season, the Cubs hired Maddon away from the Rays, and his success continued in a new uniform. In 2016, Maddon led the Cubs to 103 regular season victories and a long-awaited World

Series title. Although Maddon presided over the end of the supposed curse that hung over the Cubs, it wasn't enough to keep him in Chicago past 2019.

Once Maddon became available, he was an obvious candidate for the Angels because Moreno was desperate to recapture some of the club's successful past to appease a disgruntled fan base. "Our target is to win another World Series," Moreno said the day Maddon was introduced as manager. "We need to get back on the winning train. The last few years have been tough."

Maddon had not been a part of any of that, and he also hadn't seen what had become of Shohei Ohtani. Though Maddon had been part of the Cubs contingent that met with Ohtani just before he picked the Angels, since then he'd only seen highlights of Ohtani's exploits in 2018 and 2019. Maddon brought fresh eyes and no preconceived ideas to the standard "How are you going to use Ohtani?" questions. At the Winter Meetings in San Diego, months after Maddon had been hired, he was asked if he would consider using Ohtani to hit on days that he pitched, something the Angels never did before Ohtani hurt his elbow. "Why wouldn't you?" Maddon said. "That's another 50 at-bats a year that you're going to get out of the guy that you wouldn't get otherwise." Later that day General Manager Billy Eppler pumped the brakes on that idea. Ohtani had undergone two surgeries since he last pitched. At that moment Ohtani had barely resumed his throwing program after his knee surgery, so Eppler did not want to heap any more expectations onto him. It was nonetheless the first sign of Maddon's desire to put fewer restrictions on Ohtani.

As the Angels began Spring Training in 2020, though, Maddon was still relatively new to the job, so he went along with the organization's conservative plans for Ohtani. That included an innings limit. Ohtani had pitched just 26⅓ innings in 2017 with the Hokkaido Nippon-Ham Fighters because of ankle and thigh injuries. In 2018, he pitched only 51⅔ innings with the Angels because of the elbow injury, which cost him all of 2019 as a pitcher. The Angels certainly weren't going to use him without a limit in 2020, but they also weren't going to be painted into the same corner as the Washington Nationals in 2012.

Young ace Stephen Strasburg was returning from Tommy John surgery that season, so the Nationals put a limit on his innings. Strasburg took his normal turns in the rotation all season, only to reach his limit in September. The Nationals shut him down as they were fighting to reach the playoffs, creating a firestorm of controversy among Washington fans. In order to avoid that, the Angels decided to have Ohtani start late, so they could have him for the end of the regular season and, hopefully, the postseason.

The Angels got some help from a new rule that, in reality, applied only to Ohtani. It allowed a player to pitch in the minor leagues on a rehab assignment while remaining on the active roster as a non-pitcher. That meant Ohtani could open the season as a hitter, then leave the team for a day each time he needed to make a tune-up start in the minor leagues. Essentially, his Spring Training as a pitcher could come in April and early May in the minors.

It was a solid plan, except it went the way of just about all plans made by anyone in early 2020.

* * *

Spring Training was humming along like normal when the word "coronavirus" began to circulate through camps in late February. There was little thought that the season could be affected until March 10, when Major League Baseball finally acknowledged the threat of the virus by shutting media members out of the clubhouse. Instead, all interviews were to take place outdoors, with players at least six feet away from reporters. That day the Angels played an uneventful exhibition against the Seattle Mariners in Peoria, Arizona, with fans filling the ballpark. The next day rain pelted the Phoenix area in the morning, and the Angels game was canceled. Players dispersed for the day, unaware that it would be more than a year before they could convene again in such a carefree way.

On the night of March 11, Rudy Gobert of the NBA's Utah Jazz tested positive for the coronavirus, and the game in Oklahoma City was postponed moments before the scheduled tip-off. That sparked a wave of cancellations of sports and other public events around the nation and world. The Angels did not have a game scheduled for March 12, and before they could return on the thirteenth, Major League Baseball had suspended Spring Training and pushed the start of the season back at least two weeks. Angels players were told they could remain in Arizona, head to Southern California, or return to their offseason homes. Whatever they did, they would not be playing baseball. They were supposed to continue their workouts on their own as best as they could, in order to be ready whenever they got the word. Ohtani returned to Southern California. Later he would say the shutdown only mildly affected his personal life.

"Of course, there were times when I couldn't go out, but I'm not the person who goes out anyway, so that was no bother, really," Ohtani said. "When our movement was restricted, I was still able to practice, so I didn't have much trouble."

As the shutdown extended from weeks to months, Ohtani was among a few players who participated in workouts at Angel Stadium. No one was quite sure when—or if—the season would start, but the delay was considered a benefit to Ohtani. The Angels did not have to worry about limiting his innings anymore. Major League Baseball finally reached an agreement with the players to hold a 60-game season in empty ballparks, starting July 23. The Angels planned to have Ohtani as a two-way player for the entire truncated season.

Preparation for the season would begin with *summer camp*, as it was called, at big league ballparks throughout July. Players were tested for the coronavirus just about every day, and their facilities were reconfigured to allow them to keep their distance from each other. Instead of lounging around together in the clubhouse, the Angels players were each assigned a luxury suite elsewhere in the ballpark. The workouts were split up to reduce the number of players participating. A handful of players wore masks on the field. Occasionally players would be absent for reasons the team could not disclose, which almost always meant that a player had tested positive for the coronavirus.

It was against that backdrop that Ohtani would finally crank up his pitching workouts to make his much-anticipated return to the mound for the first time since Tommy John surgery. Ohtani had faced hitters in live batting practice during workouts in May and June at Angel Stadium, and once summer camp began he pitched in three intrasquad games. He wasn't particularly sharp in any of the appearances, but the spring of 2018 had taught everyone that Ohtani was not to be judged by exhibition games, much less intrasquad games. In his rookie year he flipped the switch once the season began at the Oakland Coliseum, and in 2020 the Angels also started in Oakland.

On July 26, Ohtani faced the A's, his first time on a mound in a regular season game in 693 days. He'd had surgery twice since that Sunday night ESPN game in Houston. Now he was back, pitching in an empty ballpark, with artificial crowd noise pumped in over the public address system. Ohtani started the first inning with a 92.5-mph fastball to Marcus Semien. His second pitch was a 93.5-mph fastball down the middle, and Semien ripped it into center field for a single.

Ohtani then walked the next three hitters, pushing in a run. He gave up back-to-back singles, driving in three more runs. Manager Joe Maddon pulled him, ending his day before he could record a single out.

Ohtani's average fastball was 92.9 mph, down from the 96.7 mph he'd averaged before surgery. Maddon insisted that Ohtani's velocity was fine in the intrasquad games, and there was no reason to believe he was hurt.

Ohtani said he felt too tentative on the mound, afraid to "let it eat," which is a phrase pitchers use to describe unleashing their top velocity.

Pitching coach Mickey Callaway suggested it was normal for pitchers to have some hesitation when first coming back from an injury, but normally that bridge is crossed in Minor League rehab games. Because of the pandemic, Ohtani didn't have that luxury. The first time after surgery that he'd pitched to another team was a regular season game.

"I just have to get that feel for the game back," Ohtani said. "Right now I feel like I was throwing the ball rather than pitching. There is still a little rust. I have to come up with a game plan."

Maddon, who was still getting to know Ohtani at the time, threw his support behind him after the nightmarish debut. "You've got to be patient, man," Maddon said. "Because of a bad moment or two, you just don't throw in the towel, ever. This guy is as good as you all think he is. He's just not comfortable getting back there yet. When you come off a severe injury, sometimes you've got to fight through some of those mental roadblocks in order to get back to where you had been."

A week later, Ohtani got a second chance, this time at Angel Stadium against the Houston Astros. For a few minutes, the Angels and Ohtani fans around the world could breathe again. Ohtani started the game with a perfect, eight-pitch inning. His fastball hit 95.8 mph. He struck out leadoff hitter George Springer on one of his vintage splitters.

In the second inning, Ohtani started with an eight-pitch duel against Michael Brantley, who walked. He then threw seven pitches to Yuli Gurriel, eventually walking him too. He struggled to put away Josh Reddick, walking him on seven pitches. The sixth pitch to Reddick was a 97.1-mph fastball, the hardest that Ohtani had thrown in either of his two starts. After the pitch, he tugged at his arm, running his left hand over his right bicep and forearm.

Ohtani threw 42 pitches in the second inning before Maddon came to the mound to end his day. Ohtani's last three fastballs, on the way to his fifth walk, were 89 mph.

After the game, the Angels sent Ohtani for an MRI exam. A day later, the Angels announced that he'd been diagnosed with a grade

1–2 strain of the flexor pronator mass, which is a collection of muscles and tendons in the elbow. It's an injury that normally is resolved in two months or less, but there was no time for that in this shortened season. He was done pitching for 2020. Twenty-two months after having Tommy John surgery, Ohtani had faced just 16 batters in two discouraging games before suffering another injury.

The new injury prompted questions about whether Ohtani should give up on being a two-way player. While Maddon conceded that "it might get to that point," at that time he was not ready to give up. "From what I've seen, I believe that he can [be a two-way player]," Maddon said. "We've just got to get past the arm maladies and figure that out."

Meanwhile, the Angels quietly began to create a Plan B for Ohtani. A few weeks after they shut him down as a pitcher, Ohtani began taking some flyballs in right field and groundballs at first base. Ohtani said the Angels never gave him a specific endgame for the work in the field, just that "they wanted me to get some reps under my belt and be prepared." Ohtani had played a little outfield in his first years in Japan. Asked why he stopped, Ohtani said: "I can't really tell you, but maybe I wasn't too good at it." Maddon doubted that. He was impressed with Ohtani's athleticism as he chased balls in batting practice. He looked smooth at first base, too. The workouts were partly to see if Ohtani could handle a position if he didn't pitch again, and partly just to keep Ohtani busy when he wasn't in the cage. Ohtani didn't want to concede, though. "I'm focused on pitching," he said. "That's the plan for now."

Unable to pitch for the second straight season, Ohtani was just a one-way player. Conventional wisdom was that he could hit even better without the mental or physical demands of pitching, but it didn't work out that way. He declined slightly at the plate in 2019, and 2020 was a disaster offensively.

Ohtani struck out in 9 of his first 27 at-bats, with just 4 hits. Although he hit a homer the day the Angels announced he would not

pitch again—reminiscent of the 2 homers he hit the day he learned
he needed Tommy John surgery in 2018—the offensive highlights
were rare. On August 21 Ohtani was out of the lineup, and Maddon
addressed the slump that had dropped his average to .171 and his
OPS to .623. He was in the middle of an 0-for-19 skid. "Obviously
he's not on top of his offensive game right now," Maddon said. "I'm
trying to [give him] more time just to work on his craft and not worry
about at-bats in a game. It's going to be very important for us to get
him right."

At that point Ohtani had struck out 21 times in 76 at-bats, and he
looked bad doing it. Often he would swing so hard that his helmet
would pop off his head. He could barely keep his balance in the batter's box, with his front foot lunging toward first base. It was especially
ugly against lefthanded pitchers. "We need him to put his seatbelt
on," Maddon said, trying to get Ohtani to remain under control and
stay in the box.

In September, with his average still below .200, Ohtani was
benched for a week. Ohtani said months later he began to feel "useless" when he was not in the lineup. "I was frustrated I couldn't get
it done, and that was the hardest," he said. Maddon said Ohtani had
been doing all the necessary work in the batting cage, and he was
showing progress there, but it didn't show up in the game.

Ohtani suggested that part of the problem was that players were
not allowed to watch video during the game, as they had been before
the pandemic. It was one of the safety protocols to prevent players
from gathering in video rooms during games. "I just want to see
how I was swinging at certain pitches in certain zones," Ohtani said.
"Ideally I would like to be able to see the replays. It probably would
have helped me."

Ohtani finished the season with a .190 average and a .657 OPS. He
hit 7 homers. When he spoke to Angels beat writers in the final weekend of the season, he took full ownership of his failures. "Obviously
the numbers show that I didn't have a great year, and I'm fully aware

of that," Ohtani said. "And I found a lot of things I need to work on in the offseason. It is kind of the same for every year but this year might be a little different. I still have a lot of things to work on so I'm looking forward to getting that underway in the offseason."

In November, Ohtani spoke to the media in Japan and he was even more pointed with his self-analysis.

He used the word *nasakenai*, which translates to "pathetic."

"I couldn't hit or pitch like I wanted to," Ohtani said, adding: "I'd pretty much never experienced the feeling of wanting to do something but being completely unable to do it."

By the time Ohtani gave that assessment, he was deep into the work that revived his career.

CHAPTER

9

High-Tech Diamond Polishing

Immediately following Shohei Ohtani's self-described "pathetic" season, he was searching for answers and open-minded to changes in his training. After starring in Japan and winning the Rookie of the Year Award for his debut season in the majors, Ohtani was not accustomed to what had happened in 2019 and 2020.

"You have a player that hasn't really gone through what he went through," said Ohtani's agent, Nez Balelo. "It's a little gut check. You say 'Okay, wait a second, what happened here? What can I do differently now?'"

Balelo said he and Ohtani decided to "lift up the hood," analyzing every element of his training to see what they could do to get him back to his customary level of play. They looked at his work on the field and in the gym, and even examined his nutrition. They knew the talent was there, because Ohtani had already demonstrated he could be a successful two-way player in the majors for the first ten weeks in 2018. The offseason of 2020–21 was all about rediscovering where he'd already been.

"A lot of it was just taking this fine diamond and polishing it up again," Balelo said. "It got a little dirty. All we did was polish it up again. There wasn't this incredible magic potion that he sipped every day. It was all there. The core was all there."

Polishing that diamond required Ohtani's full investment in a new approach. "This was Shohei really wanting to own his career, and own his offseason and do something different," Balelo said. "So that's what we did."

The most important part of Ohtani's winter rebirth occurred before he even started training, though. Ohtani was healthy when the offseason began, which was a refreshing change. He had undergone Tommy John surgery in October 2018 and he had knee surgery in September 2019, so his workouts had been limited in each of the previous two winters. No one expected Ohtani to be at full strength immediately after Tommy John surgery, but the impact of the knee surgery was perhaps less understood at the time. The legs are vital for any pitcher or hitter. Ohtani, who favored high intensity and heavy leg workouts, could not do those in the winter of 2019 because of his knee surgery. In October 2020, Ohtani was a year removed from surgery, so he was again free to do heavy lifting with his legs.

Ohtani's leg strength, and his aptitude for improvement, had best been illustrated a few years earlier.

In January 2018, General Manager Billy Eppler and a few members of his staff went to Japan to spend some time with Ohtani and run some tests before his first Spring Training in the majors. One of the tests was a vertical leap. Ohtani's performance was just about average, which was surprising for an athlete who had been so extraordinary at everything else. It was a disappointment to Ohtani, too. He had never been asked to try a vertical leap, and the technique was a mystery to him.

A month later, Ohtani was in Arizona and the Angels tested him again. He had improved by nine inches, achieving one of the best leaps—literally—in the organization. Normally it's impressive if someone can add just two or three inches to his vertical leap. Ohtani had spent weeks watching YouTube videos to learn the proper technique for a vertical jump, and he quickly made a jaw-dropping improvement, showing explosive power with his legs.

Starting the winter of 2020–21 with healthier, stronger legs, Ohtani began the rebuilding—polishing, from Balelo's perspective—with a trip to Driveline Baseball.

Driveline was the brainchild of Kyle Boddy, a math whiz and onetime Microsoft software developer who decided to apply that background to improving the performance of baseball players. Boddy learned all he could about biomechanics. He began a blog, which led to opening a Seattle-area warehouse that, over the years, has come to be filled with computers, high-speed cameras, and weighted baseballs. Major leaguers, and those with major league dreams, flocked to Driveline.

While big league teams are focused mostly on wins and losses, at Driveline the staff is entirely focused on improving the performance of its clients. The coach-to-athlete ratio is much lower at Driveline than with a big league organization. The technology is often more advanced, too, because that's all they do at Driveline.

Bill Hezel, Driveline's director of pitching, said that some Major League organizations are highly advanced, but others don't even have a basic pitch-grading system. Pitch-grading is a way of evaluating the quality of a pitch using objective data like spin rate and movement. At Driveline, they use Rapsodo devices and Edgertronic cameras to measure and optimize the way a pitcher throws the baseball. The Rapsodo is a triangular sensor, about six inches high, that sits on the ground between the pitcher and catcher. It tracks the number of revolutions per second for the ball and the axis on which the ball spins. It also shows how much the ball breaks. A pitcher can then experiment with different grips to maximize spin, which makes a breaking ball break more sharply and a fastball stay on its line longer, seemingly defying gravity and giving the hitter the illusion that the ball is actually rising.

The Edgertronic cameras provide high-resolution, slow-motion images, allowing pitchers to see in crystal clear detail what would be nothing but a blur to a normal camera. The Edgertronic cameras are focused on a pitcher's hand at the release point, so the pitcher and his coaches can see exactly how different finger positions impart different types of spin and movement. The combination of the Rapsodo and the Edgertronic devices gives the pitcher more actionable information than simply relying on "feel."

Driveline's pitching "laboratory" is one of the attractions that has brought so many Major League pitchers to Seattle to hone their craft. Cy Young winners Trevor Bauer and Clayton Kershaw are among the big leaguers who have spent time at Driveline. Every year the majors are filled with players who report to Spring Training after unlocking a new part of their game at the facility. Others likely would not have been in the majors at all if Driveline hadn't helped them improve as minor leaguers or even amateurs.

Most of the narrative surrounding Driveline, since it became a part of the baseball lexicon around 2016, has focused on increasing velocity. For much of baseball history, scouts and coaches assumed that velocity was an innate skill that could not be taught or improved to any significant degree. Boddy and the staff at Driveline began to challenge that notion.

Most notably they use high speed cameras to track the way a player moves. The player wears sensors at various points on his body so computers can mine the data and reveal the mechanical movements that produce the best results.

"Pretty much every athlete we work with, it always starts with that," Hezel said. "We go through some sort of motion-capture analysis. That's the foundation for everything. Where are their inefficiencies of movement? Better mechanical efficiency, better movement on the mound, typically does lead to either more velocity or the ability to produce velocity more efficiently, which is good for long-term health."

Driveline also uses weighted balls to improve mechanics and velocity. The brightly colored balls came in a variety of weights, mostly heavier than the standard five-ounce baseball. Hezel explained the weighted ball approach by going to an extreme. "If I gave you a bowling ball and I told you to throw it, you wouldn't move the implement farther away from your body," Hezel said. "You'd keep it close to your body. That's similar to throwing a baseball. Generally we don't want the hand to get really, really far away from the body and the throw. We don't want the elbow to fly out." Hezel added that the heavier balls are more difficult to throw, so pitchers need to use more precise, more efficient mechanics to get the job done. The use of Driveline's weighted balls had become prevalent enough that by 2021 it was common to see a big league pitcher—including Ohtani—chucking a colored ball at a padded wall as part of his daily routine.

* * *

Ninety-five years before Shohei Ohtani stepped into Driveline's gym full of high-speed cameras, Babe Ruth stepped into former boxer Artie McGovern's gym to get in shape with sprints and medicine ball throws and more, a concept that was just as cutting-edge at the time.

Back in the 1920s, baseball players didn't work out in gyms in the winter because most of them had to work other jobs to pay their bills. As a result, their conditioning was forced to wait until the start of Spring Training. Ruth, however, was one of the few players who made enough money that he didn't need another job. Free time, though, was also a curse for Ruth, who was legendary for indulging his desires, from food to alcohol to women. It was already catching up to him by the time he was thirty. Ruth described himself in an interview with *Collier's* magazine as "the Babe and a Boob" after the 1925 season, in which he felt his life choices had led to a disappointing performance.

In Ruth's first five seasons as a full-time hitter with the New York Yankees, he had hit .370 with a 1.288 OPS. He had averaged 47 homers per season. In 1925, though, Ruth had missed the first two months of the season after surgery for an intestinal abscess, which he believed was the result of his lifestyle. Ruth hit .290 with 25 homers and a .936 OPS. While those numbers were certainly better than respectable, it nonetheless marked a steep decline, and Ruth was concerned about the trajectory of his career.

That brought Ruth to Artie McGovern, a former professional pugilist who ran a gym that catered to celebrities and other wealthy New Yorkers, including Ruth's Yankees teammate, Lou Gehrig. McGovern was a taskmaster who would send trainers to the apartments and homes of his clients to make sure they did the work he required. McGovern told *Collier's* that Ruth "was a physical wreck" when they began working together. "His blood pressure was low and his pulse was high. He was as near to being a total loss as any patient I have ever had under my care. He had lived a life of excess and was suffering the inevitable consequences."

McGovern changed Ruth's diet, eliminating red meat and sweets. Under the new meal plan, Ruth would typically have poached eggs and toast for breakfast, a salad for lunch, and lamb or chicken with vegetables and a salad for dinner.

McGovern began Ruth on a daily regimen of exercises, starting with leg lifts and crunches that he could do while laying in bed first thing in the morning. He took long walks, worked the rowing machine, rode a stationary bike, and boxed. Ruth improved quickly in his work with McGovern's trainers.

"At the beginning the Babe was quite sluggish and went to his work in a dull way," McGovern said. "Now he is more alert and keen; he has more snap and pep. He kids and jokes with the boys, whereas previously he had very little to say."

Ruth also played handball. Lots of handball. When Ruth started working with McGovern, he was exhausted after one game of handball, but he was soon able to play five or six in a row. As reporters grew more curious about the work that Ruth was doing with McGovern, writer Paul Gallico showed up at McGovern's gym to play handball with the Sultan of Swat.

"He is amazingly fast on his feet," Gallico wrote. "Baseball fans realize that for a big man he is speedy, but not until you get him inside a small, enclosed court do you realize how he carries those 220 pounds about. He gets his hands on shots he had no business making."

Ruth lost 44 pounds in just six weeks working out with McGovern. He reduced his waist size by 8½ inches, to 40 inches. The results showed in his numbers on the field, too.

In 1926, Ruth returned to form with a .372 average, 47 homers and a 1.252 OPS. Ruth continued working out with McGovern each winter, and in 1927 the Bambino had a record-breaking season. He blasted 60 homers, one more than the record he'd set in 1921. Ruth continued putting up otherworldly numbers into his late thirties, in large part because of the physical turnaround that started in Artie McGovern's gym.

* * *

Shohei Ohtani certainly didn't need a fitness makeover when he arrived at Driveline. What he needed most was information. "I felt like it's a good idea [to go]," he said months later. "It won't hurt to get opinions from a third party. And they have really good opinions, some good data, some good intake, and I think there's a lot I could take away from it."

The data provided by Driveline could help Ohtani learn more about his fatigue levels, which would not only help him train over the winter but also help him learn how much rest he really needed during the season. The Angels had spent the first three seasons essentially experimenting with Ohtani. They gave him days off before and after he pitched. Sometimes they had him skip batting practice on days he threw bullpen sessions. Ohtani had insisted that he could do more. He had said as much in his first month in the big leagues, back in 2018. But Ohtani went along with the Angels' restrictions, at least in part because he didn't have the empirical data to support his belief that he could do more. That was what Driveline could provide, though.

"I think we've now been able to collect more data to know when he is really tired and when he's not tired," Balelo said after Ohtani worked at Driveline. "Gathering that was one of the things we did this offseason. So we know when he's peaking, when he's not peaking, when he needs to rest, when he doesn't need to rest."

Driveline took measurements of Ohtani's strength levels using a variety of tests, and they also used technology specifically designed to measure the stress on a pitcher's arm. Around 2010, a company called Motus began marketing a sleeve that a pitcher could wear on his throwing arm while he was pitching or even playing catch. The sensors in the sleeve recorded data that provided the pitcher and his coaches with objective numbers to quantify the stress on his arm, much more accurately than simply counting throws. Driveline subsequently purchased the patents for the Motus sensor products, rebranding them as Pulse. Driveline modified the product, turning it from a sleeve into a band that is worn around the bicep. The data is now more precise, as the device can measure different stresses based on what type of ball or implement was being thrown.

The Pulse allows pitchers to train their arms at a higher intensity, because they have more quantifiable data about when they are reaching the danger point.

"We generally see that a lot of athletes are actually undertrained when it comes to throwing fitness," Hezel said, speaking generally and not specifically about Ohtani. "Just because of the nature of the game now, there's a lot of talk about them being overtrained and throwing too much. What we find, in a lot of cases, [is that] their throwing in the offseason is extremely conservative, or extremely low and moderate intensity and they're just not prepared when the season starts to throw at the velocities they need to. I think just generally you see that a large amount of athletes just don't totally understand the best way to get themselves prepared for the season and the amount of throwing that they have to do. What you often see a lot more than the throwing volume issues is a lot of pitchers who spend their offseason throwing in this low to moderate intensity range, so they'll never really push the intensity all that much before they report to Spring Training and that is typically a pretty big issue. It's very hard for your body to be prepared for the stresses of throwing 95, 96, 97 mph if you never do it in training at all, and the only time you do it is in the competition."

Further increasing the intensity of the workouts at Driveline, pitchers and hitters often have the opportunity to work against each other. In a simulated game, a pitcher faces hitters with someone calling balls and strikes. The pitcher will work to a hitter as he would in a game, setting him up with different pitches and different locations. An 0-and-2 pitch is different from a 2-and-0 pitch. A pitch with a runner in scoring position is different from a pitch with the bases empty. The pitcher might need to summon extra adrenaline to get that extra velocity when the situation calls for a strikeout. It's the same for a hitter, who needs to protect the plate with two strikes. He might be trying to hit a flyball or a groundball to the right side to simulate when the game dictates that approach. Such simulated games are common during the season or even in Spring Training—more for pitchers than hitters—but players don't often rise to that level of intensity in the offseason. Ohtani hadn't, but he and Balelo decided to give it a try in the winter of 2020–21.

"People train in different ways," Balelo said. "What I believe and others believe is that in order to train properly, to get you ready for the most game-like situation, you have to put yourself in a situation that is very game-like. Just speed up the clock. You've got to turn it up. Let's get to it. When you put a player like Shohei in a game-like situation, and you say, 'Okay, here you go,' he's going to figure out a way to get better and compete. At the end of that game-like situation, he's going to come out on top. And I think that was the key."

In 2018, Ohtani performed poorly in Spring Training, which led many observers outside the Angels organization to question whether he was ready for the big leagues. After Ohtani put that to rest with his success in the regular season, one of the explanations was that Ohtani was simply lacking the adrenaline of real games in those workouts in Arizona.

The increased intensity of his pitching and hitting workouts in the winter leading up to 2021 were clearly going to make a difference.

Ohtani was ready to hit the ground running in Spring Training.

Ohtani starred at Hanmaki Higashi High School in Iwate Prefecture, in Northern Japan. He was considered a top prospect as a pitcher and as a hitter.

Although Ohtani had planned to skip professional baseball in Japan and go straight to the United States, he instead spent five seasons with the Hokkaido Nippon-Ham Fighters. He was the MVP of Nippon Professional Baseball in 2016.

When Ohtani picked the Angels in December 2017, his introductory press conference was a major event for American and Japanese media. Since then, dozens of Japanese journalists have tracked Ohtani throughout his American career.

Former Angels manager Mike Scioscia, left, and general manager Billy Eppler, right, helped to convince Ohtani to pick the Angels when he came from Japan. Ohtani played under three managers and two general managers in his first four seasons.

Although there was some speculation that Ohtani might not be ready for the majors in 2018, he was on the team on Opening Day, with a horde of journalists there to chronicle his historic debut.

Mike Trout was considered the best player in the major leagues, but the Angels had failed to win a playoff game in his first nine seasons. The pressure to win increased as the Angels added Ohtani, a second player of historical significance.

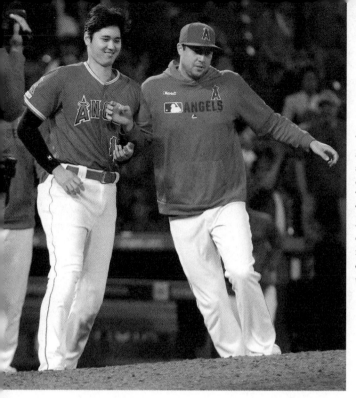

Tyler Skaggs and Ohtani shared the same agent and had lockers near each other at Angel Stadium. They also each underwent Tommy John surgery. Skaggs and Ohtani were close when Skaggs was found dead in the middle of the 2019 season. He was twenty-seven.

Joe Maddon took over as Angels manager prior to the 2020 season, and he oversaw Ohtani's worst season and then his best. One of the keys for Ohtani's improvement was the decision by Maddon and General Manager Perry Minasian to remove the restrictions on his playing time.

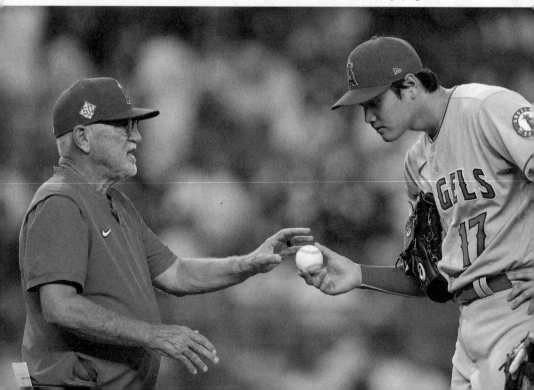

In Ohtani's first outing of Spring Training 2021, he threw 100 mph, demonstrating that he had moved beyond some of the issues that caused him to struggle in two games before he was hurt in 2020.

Ohtani labored at the plate in 2020, but a new offseason workout regimen prior to the 2021 season helped him improve his swing. He lifted his OPS from .657 in 2020 to .965 in 2021.

Ohtani came to the plate 639 times in 2021, proving that he did not need to rest the day before and after he pitched, as he did in 2018. Ohtani played in 155 of the Angels' 162 games.

Ohtani takes a cut against the San Diego Padres in August 2021. Ohtani blasted 46 homers that year, tied for third most in the major leagues.

Shohei Ohtani pitches during the first inning of the 2021 All-Star Game. He was the first player ever to be selected to the All-Star team as a pitcher and a hitter. Ohtani started at DH in the All-Star Game, in addition to starting on the mound. He went hitless in two at-bats, and he pitched a scoreless inning, picking up the victory.

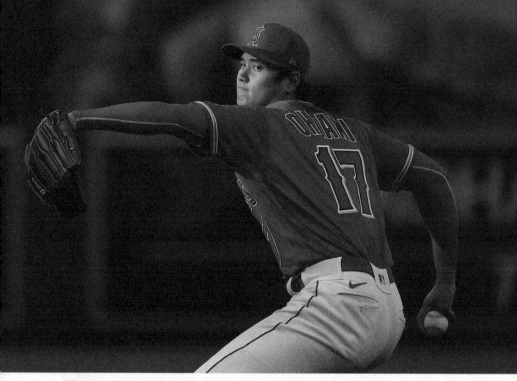

Ohtani was able to remain healthy for the entire season, allowing him to start 23 games and pitch 130⅓ innings, with a 3.18 ERA. He struck out 156 hitters.

Ohtani fans in Ōshū, Japan, his hometown, celebrated when he was named the American League MVP in November 2021. In Ōshū, they now celebrate Ohtani Day on the 17th of every month.

CHAPTER 10

New Approach, New Hope

After two seasons that had been filled with the physical pain of injuries and the emotional pain of a lost teammate, capped by a performance that cast doubt on his future as a two-way player, Shohei Ohtani arrived at Spring Training in 2021 and said change had already begun. His mindset was new, and the way the Angels planned to use him was new.

"It's kind of how I felt in 2018," Ohtani said. "Rather than have pressure, I just want to have fun and feel good out there, and just do my job when it's given. Hopefully, I want to make [Manager] Joe [Maddon] use me as much as possible."

The Angels had treated Ohtani like a fragile artifact for most of his first three seasons in the big leagues, and you couldn't blame them. It had been a century since anyone had been able to pitch and hit at a high level in the majors. Even when Babe Ruth did it in 1918 and 1919, he said the physical demands were too great. Ruth was a two-way player just temporarily, while transitioning from pitching to hitting. Ohtani, by contrast, came to the majors specifically to be a two-way player, and it was up to the Angels to ensure that he could handle the workload.

General Manager Billy Eppler sat at the top of the Angels decision-making chain when it came to Ohtani's use. Based on what they knew of Ohtani's career in Japan, the Angels believed they needed to place firm limits on his playing time. The Fighters typically rested Ohtani the day before and the day after he pitched, which reduced the days he could be the DH. He also rarely hit on the same day that he was pitching. The Angels stuck to that blueprint with Ohtani in his rookie year. Ohtani said just two weeks into that season that the Angels were being too cautious with him, but he was deferential to their judgment. "I would like to play more," he said in April 2018. "If not, that's what it is. I have to follow what they have to say."

Despite their best intentions, the Angels' careful treatment of Ohtani wasn't enough to keep him from blowing out his elbow. Then after Tommy John surgery he had lasted just two games before getting hurt again. At that point many outside the Angels organization said it was time for Ohtani to give up on being a two-way player. While the Angels said publicly that they weren't ready to go there, privately there were plenty of skeptics within the organization. It was likely that 2021 was going to be Ohtani's last chance to show what he could do on the mound.

Eppler, however, was not going to make that decision. After the Angels finished the coronavirus-shortened 2020 season with a losing record for the fifth time in Eppler's five years running the team, the Angels fired him. Two years after Mike Scioscia had stepped down, the team was now without both the manager and general manager who had convinced Ohtani to pick the Angels.

The six-week search for Eppler's replacement included interviews with at least seventeen candidates. The team eventually selected Atlanta Braves assistant general manager Perry Minasian, whose background was unique among the thirty-member club of people who ran baseball operations for big league teams. Minasian was not an Ivy Leaguer or a former Major League player. He hadn't even played in the minors. Or college. But he did have a unique insight into Major League players, which would be key to a decision that revitalized Ohtani's career.

* * *

Perry Minasian's grandfather was a close friend of Tommy Lasorda, who in 1966 was working his way up the managerial ladder by running the Los Angeles Dodgers' rookie-league team in Ogden, Utah. When Lasorda needed someone to work in the clubhouse, he hired his friend's thirteen-year-old son, Zack. The job entailed doing players' laundry, getting them food, cleaning their shoes, and generally doing anything that anyone wearing a uniform needed done. Zack spent three summers working under Lasorda, whose career would take him to the manager's office in Los Angeles and—decades later—the National Baseball Hall of Fame. Zack followed Lasorda, spending a couple years working the clubhouse at Dodger Stadium. He then took a detour from life in baseball. He got married and started a family in Chicago.

Bobby Valentine was one of the Dodgers players who shared a clubhouse with Zack in the late 1960s before beginning his own rise as a manager. Valentine got his first job as a big league manager with the Texas Rangers in 1985. A few years later, the Rangers needed someone to run the visitor's clubhouse at Arlington Stadium, so he called Zack Minasian. In 1988, Minasian returned to baseball, packing up his family and moving to Texas.

All four of the Minasian boys—Rudy, Perry, Calvin, and Zack Jr.—helped in the clubhouse as soon as they were old enough. Perry started when he was eight. They each had specific jobs. Perry, the second-oldest, was responsible for cleaning the bathrooms. While the boys had plenty of work to help their father meet the needs of a different team every three or four days for eighty-one days during the baseball season, they also had a good time. They wrestled with Kansas City Royals multi-sport athlete Bo Jackson and played baseball using tape balls with Seattle Mariners star Ken Griffey Jr. The boys also got to experience big league baseball from the dugout, working as batboys for the Rangers and for visiting teams. The *Dallas Times Herald* ran a front-page photo of eight-year-old Perry Minasian blowing a bubble while standing in the Rangers dugout next to future Hall of Famer Nolan Ryan, who was in the middle of his seventh no-hitter.

A few years later, young Perry abandoned his own dreams of becoming a big league player when he watched in awe from the field as future Hall of Fame pitcher Randy Johnson warmed up. He realized he'd never be able to compete at that level.

Minasian did aspire to do more than clean bathrooms, though, so he eventually shifted toward baseball operations. During college, Minasian had an internship in Spring Training with the Montreal Expos. He was then named a coaching assistant under Rangers manager Buck Showalter. Essentially, his job description was to do whatever the manager needed. "If we need a stack of pencils from Office Depot, you're going to get them," Showalter recalled. "If we ask you about a guy from Seattle, you're going to find out. If we want to know a stat, you're going to find it." Minasian served in a variety of roles with the Rangers before leaving to take a scouting job with the Toronto Blue Jays. After he worked his way up in the Blue Jays front office for six years, the Braves hired him.

Three years later, the Angels hired Minasian to run their show. It was the first time he'd ever interviewed for a big league general manager position.

As he was making the rounds with the media in his first days with the Angels, Minasian often said that growing up in a clubhouse—literally—helped him understand how Major League players think and what they feel. Braves GM Alex Anthopoulos, who had known Minasian since they were interns together with the Expos, said that experience was invaluable. "It's a difference-making perspective that is a competitive advantage," Anthopoulos said. "Most people don't have the perspective on players and coaches that he has." That perspective colored Minasian's attitude toward Ohtani. He wanted to change the way the Angels were using him.

"In my experiences with players, I do not like limitations, especially on Major League players, because it is so hard to get here," Minasian said. "You have to be not only physically talented, but mentally you have to be built a certain way. My thought was, he's one of those guys."

In his first weeks on the job, Minasian suggested to Manager Joe Maddon that they loosen the Ohtani restrictions. Maddon had demonstrated he was open to the idea nearly a year earlier, when he spoke about Ohtani at the Winter Meetings in December 2019. Minasian also spoke to Ohtani's agent, Nez Balelo. "Talking to Joe about it, he was 1,000 percent on board," Minasian said. "He loved the concept. Nez loved the concept. I think he had similar thoughts."

Ohtani was preparing himself to be used more. One of his main objectives at Driveline was to use their technology to study his fatigue levels, so he'd have objective data to show when he truly needed rest, and when he didn't. That sort of information would be vital for Ohtani to increase his workload without jeopardizing his health or hurting his performance.

"We were all about it," Balelo said of Minasian's new approach for Ohtani. "Of course Shohei was all about it. And it was something that they wanted to do. I really liked Perry's no-nonsense, no BS. This is the way we're gonna do it. Let's talk through it. And if everybody's comfortable, let's go. Let's do this." For as much as the idea appealed to Ohtani, Balelo said he emphasized to his client that it only would work if he could be honest about how he was feeling. Although Ohtani's manager in Japan had doubted that he would ever be willing to admit when he was tired, Balelo said much had changed since 2018. "From what he went through the last three years," Balelo said, "he had a better understanding of what you need to do to be honest with yourself."

* * *

Before Spring Training 2021 even began, the Angels were already expressing cautious optimism about Shohei Ohtani. Manager Joe Maddon said that Ohtani's fastball had hit 95 mph in workouts, which was certainly a reason to be encouraged. In the two games he pitched in 2020, he had trouble getting to full velocity, which he and his pitching coach explained was because of reluctance following surgery. If he was already throwing 95 mph without the adrenaline of a game, there was hope. "His workouts have been fabulous," Maddon said. "The reports I've been getting are really good, honestly really good, so I'm eager to watch this like everybody else is. If we get Shohei in the right direction, that'd be a pretty good offseason acquisition right there." A few days later Ohtani threw live batting practice in Tempe Diablo Stadium and he hit 100 mph in his 35-pitch workout, according to data the Angels provided to the media.

Beyond the improved velocity, Ohtani was also showing Maddon better mechanics than he'd seen at any point in 2020. Ohtani had refined everything at Driveline over the winter. "I'm just watching him throw, watching BP the other day, my God," Maddon said. "I know it's batting practice, but I'm talking from a functional, mechanical perspective, everything he's doing, the way his body's working right now, exceeds what I saw last year."

The media and the public didn't get a chance to see what Maddon was seeing until the Cactus League games began. Up until then, Ohtani's workouts had been confined to closed sessions in Tempe. On March 1, Ohtani stepped to the plate for the first time in an exhibition game and he yanked a single into right field. On his next trip, he singled into left. "I think I'm able to make good swings right now," Ohtani said. "I'm where I should be. I'm feeling good right now." Two days later, Ohtani blasted a 468-foot homer over the batter's eye at Tempe Diablo Stadium, the ball rocketing off his bat at 107 mph. It was an *I told you so* moment for Maddon. "That's what we've been seeing in batting practice," Maddon said. "Better balance, a better overall approach. And that's a pitch that's been tough for him in the past, an elevated fastball with good velocity. He's doing so many things better, a better place mentally, a better place physically."

Ohtani's bat seemed fine at the start of the spring. On March 5 he finally had a chance to show his progress on the mound against the division rival Oakland A's at Hohokam Park in Mesa. The A's had seen the high and low points of Ohtani's pitching career. In 2018, he took a perfect game into the seventh against Oakland. In 2020, he couldn't record an out in his first game after Tommy John surgery. On this day in Spring Training, Ohtani was sharp. His fastball hit 100 mph on a pitch that struck out Oakland first baseman Matt Olson. He threw a splitter that dove away from Mark Canha, striking him out. All told, Ohtani struck out five of the ten hitters he faced. Maddon said something else about Ohtani that was telling that day. As Ohtani stood on the mound between pitches, he casually flipped the baseball in the air. Maddon said that's one of his litmus tests for when Ohtani is feeling comfortable and relaxed on the mound.

Around the five strikeouts Ohtani gave up three doubles and two walks, but none of that mattered to Maddon or Ohtani because he'd shown that his problems from 2020 were behind him. "He's looked this way the whole camp," Maddon said. "The delivery is good. I can't emphasize that enough. Last year he was pushing the ball so much. He was just off. Once he's ironed that out and his arm is working like it can, you're seeing the big numbers."

The 41-pitch outing marked the first time in more than 1,000 days—since June 2018—that Ohtani could walk off the mound following a successful performance. He'd pitched only three times since then, once failing to record an out and twice getting hurt. He was satisfied this time, even surprising himself with the velocity he reached. "Since it was my first game I was not planning on letting it go in the beginning, especially early in counts," Ohtani said. "As the game went on, I felt better. I started throwing harder, but I think that led to me cutting the ball a couple times, so that's another thing I need to work on for my next start."

The next time he took the mound his fastball reached 99 mph, which was encouraging, but his command was lacking. The Chicago White Sox nicked him for 5 runs, including 3 that scored after he left the game. One of his 4 strikeouts was against the reigning MVP, White Sox first baseman José Abreu.

Ohtani got a shot at the reigning Cy Young winner three days later, blasting a homer against Cleveland righthander Shane Bieber. It was Ohtani's second homer of the spring that cleared the batter's eye at Tempe Diablo Stadium, this one measuring 464 feet. He had also hit 2 homers the day before against the Cincinnati Reds, both of those clearing the left field fence in Tempe. "The ball just kind of tapped the bat and it made it over the fence," Ohtani said of his first homer that day. "So that means if I were to pull that ball it would have still made it over the fence, so that's a good sign."

The signs were all good. After the Cleveland game, Ohtani was 11 for 19 with 4 homers in the Cactus League. "Bottle this and keep it for the next ten years," Maddon said. "He's feeling really good about himself."

Ohtani was swinging the bat well and showing encouraging signs on the mound, most notably his velocity. His command wasn't what he needed it to be, but he had barely pitched in three years, so that was to be expected.

Maddon decided it was time to put Ohtani to a new test.

* * *

The Angels disrupted a nondescript Sunday morning with an announcement via Twitter at 8:40 a.m. on March 21. "Shohei Ohtani pulls double duty today," read the tweet, which included a photo of the lineup sheet for that day. The Angels were set to play the San Diego Padres in Peoria, and the lineup had Ohtani in the leadoff spot. There was a "1" in the position column next to his name, indicating that he was pitching. It was a jarring sight because pitchers don't hit in the American League. Even for a Spring Training game at a National League park, an American League team would always use the DH. The only time an AL team would have its pitcher hit was a regular season game in an NL park, and in that case the pitcher certainly wouldn't hit leadoff. Although Ohtani is no normal pitcher, the Angels still had not crossed the line of having him hit when he was pitching. He had done it on a few occasions in Japan, but never with the Angels. In December 2019, when the Angels believed that they would have a healthy Ohtani as a two-way player for most of 2020, Maddon had suggested they might try it, but Ohtani's season as a pitcher lasted just two games. They never got the chance.

The spring of 2021, though, was supposed to be the start of a new era for Ohtani. The restrictions were gone, Maddon had said repeatedly. "I don't want to tell him what he can or cannot do, and neither does [General Manager Perry Minasian]," Maddon said at the start of camp. "So let's watch him. Let's talk to him. Let's communicate with him. Let's permit him to go out there. He was very successful in Japan. Let's just see what he does and watch and make our evaluations and adjustments based on what we're seeing, and not be kind of prejudiced or predisposed in advance."

For more than a month, the Angels evaluated Ohtani's performance and his communication. Just a few days before Maddon took the plunge of having Ohtani pitch and hit, Ohtani had told Maddon that he needed an extra day off. Ohtani's honesty about his fatigue level was an important piece of the puzzle. If the Angels were going to push Ohtani, they needed to be confident that he would speak up if it was too much.

Maddon was ready to see how it looked with Ohtani pitching and hitting. How would he hit if his normal pregame batting practice was limited by his pitching preparation? How would he fare when he went to the mound immediately after running the bases? How tired would he be afterward?

"It's important that we experiment right now," Maddon said. "Because it's all about how he feels. It's not about how I feel."

Ohtani took about ten minutes worth of batting practice at the Angels complex in Tempe, then he and his teammates made the thirty-minute trip to Peoria, on the other side of the Phoenix area. He did all of his stretching and throwing in the outfield, followed by a warmup in the visitor's bullpen. He then returned to the dugout just in time to lead off the game in the batter's box. Facing lefthander Blake Snell, a former Cy Young winner, Ohtani punched a single into center field. He remained at first for the rest of the inning, sliding into second on a force play for the third out.

Ohtani then jogged into the dugout, grabbed his glove and cap, and headed to the mound to begin pitching. He worked 4 innings and gave up just 1 run, with his fastball mostly sitting at 94–96 mph. Although it dropped to 92–93 mph at times, he was also able to crank it up when he needed it. Padres young star Fernando Tatís Jr. was at the plate with two on and one out in the third, and Ohtani ramped his fastball up to 102 mph, getting Tatís on a popout. He threw another fastball 100 mph on his way to an inning-ending strikeout of Jurickson Profar. "He definitely has another gear when the other team is threatening," Maddon said. "There is another level of all his pitches. It's just a matter of him figuring out how to get to that point a little more consistently to not put himself in that position. He definitely has another gear when it gets hot."

Ohtani threw 62 pitches in the game, and at the plate he managed a second hit, a double off the fence against San Diego closer Mark Melancon. Afterward, Ohtani said he came through the game without any physical issues. "I didn't feel much extra fatigue or anything," he said.

All things considered, the experiment could not have gone much better. As the Angels approached their final days in Arizona, Ohtani was providing more reason every day to believe that 2021 might be different. He was healthy. His swing and his delivery were solid. He was responding well to an increased workload.

"I'm very excited to show what I can do," Ohtani said after doing double duty against the Padres. "That's why I came here back in 2018. I'm sure I disappointed a lot of people the last two years by being hurt. I am looking forward to showing everyone what I'm capable of."

Ohtani didn't show much in his final tune-up before the season, though. He got the ball against the Dodgers in the Freeway Series, the traditional final three exhibition games against their Southern California neighbors.

In the first inning at Dodger Stadium, Ohtani walked 3 and uncorked a wild pitch, pushing home a run. In the second, he issued another walk, as he struggled to dial in the location with his fastball. Ohtani then switched to more breaking balls, including a hanging slider that Chris Taylor blasted for a two-run homer. An out later, Ohtani fell behind Corey Seager, 3-and-0, so he grooved a 93-mph fastball over the middle and Seager homered. In the third, Ohtani walked A. J. Pollock, gave up a single to Max Muncy, and then hung a curveball that Will Smith hit over the right field fence. As Smith circled the bases with the Dodgers' seventh run, Ohtani looked at the middle finger on his right hand. Ohtani then trudged off the field, his night ended and the optimism of so many Angels fans dampened days before Opening Day.

Ohtani later explained to reporters that a blister had developed on his middle finger during his previous outing against the Padres, and it was worse against the Dodgers. It prevented him from controlling his fastball. He shrugged off the ugly results. "I'm not too worried for my next outing," Ohtani said. "I'm glad the blister peeled off today before the games actually matter." Ohtani had five days to let his finger heal before he was to make his first start of the regular season. Maddon said that Ohtani and athletic trainer Adam Nevala had both advised him that there was time for the blister issue to be resolved.

Although the performance against the Dodgers was enough to bring out many of the Ohtani critics who had been quiet throughout Spring Training, the Angels were undeterred.

Superstar Mike Trout was certainly ready to believe in Ohtani. Trout had been to the playoffs just once in his first nine seasons because the Angels lacked a strong supporting cast, so he was eager to see if Ohtani could be the difference-maker.

"It's like you're adding two stars," Trout said. "You're adding an ace and you're adding a guy to the middle of the lineup who can bang."

Maddon also repeated what he'd been saying all spring. Forget the results of the Dodgers game. Forget the blister. Ohtani finally looked different. What Maddon had seen over six weeks of Spring Training convinced him that 2021 was going to be nothing like the disappointment of 2020.

"The stuff that he's doing in the box, and the stuff that he's doing on the mound, I'm seeing with my own eyes for the first time," Maddon said. "I saw some good performances before I got here, via television, but in person, mechanically, technically, mentally, being under control . . . this is a new look for me, and it's spectacular."

CHAPTER

11

The Start of Something Extraordinary

Under normal circumstances a crowd of 13,207 at Angel Stadium would have been embarrassingly small. On Opening Day 2021, though, the players were thrilled to see a quarter of the ballpark full. They had played the previous season in empty stadiums because of the coronavirus pandemic. Instead of paying customers, there had been cardboard cutouts of fans in the seats. There had been artificial crowd noise pumped over the public address system. Now, in the Angels' first game in front of fans since 2019, they came from behind to beat the Chicago White Sox. Afterward, Manager Joe Maddon said the crowd sounded more like 40,000 than 13,000. It was an important step toward normalcy after a year in which so much of the world had been turned upside down.

Many of those fans came to the ballpark to see Shohei Ohtani, who was also looking for a return to the life he'd known. In Japan and in his first year in the majors, Ohtani had become accustomed to being one of the best players on the field. Since then, in 2019 and 2020, he was hardly "The Babe Ruth of Japan." He barely pitched in those two years, and his hitting had declined sharply.

Spring Training always brings new hope, and for fans of the Angels and Ohtani, the spring of 2021 had been mostly hopeful. Ohtani had finished the Cactus League with a rough outing on the mound, which he attributed to a blister, and then he started the regular season with 4 strikeouts in his first 9 at-bats. Although he had 2 hits, including a homer, his early swings could have been concerning to anyone looking for a reason to be concerned. He bailed out with his front foot on the strikeouts, as he had in 2020, and even the hits were balls he had pulled. Ohtani is at his best when he is driving balls up the middle and into the gaps.

Maddon didn't bite at an early question about Ohtani's performance at the plate. "What you're seeing I think is a function of where the ball is being pitched," Maddon said. "I don't see him bailing like I saw last year. I'm still seeing a swing with a lot of good force in it. For me, it's completely different than when he spun off the ball a lot last year."

Maddon was also committed to using Ohtani in a completely different way. Although Ohtani was scheduled to pitch the fourth game of the season, on a Sunday, he was in the lineup at designated hitter that Saturday. He had not been in the lineup the day before any of his previous big league starts.

The next day, Ohtani was on the mound. And in the lineup. Although he'd done it in a couple test runs in Spring Training, it was another first for Ohtani in a Major League regular season game.

The Angels forfeited the use of the DH for the first time in their history when they had Ohtani pitching and hitting second for the April 4 game against the White Sox, which was the ESPN Sunday Night Baseball broadcast.

In the top of the first inning, Ohtani had none of the issues with his velocity or his control that plagued him the last time he pitched in the majors, in 2020. His first pitch was a 98.2-mph fastball, and he had cranked a pitch up to 100.6 mph before the inning was over.

In the bottom of the inning, Ohtani stepped to the plate and interrupted the quiet murmur of a sparsely filled ballpark with a loud blast. He hammered a Dylan Cease fastball 451 feet, a no-doubt homer into the seats beyond the right field fence. The ball left his bat at 115.2 mph.

Ohtani had thrown a pitch 100 mph and hit a ball 115 mph within a span of fifteen minutes. No one else in the big leagues accomplished both of those milestones in the season, and Ohtani did it in the first inning of his first start.

Ohtani shut out the White Sox for the first 4 innings, throwing 64 pitches. He continued to hit 100 mph throughout the game, with 7 pitches in those 4 innings registering at triple digits. In the fifth inning, Billy Hamilton led off by hitting a sharp line drive into right field, but Juan Lagares dove to make the catch. Ohtani then gave up a single to Nick Madrigal. An out later, he made an errant pickoff throw and walked Adam Eaton. The Angels were up 3–0, but there were two on, one out and reigning MVP José Abreu was coming up to face Ohtani for the third time in the game.

The third time through the lineup sends up red flags for managers in this age of analytics, with statistics showing that a pitcher's effectiveness decreases when hitters see him a third time. Ohtani was at 78 pitches. Considering what had happened so far in the inning—a walk, a hit, and a hard out—and where the White Sox were in the order, conventional wisdom would have been for the Angels to yank Ohtani from the game.

Maddon, though, was willing to give Ohtani a longer leash than he'd had in the past. Ohtani threw 7 pitches, including a 99.6-mph fastball, before walking Abreu to load the bases. Maddon kept Ohtani in the game to face Yoán Moncada. Ohtani's first pitch was a splitter that got past catcher Max Stassi, allowing a run to score. Five pitches into the duel with Moncada, Ohtani had already gotten him to swing and miss at a pair of 99-mph fastballs. The 2-and-2 pitch was 100.9 mph, and Moncada fouled it off. Ohtani's next pitch, his ninety-second of the night, was a fastball over the inner half of the plate and Moncada swung through it. The ball ticked off Stassi's glove.

The catcher scrambled back to pick it up, then uncorked a wild throw to first. One run scored, and Abreu—who had started at second—was rumbling home. Ohtani raced to cover the plate, and the 6-foot-3, 235-pound Abreu slid into him, taking out his knees and knocking him to the ground as he scored the tying run.

In a matter of five pitches, Ohtani had gone from having a 3–0 lead to laying on the ground in pain in a 3–3 game. The feel-good story of his return to the mound didn't feel so good anymore.

Ohtani got up slowly and walked off the field. It was a frightening end to his start. Hours later, after the Angels won the game on a walk-off homer by Jared Walsh, Ohtani said he was okay. "When the collision happened the impact was kind of big," Ohtani said. "I couldn't get up right away, but after time I felt much better. . . . It wasn't as bad as it looked."

Once beyond the concern of Ohtani being hurt on that play, the question was why Maddon had left him in the game for those last two hitters. Maddon said it was part of the Angels' plan to let Ohtani play without so many restrictions. They were not going to treat him like some glass figurine.

"That's how a guy becomes *a guy*," Maddon said. "You gotta give him that opportunity, especially this time of year. If he does that now and is able to fight through it, he will know what he's capable of. If you are constantly taking guys out of troubling situations they are never going to find out." Maddon pointed out that Ohtani's stuff was still good, despite allowing the baserunners in the fifth. He had still cracked 100 mph with his penultimate pitch of the night. "The stuff didn't wane," Maddon said. "That's what you're looking at. I'm looking at him throwing the ball. I'm looking at the numbers. It's pretty good. I couldn't, in that moment, bring anybody in that I felt more confident about than him." Besides, Ohtani had still made the pitch he needed to escape the inning. He struck out Moncada. If Stassi had caught the ball, the conversation wouldn't be happening. Ohtani would have finished 5 innings with a 3–1 lead. Ohtani said he was "grateful" that Maddon had shown faith in him.

Ohtani had passed the first test of his new restriction-free baseball life, but it wasn't a perfect grade. A day after that collision at the plate, Ohtani was uninjured but just sore enough that Maddon decided it was best to give him the day off. A couple days later, Ohtani was hitting again, but Maddon revealed that the blister had started to become an issue late in his first start, so his next game on the mound was uncertain. "It's gotten a lot better," Maddon said. "That's why we're holding him back. We want this to be totally well." The Angels ended up giving Ohtani more than two weeks off before sending him out to pitch again on April 20.

In the meantime, though, he was in the lineup every day as the DH, and he was swinging a hot bat. Ohtani was 13 for 39 (.333) in the nine games leading up to his next start on the mound. On April 12 at Kansas City, Ohtani had the first of back-to-back three-hit games. The Angels were clinging to a 4–3 lead in the seventh inning when Ohtani rocketed a two-run double at 119 mph off the wall in right field. It was the hardest Ohtani would hit a ball all season. Only two players in the majors hit a ball harder: New York Yankees slugger Giancarlo Stanton (ten times) and San Diego Padres third baseman Manny Machado (once). To Ohtani, that line drive was the tangible demonstration of the leg strength he'd regained with a winter of work that was unrestricted by rehab. "I have my lower body there; it's strong," Ohtani said. "That's the biggest difference from last year. If it was last year I wouldn't have been able to pull that ball that hard."

By the time Ohtani's blister fully healed, he had missed enough throwing that they had him take a step back. He was on a limit of 75 pitches for a start at home against the Texas Rangers. Because of the limit, Maddon used Ohtani as a pitcher only. One of the issues of forfeiting the DH to have Ohtani hit and pitch is that the Angels would then need pinch-hitters for the relievers who follow Ohtani to the mound. If Ohtani didn't pitch deep into the game, which seemed likely given his pitch-limit, that could be a problem. American League rosters aren't built for many pinch-hitters. With that in mind, the Angels were content to simply test Ohtani on the mound and not worry about his hitting.

Ohtani made a couple adjustments because of the blister. He threw fastballs with just 39 percent of his pitches, down from 56 percent in his first start. He also turned the velocity down a notch. He had averaged 98.1 mph with his fastball in the first game, hitting 100 nine times, but this time he averaged 95.6 mph. With those tweaks to his game, Ohtani had no issues with the blister during an 80-pitch outing. He also had no trouble when the Rangers put the ball in play. He allowed only 1 hit and no runs in 4 innings. The problem was his control. Ohtani issued 6 walks and he hit a batter. He walked the bases loaded in the first inning, escaping the 28-pitch inning unscathed after he recorded 2 of his 7 strikeouts. Afterward, Ohtani was asked to assess his control. "I would give it a zero out of 100," he said. "It's definitely something I need to improve on with my next outing."

Ohtani had also walked 5 in 4⅔ innings in his first start, a troubling development alongside the mostly encouraging story of his finally being healthy and effective as a two-way player. Maddon did his best to defuse the issue of Ohtani's poor control. Besides the blister affecting his command, he had barely pitched in three years. "It's all about feel," Maddon said. "When your fingertip is messed up, the feel can kind of evade you. Just give him some more time. I think whatever's getting in the way is definitely workable to make him become better with his command."

The Angels were willing to be patient with Ohtani's command because he was still showing so many signs—on the mound and at the plate—of what he could be. He homered 3 more times in the next week, and held the Major League lead with 7 homers by April 25. When he started the next day, he made history.

For the first time in nearly a hundred years, a player started a game at pitcher while leading the majors in homers. On June 13, 1921, Babe Ruth made a rare start on the mound for the New York Yankees, while leading the majors with 19 homers. By that time Ruth was no longer a full-time two-way player, having mostly abandoned pitching after the Yankees acquired him prior to the 1920 season. That was one of the reasons that all of the Shohei Ohtani–Babe Ruth comparisons missed the mark.

But there was another reason that the discussion was historically incomplete: the other two-way players who had come between them.

* * *

As Shohei Ohtani's accomplishments sparked more and more examination of Babe Ruth, Bob Kendrick found himself reminding more and more people of the hole in their knowledge of baseball history.

Since 2011, Kendrick had been the President of the Negro Leagues Baseball Museum in Kansas City, which shines a light on the professional baseball leagues that existed before Major League Baseball was integrated in the late 1940s. In December 2020, Major League Baseball announced that the Negro Leagues would be reclassified as major leagues. They would go into the record books just like other top tier leagues, like the American Association or the Federal League from the early part of the twentieth century. In the Negro Leagues there had been plenty of two-way players in the decades after Ruth mostly stopped pitching.

Negro Leagues stars like "Bullet" Joe Rogan, Leon Day, Martín Dihigo, and Ted "Double Duty" Radcliffe were all known for regularly pitching and hitting. Rogan, Day, and Dihigo have all been inducted into the National Baseball Hall of Fame in Cooperstown, New York. Although those players are largely unknown to all but the most serious baseball fans, the performance of Ohtani in 2021 provided a platform for Kendrick and other Negro Leagues experts to share their stories.

"It's obviously a teaching moment," Kendrick said of Ohtani's sensational 2021 season. "It shines a very bright light on the history of the Negro Leagues and the immense talent that was in the Negro Leagues. It's been refreshing for me to see this kid from Japan, to basically defy what skeptics probably thought. Most people thought that he couldn't do it. He did it, and he did it in dramatic fashion."

Kendrick said the Negro Leagues and baseball in Japan have been intertwined for nearly a century. The Philadelphia Royal Giants of the Negro Leagues visited Japan in 1927, seven years before the more famous Major League tour led by Babe Ruth in 1934. Kendrick said the Royal Giants' two visits "sparked the fire of professional baseball in Japan."

Decades later, players from the Negro Leagues would integrate the major leagues, answering critics who didn't believe their talents would translate to a different league. Japanese players faced a similar challenge. That's why Kendrick believes that Buck O'Neil—a Negro Leagues player and manager who would become one of the legendary storytellers of that chapter of baseball history—developed such a bond with Ichiro Suzuki. A former star from the Orix Blue Wave, Suzuki came to the majors in 2001 and amassed more than 3,000 hits in a career that will land him in Cooperstown when he becomes eligible in 2025.

"Buck O'Neil saw so much of the Negro Leagues in Ichiro," Kendrick said. "I think he would feel the same thing about Shohei Ohtani. When Ichiro announced that he was coming over to the United States to play Major League Baseball, what's the first thing that came out of people's mouths? *You did that in your league but you won't do that in our league.* It was the same way for the Negro Leagues players, as they were transitioning into the major leagues. Despite how good they may have been, there was this prevailing belief that you might have accomplished that in your league, but you get to this league and you won't do it. But they lit that league up, too. Because a great player is a great player."

While Ohtani was lighting up the major leagues as a two-way player, he was providing a "teaching moment," as Kendrick said, for retelling the stories of the two-way stars of the Negro Leagues.

Ted Radcliffe earned the nickname "Double Duty" while playing for the New York Black Yankees in 1932. He caught Satchel Paige's shutout in the first game of a doubleheader. He also hit a grand slam in that game. In the second game of the day, Radcliffe took the mound himself and pitched a shutout. Radcliffe stands apart from the other great two-way players in the Negro Leagues because he was the only one who was primarily a catcher when he wasn't pitching. He made the Negro Leagues All-Star Game as a pitcher three times and as a catcher three times. Radcliffe was a better pitcher than he was a hitter, but he made up for the latter with his defensive work behind the plate. "Duty's impact cannot be denied, because number one, he's probably pulling the most difficult of a two-way role, when you talk about pitching and catching," Kendrick said. "We know what catching does to the body. It just beats you up."

Leon Day was so well regarded during his Negro Leagues career in the 1930s and 1940s that there was talk that he would follow Jackie Robinson to the major leagues.

Day was best known as a pitcher. According to the SeamHeads.com database, which is the most complete reconciling of Negro Leagues statistics, Day posted a 3.40 ERA in 113 games pitched in the 1930s and 1940s. He also hit .308 over 728 plate appearances. Monte Irvin, who began his career as an outfielder in the Negro Leagues and later played alongside Willie Mays for the New York Giants, famously said that Hall of Fame pitcher Bob Gibson "had nothing on Leon Day." O'Neil also said that Day was actually a better center fielder than he was a pitcher. "To be compared in one breath to Bob Gibson and then also that he was a better center fielder, he had to be some kind of ballplayer," Kendrick said.

The Negro Leagues two-way star who most stacks up to Ohtani physically was Martín Dihigo. "He was six-four, six-five, probably about 210 and movie star good looks," Kendrick said. "He had *super-star* written all over him." Dihigo was born in Cuba and also played in his home country and Mexico. He was nicknamed "El Maestro." Kendrick said he earned the moniker "because he did it all. He played all nine positions, and he played all nine of them well." The SeamHeads. com statistics for Dihigo are limited to just nine seasons because of his time in leagues outside of the United States, but in the recorded Negro Leagues seasons he compiled an ERA+ of 141 and an OPS+ of 138. That means he was 41 and 38 percent better than average for his league as a pitcher and hitter, respectively.

The best two-way player of the Negro Leagues, though, is generally considered to be "Bullet" Joe Rogan. Phil S. Dixon, who wrote a biography of Rogan, said his research led him to the conclusion that Rogan was, in fact, "the greatest all-around baseball player that ever lived." Dixon believes that Rogan was lost in the shuffle among better known Negro Leagues players because most of them played in the East. Players like Rogan, who spent most of his career with the Kansas City Monarchs, were underappreciated.

Rogan was just five-seven, 160 pounds, but packed a lot of talent into a small frame. "While he didn't look like an exceptional athlete, he was a great athlete," Kendrick said. Rogan was a catcher when he first started playing before his military service, but when he emerged from World War I at age twenty-seven to play for the Monarchs, he had begun pitching. His nickname of "Bullet" was because of his blazing fastball, another similarity to Ohtani. Rogan starred for Kansas City from 1920 to 1930. His career ERA+ was 161 and his OPS+ was 152.

According to SeamHeads.com, in 1925 Rogan was 18–2 with a 1.84 ERA on the mound, and at the plate he batted .372 with a 1.007 OPS. It was arguably the best of several seasons in which Rogan excelled as a pitcher and hitter. SeamHeads.com shows Rogan posting an OPS of .990 or better in seasons with at least 50 games five times. He had eight seasons in which he had an ERA of 3.10 or better over at least 100 innings.

While Radcliffe, Day, Dihigo, and Rogan were the best of the two-way players in the Negro Leagues, they were not the only ones. Because rosters were typically only sixteen or seventeen deep, teams could not afford to have pitchers specialize, so most of them played other positions. "You needed that level of versatility," Kendrick said. "But what it also speaks to is the great athletes who were playing in the Negro Leagues. I described them as having been some of the greatest *athletes* to play baseball, because by and large, they could have played any sport."

* * *

When Shohei Ohtani took the mound against the Rangers in Arlington on April 26, he was still faring better as a hitter than as a pitcher. He threw 29 pitches in the first inning and gave up 4 runs. His control was lacking, with 2 walks, a hit batter, and a wild pitch. Most of the damage came on a three-run homer by Nate Lowe, who hammered an Ohtani cut fastball over the right field fence. Ohtani had never thrown many cutters, but he had started trying to incorporate the pitch because of the control issues he was having with his four-seam fastball. After that difficult first inning, though, Ohtani went with more four-seamers, and he found his splitter, the signature pitch that he often uses to put away hitters with two strikes. Ohtani did not allow a run through the next 4 innings. He struck out 8 and didn't walk any over those 4 scoreless innings.

At the plate, Ohtani had walked and scored in the top of the first. Just after his rough inning on the mound, he came up in the top of the second and yanked a two-run double down the right field line, cutting the deficit to 4–3. He then scored the tying run on a Mike Trout single. Ohtani's second hit of the game was a bunt single. The Rangers—like most teams—had pulled their infielders to the right side in a shift against Ohtani, leaving a hole near third base which he exploited with the bunt. The Angels went on to win the game, 9–4, with Ohtani picking up his first victory as a pitcher since May 2018, before Tommy John surgery.

"If you weren't entertained by watching him tonight," Manager Joe Maddon said, "you can't be entertained watching the game of baseball."

Maddon pulled Ohtani after just 75 pitches because the pitcher had begun to develop a blister—in a different spot from the one that had affected him earlier in the month. He nonetheless put Ohtani right back in the lineup the next day. Ohtani was the Angels' DH for the next seven games, at that point playing in 27 of the first 28 games. Ohtani took a 93-mph fastball from Seattle Mariners lefthander Justus Sheffield on the elbow on May 2. Although the pitch hit Ohtani in the protective pad he wears, it was still enough for the Angels to give him a couple extra days off before his next start. (He had been scheduled to pitch the following day.) It was exactly the type of situation that had prompted the Angels to give him the day off before he started when they first used him as a two-way player in 2018.

The Angels were using a six-man rotation, which meant that any-time they needed to scratch any of their starters, they would have at least one other starter who had the standard four days of rest since his previous outing. When Ohtani couldn't pitch on May 3, the Angels instead went with lefthander José Quintana, who still had five days rest. Also, Maddon reasoned that Ohtani could just as easily suffer some kind of injury *two* days before a start that would prevent him from pitching, so they were already taking a risk merely by using him as a two-way player. They were willing to accept a marginal extra risk in order to get his bat in the lineup. "I'm not going to take different days away from him just because of a freak accident," Maddon said. "I'm not normally knee-jerk with all my stuff. That's just part of the game." Maddon also pointed out that Ohtani wanted to play, and the whole basis for the change in approach with Ohtani was to get better production out of him by letting him play as he saw fit. Ohtani responded to getting hit by stealing two bases, which showed Maddon his competitiveness. "That's a growth moment for him," Maddon said. "He said, 'You hit me, I'll steal two bases.' I could not have loved that moment any more than I did yesterday." Ohtani was in the lineup at DH on May 3, the day he was supposed to pitch, as well as May 4, the day before his rescheduled outing.

Neither Ohtani's elbow nor that developing blister were issues when he did pitch again, but the control trouble persisted. Repeating a familiar theme, Ohtani walked 2 in a 21-pitch first inning. Ohtani walked six in the game. Even though he didn't give up any runs, and only 1 hit, the walks raised his pitch-count enough that he could only last 5 innings, and the Angels' bullpen then gave up 3 runs in a game they lost.

Four starts into the season Ohtani had a 2.41 ERA and he had struck out 30 in 18⅔ innings. Ohtani had also issued 19 walks, a staggering number that was not sustainable. Offensively, Ohtani had 9 homers and a .264 batting average in his first 27 games. His OPS was .938. The troubling undercurrent to his offensive performance was the fact that he'd struck out 28 times and only walked 5 times. Although Ohtani had given plenty of reason for optimism in his first month, his control of the strike zone—on the mound and at the plate—was threatening to drag down everything else if he didn't make changes. Ohtani, however, had shown throughout his career on both sides of the globe that he knew how to adjust.

CHAPTER

12

"The Gold Standard"

Shohei Ohtani without restrictions cost a future Hall of Famer his job. When the Angels were planning for 2021, they had to account for Ohtani having days off around his pitching schedule because that's what he'd done in the past. As they went through Spring Training and the first month of the season, they learned those breaks were not necessary. Ohtani could be the DH the day before and the day after he pitched, and he could hit and pitch on the same day. That meant there was no longer much opportunity at DH for Albert Pujols, a forty-one-year-old at the tail end of a brilliant career. Pujols was hitting .198 on May 6, when the Angels cut him loose. Although Pujols was clearly no longer productive, the manner in which the Angels let him go was a surprise. Pujols had spent the previous nine seasons with the Angels, passing the 600-homer and 3,000-hit milestones and adding to his resume for Cooperstown while wearing their uniform. The Angels were still on the hook for the last $25 million of his $240-million deal because no team claimed Pujols on waivers (which would have meant also taking over his contract). After the Angels officially released Pujols, he signed with the Los Angeles Dodgers, who paid him the minimum salary to fill a bench role while the Angels owed him the rest.

Although the Angels could have kept Pujols as a pinch-hitter and mentor, they certainly didn't have many starts for him. Jared Walsh, a rising young player, was their first baseman, and Ohtani was the DH. Both players were much more productive than Pujols, something the Angels couldn't have been sure of before the season began. Walsh had one hot month at the end of 2020 and a bad spring, while Ohtani had struggled the previous season.

And then Ohtani's 2021 breakout began. For all of the encouraging signs that he showed the Angels at the plate and on the mound in April, starting in May his game rose to a new level.

On May 11, Ohtani took the mound at Houston's Minute Maid Park, the same ballpark where his dreams of avoiding Tommy John surgery had died two and a half years earlier. Ohtani had faced the Astros on September 2, 2018, after three months of rehabilitating a damaged ulnar collateral ligament. He threw 49 pitches, and days later he learned that he'd torn his UCL. Ever since then, the baseball world had been waiting to see if Ohtani could again be the kind of frontline starter he was before surgery. This time, he was.

Facing a dangerous lineup in a hitter-friendly ballpark, Ohtani gave up one run in 7 innings. More impressive, the control problems that had haunted him in his first four starts of the season were gone. He walked 1 and struck out 10. Ohtani needed just 88 pitches to record 21 outs. "Spectacular," Manager Joe Maddon said. "To see Shohei find his fastball command, this is what we've been talking about. That's what it's going to look like most of the time. . . . That's the gold standard. He was outstanding."

Although Ohtani said afterward that his body felt "heavy and sluggish" during his pregame warmups, he nonetheless found enough of a groove to pitch his best game in three years. "My mechanics felt very efficient and there was no useless movement," Ohtani said.

The game also marked a new milestone in the way the Angels used Ohtani. The Angels had forfeited the DH to have Ohtani in the lineup while he was pitching, slotting him into the second spot in the order.

In the late innings, they made a rare move to keep Ohtani's bat in the game. Angels number nine hitter Kurt Suzuki made the final out in the top of the eighth, leaving Ohtani two spots away. Although Maddon decided Ohtani had done enough on the mound after he pitched the bottom of the seventh, the game was tied and he wanted to get him to the plate again. Ohtani moved to right field as righthander Aaron Slegers took the mound in the bottom of the eighth. It was the kind of reverse double-switch that was only useful for a player like Ohtani. Unfortunately for the Angels, Slegers and two subsequent relievers allowed the Astros to score 4 runs, so the game was no longer close when Ohtani came to bat again.

The Angels lost the game and the extra at-bat they got out of Ohtani was not significant, but the moment was. It was yet another example of the loosened restrictions on Ohtani. Even though Ohtani had not practiced in the outfield, the Angels sent him out there, figuring his natural athleticism would be sufficient. They did it even though they were subjecting Ohtani to the risk of an injury. He could run into a wall or hurt his arm uncorking a throw. The Angels were willing to take that chance because Ohtani assured them he could do it if it meant another at-bat. "It was a close game," Ohtani said, "and if I could make a difference with the bat I was all for it."

Ohtani got the chance to make a difference several days later, on May 16 in Boston. The Angels trailed the Red Sox, 5–4, with two outs in the top of the ninth inning in the series finale on a Sunday afternoon. Facing closer Matt Barnes, Mike Trout dropped a bloop single into right field. Ohtani, who had been hitting in front of Trout until Maddon flip-flopped them that day, then yanked a 97-mph fastball just inside the famed Pesky Pole, down the right field line. It was the first time in eight years that the Angels had hit a go-ahead homer when they were down to their final out. Ohtani called it the biggest of the 59 homers he had hit to that point in his career, particularly because the Angels had lost the first two games of the series in ugly fashion. They'd blown a seventh-inning lead on Friday and had been blasted,

9–0, on Saturday. "The first two games of the series, it wasn't a good way to lose," Ohtani said. "It was huge for us to come up with this one. We showed that we could beat any team and get things rolling."

The good feelings lasted just a day, though. On May 17, in the first inning of the first game of a series against the Cleveland Indians in Anaheim, Trout felt something in his right leg as he was running the bases. At first, the pain was so sharp that Trout assumed he'd been hit by the ball. His next thought was that he'd blown out his Achilles. Although Trout was relieved to learn that he had only a Grade 2 calf strain, that injury was expected to cost him six to eight weeks. But it would be much worse. Trout suffered a setback in July and didn't play again for the rest of the season.

At the time of the injury in May, though, the Angels still had hopes of withstanding Trout's absence, largely because of the way Ohtani was adjusting and improving week by week.

* * *

Righthander Alex Cobb was a veteran in his tenth big league season when he pitched for the Angels in 2021. He had seen a little of everything in a rollercoaster career. Cobb had ascended to the Tampa Bay Rays as a phenom at twenty-three, undergone Tommy John surgery at twenty-seven, battled back to earn a $57-million contract with the Baltimore Orioles at thirty, and then had his contract dumped to the Angels at thirty-three. Cobb had not seen much of Shohei Ohtani as an opponent, but once they were wearing the same uniform, he quickly became a fan. A few months into the season, Cobb began to appreciate Ohtani in a new way.

Cobb said it hit him one day when he noticed that Ohtani was setting up opponents the way veterans do when they no longer have overpowering raw stuff. Except Ohtani still had that, too. "He has an elite-type feel for the execution of pitches," Cobb said. "He's turning into not only a top *plus-stuff guy*, but a top *pitchability guy*. . . . It's going to be really scary to see what he turns into. This is really his first full season [pitching] in the big leagues. It takes a long time to learn how to set up guys. A lot of guys have the stuff, but when you combine that with the pitchability, then you're talking about a top-five pitcher in the league."

Ohtani's ascent as a pitcher could largely be traced to the fact that he was finally getting the mound time he needed. In the 2019 and 2020 seasons, he had faced a total of 16 batters in two big league games. He needed the time *off the mound* to regain the strength in his arm, and he needed time *on the mound* to regain everything else. "There has to be some patience," pitching coach Matt Wise said in June 2021. "He didn't have a lot of innings under his belt last year."

Even when Ohtani had been healthy as a pitcher, he'd often had his routine interrupted. He had blister issues and a minor ankle injury in April 2018. In April 2021, he again had blister trouble. The next month, a start was pushed back when he was hit in the elbow by a pitch. After that, though, Ohtani went months without any physical issues keeping him from taking his turns on the mound. The only time he had a start delayed was when the Angels were in Oakland on May 27 and Ohtani was on an Angels charter bus that got stuck in traffic near the team's San Francisco hotel. The bus couldn't make it across the Bay Bridge in time, so Ohtani, interpreter Ippei Mizuhara, and catcher Kurt Suzuki instead hopped on the Bay Area Rapid Transit—the region's subway system. They took the wrong train, delaying their arrival at the ballpark by enough time that the Angels simply pushed Ohtani's start to the next day.

Transportation issues notwithstanding, Ohtani got enough regular innings over that two-month span to refine his mechanics and his pitch repertoire. His cut fastball, which he had barely thrown since leaving Japan, showed significant improvement during that period.

The cutter. It was the signature pitch for Mariano Rivera and Roy Halladay, who began their paths toward the Hall of Fame when they added the pitch early in their careers. A cutter is thrown with a slightly different grip than a traditional four-seam or two-seam fastball, giving it more horizontal movement. Ohtani had thrown a cutter in Japan, but he had not used the pitch at all in the majors in 2018 or in his two starts in 2020. In April 2021, he experimented with it, and by May the cutter had become a meaningful part of his arsenal. "It's just another toy," Suzuki said. "He's got so many weapons." Ohtani began throwing his cutter 20 to 30 percent of the time. The cutter typically induces weak contact, which makes it a useful pitch for getting quick outs, rather than relying on strikeouts that can drive up a pitch count. Ohtani's cutter averaged 86.9 mph in 2021, and opponents hit just .241 when they put it in play. By contrast, his four-seam fastball was much harder—95.6 mph—but opponents hit .294 against it. As a two-way player, Ohtani constantly faced the issue of preserving his energy, and the cutter helped him do just that. He could get outs without resorting to his maximum velocity fastball or breaking balls that stressed his arm. More efficiency with his pitches helped him get deeper into games without cracking the 100-pitch threshold.

Ohtani also continued to demonstrate an ability to manipulate the velocity of his four-seam fastball. In his first start of the season, he had hit 100 mph nine times. He didn't do it again until September, other than one crowd-pleasing pitch at the All-Star Game. His reduced velocity coincided with better control and an end to the blister issues that had nagged him in April. Ohtani said he backed off on the velocity in one game because of the blister, but otherwise he said the change was not intentional. His catcher thought otherwise.

"He's a very smart guy," Suzuki said. "I think he understands his body better than a lot of the guys I played with. He knows when he has to subtract and add. You see a couple times when he'll pump a couple 98s in there in a big situation when he needs it. But he knows if he throws strikes, he can still throw hard enough to get guys off his split, his breaking balls, and all that kind of stuff."

Wise, who had pitched in the big leagues for nine years and been a coach in the minors and majors for ten years, said Ohtani "has the ability to add and subtract during the game better than anyone I've ever seen. He'll go 91 to 99. That's a skill that not many people possess."

Baseball researcher Eric Fridén began tracking a stat he called "reserve power," which measured the way a pitcher's velocity increased with the pressure of the situation. Ohtani's average fastball in 2021 increased from 95.3 mph with no runners in scoring position to 96.8 mph with runners in scoring position. Fridén had been tracking the statistic since 2008, and by his measure Ohtani's reserve power over the course of the 2021 season was surpassed by only future Hall of Famer Justin Verlander and reliever Andrew Miller. Miller had done it just once, and Verlander had done it for seven seasons. Ohtani was well aware of this phenomenon. "I feel like my velo goes up once guys get on," Ohtani said. "It's something natural. I'm not really controlling it."

Fridén also tracked "staying power," which is when a pitcher can increase the velocity of his fastball later in the game. Ohtani's 2021 season ranked seventh on Fridén's list. Suzuki said Ohtani was "pacing himself," by manipulating his velocity.

More important than the velocity of his fastball, though, was Ohtani's control. Manager Joe Maddon had described Ohtani's fastball in April as "all over the place." Ohtani walked 9.2 hitters per 9 innings in his first 4 starts, and 2.0 over his final 19. When Ohtani missed the strike zone and fell behind in counts, it was more difficult to get hitters to chase his signature split-finger fastball.

It all came together on June 4, when Ohtani struck out 10 and did not walk a hitter in a victory over the Seattle Mariners. It was the first time in Ohtani's 20 career starts that he didn't issue a walk. He threw eight splitters, and the Mariners struck out on seven of them. "He's got one of the special pitches in our game," Mariners manager Scott Servais said. "The Ohtani split-finger is about as good as it gets. When he's commanding it like he was tonight, it's a real challenge. It's as good a pitch as you're gonna see in the league."

Two starts later Ohtani further demonstrated how much his game had advanced on the mound. Ohtani went into his June 17 start against the Detroit Tigers aware that he hadn't been throwing his slider much. "I was originally planning on throwing more sliders to lefties, because I saw my percentage was really low," Ohtani said. "Once I started throwing it, it felt better and better so I stuck with it." Ohtani ended up throwing sliders with 41 percent of his pitches that night, up from just 2 percent in his previous start.

It was an example of another of Ohtani's special qualities. From one game to the next, you never knew which pitch he'd be featuring. During the 2021 season his fastball usage ranged from 76 percent to 19 percent. His cutter use peaked at 29 percent, while he didn't throw it at all in other games. Among pitchers who threw at least four different pitches and faced at least 500 hitters in 2021, Ohtani had the highest standard deviation of his pitch usage, according to Ben Lindbergh of *The Ringer*. Suzuki said Ohtani would often develop a game plan on the fly, based on how each pitch felt in that game.

Against the Tigers, Ohtani rode the slider to a 6-inning performance in which he gave up just 1 run. The Angels broke open a close game on a Taylor Ward grand slam in the seventh inning, which caused an eruption among the 30,790 fans at Angel Stadium.

It was the first time in 627 days that the ballpark had hosted a game without restrictions on the crowd size. In 2020, Major League games were played in empty ballparks because of the COVID-19 pandemic, and local regulations allowed for limited crowds for the start of 2021. When the restrictions were finally lifted for "Reopening Day," as the Angels dubbed it, the stands could once again be filled. It was a coincidence that Ohtani pitched the Angels' first game in two seasons when they could fill the ballpark, but it was fitting. Ohtani had been a turnstile-mover when he debuted as a two-way player in the majors in 2018, and his game was peaking again when the gates fully opened in 2021.

* * *

Kaoru Iwase, a thirty-eight-year-old wedding planner who had moved from Japan to Orange County in 2014, regularly attended Angels games in her first few years in Southern California. Once Ohtani arrived in 2018, though, it became a borderline obsession. Iwase said she attended about sixty games per season in Ohtani's first two years. In 2021, once the ballparks were again open to fans after the pandemic, Iwase had a bolder plan. She wanted to go to all 162 games.

"Watching Shohei Ohtani play is kind of my motivation in life right now," Iwase said through an interpreter after the 2021 season. "Every time I see him, he does something great. Home runs, stealing bases, breaking records. If I missed games, I would miss something."

Iwase ended up seeing 136 games in 2021, including the vast majority of the road games. She and her husband, Tomoyuki, spent about $50,000 traveling around the country to follow Ohtani. She went to many of the games herself, leaving her husband to run their wedding planning business while she worked remotely. "To be honest, I wasn't doing much as a wedding planner this year," she said.

What Iwase did was build a brand as the self-proclaimed number one Ohtani fan in the world, arguably the leading face of Ohtani-mania, which had gripped the major leagues soon after his arrival in 2018. Early in the 2021 season, Iwase created an Instagram account and a YouTube channel to document her journey following Ohtani. The YouTube channel went viral when she posted a video of Ohtani hitting his go-ahead homer in the ninth inning at Fenway Park in May. By the end of the season she had more than 150,000 subscribers, and a handful of videos that had been viewed more than 2 million times apiece.

Iwase said she was getting only one or two hours of sleep per night because of the time she spent traveling and editing videos. She also tried to get into the ballpark as soon as the gates opened, so she could have the maximum opportunity to get a glimpse of Ohtani doing pregame workouts, or maybe even get his autograph. She said she nearly got him to sign in New York, but he stopped signing just before her turn. Iwase normally sat in right field, which she figured allowed her the best chance to get one of his home runs. Although she never got a home run ball, Ohtani did throw her two balls during his pregame workouts. She proudly displayed the balls in plastic cases after the season.

Along the way, Iwase said she helped convert fans of other teams into fans of Ohtani. "I was booed at the beginning, but we would communicate and by the end of the game I was accepted and we were high-fiving," Iwase said. She also developed friendships with other Angels fans and Ohtani fans that she met in Anaheim and on the road.

While Iwase may have been one of the most hardcore Ohtani fans, she had plenty of company. Fans from Japan streamed into Angel Stadium. A group of fans began regularly showing up in right field, holding placards that spelled out OHTANILAND. One of the early examples of Ohtani's road following occurred in April 2018 in Kansas City, when three female college students from Japan were screaming so loudly that a security guard asked them to quiet down when Ohtani was batting. Ohtani, who had been accustomed to that treatment from his days in Japan, insisted that he hadn't requested the women stop screaming. Wherever the Angels played, the ballparks were dotted by groups of fans, many of them Japanese, in Ohtani jerseys.

Throughout the season, Ohtani sparked a boost in tourism from Japan to Orange County. Visit Anaheim, an organization that promotes tourism and conventions in Orange County, reported that the number of visitors from Japan increased 4 percent in 2018 from the previous two years. It continued in 2019 once Ohtani was activated from the injured list in May. "We have seen last year—and now that he has been activated this year—that there is a boost in visitation to games because of Shohei Ohtani," Charles Harris, senior vice president of marketing for Visit Anaheim, said in 2019.

Kihei Otani, the president of the Orange County Japanese American Association, said in 2021 that Ohtani was a source of pride for everyone from Japan, baseball fan or not. "He's definitely a bright spot in our community," Otani said. "Japanese Americans here are all excited to see him playing. I can't imagine any Japanese American not rooting for him and not going to his games to support him."

Of course, Ohtani wasn't just the pride of Japan. He was a unique baseball star, succeeding as a pitcher and hitter like no one had in a century. He created an attendance bump when he took the mound in 2018, and that continued in 2021. Around midseason, the Angels were averaging more than 3,000 extra fans on the days that Ohtani pitched, according to Robert Arthur of Baseball Prospectus.

When the pandemic restrictions were finally lifted in June to allow for the Angels to sell all the seats at Angel Stadium, they sold 30,709 tickets for "Reopening Day," a Thursday night with Ohtani on the mound. The next three games of the weekend series, with Ohtani only DHing, drew a maximum of 23,175. It happened on the road, too. When the Angels were in New York in late June, the Wednesday night game that Ohtani started drew 30,714 fans. The Monday and Tuesday games each drew at least 5,000 fewer fans. The Angels played a four-game series in Texas, August 2–5, and the Ohtani start attracted 27,360 fans, 6,000 more than any of the other three games in the series.

The extra fans also wanted to see Ohtani get a chance to hit. At least twice in 2021, in Minnesota and Baltimore, the home crowd booed when Ohtani was intentionally walked.

Meanwhile, fans on the other side of the globe also had their attention fixed on Ohtani. In Oshū, the town in Northern Japan where Ohtani was born, the city celebrates "Ohtani Day," on the seventeenth of every month, a nod to his uniform number. All around the city, people wear Ohtani jerseys in banks, restaurants, and doctor's offices. The tradition has grown ever since 2018.

In Ohtani's first two years, there were rice paddies around Oshū that were painted and cut to create likenesses of Ohtani. (They abandoned the artwork in 2020 to discourage tourists amid the pandemic.) The Oshū City Hall includes a sculpture with a laser-created replica of Ohtani's hand, allowing visitors to "shake the hand" of the town's most famous son.

The pride in Ohtani's accomplishments swelled in Oshū throughout his historic 2021 season.

"We've been cheering on Ohtani for a very long time," said Katsuyoshi Ohkoshi, the head of the Oshū City Promotion Division. "But he's kind of ascended to a different level this season. Talking with friends, talking with people around the city, he's become so great that we ask ourselves: Did he really grow up here? Is he someone from this city?"

• • •

As fans lapped up everything that Ohtani did in the first half of the 2021 season, it was no surprise that he began to run away with base-ball's ultimate popularity contest. Ohtani had nearly twice as many votes as any other designated hitter when the first All-Star voting results were released on June 14. Ohtani was first with just over 525,000 votes. J. D. Martinez of the Boston Red Sox was a distant second with just under 300,000. In 2021, the All-Star election was a two-step process, though. Ohtani finished the first round with nearly 2 million votes, while Martinez had just over 750,000. Ohtani then went into a four-day run-off election against Martinez and third-place finisher Yordan Álvarez of the Houston Astros. Ohtani won that round, too, on July 1, officially earning the All-Star spot at DH. "It is a pretty big milestone," Ohtani said. "I want the team to win first. That's the main priority for me. As long as I'm performing and helping the team win, it should come naturally to be selected as an All-Star."

That was just a part of the story, though. All along there was a sec-ondary question of whether Ohtani would also pitch in the All-Star Game. Pitchers for the All-Star Game are determined by a vote of the players, not the fans, with a few extra spots filled by the Commission-er's office. The complication was that standard baseball rules don't allow a player to DH and pitch in the same game. When the Angels had Ohtani pitch and hit, they had to forfeit the use of the DH. The questions of whether Ohtani would pitch, and whether Major League Baseball would bend the rules to accommodate him, would all be answered closer to the July 13 game at Denver's Coors Field.

Another question about Ohtani's All-Star week participation was decided before Ohtani was even officially selected for the game. Days after the first voting results were released, with Ohtani comfortably ahead, he was selected to participate in the Home Run Derby.

Ohtani and the Home Run Derby had been connected ever since he started hitting tape-measure homers as a rookie in 2018. Even though he was not certain to make the All-Star team as a pitcher or a hitter back in his first year, there was plenty of discussion of whether Ohtani should be selected for the Derby. Ohtani said at the time he'd be interested, but the call never came. He had injured his elbow about a month before the All-Star Game, and only returned to the lineup as a hitter about a week before the game.

In 2021, though, there were no such health issues. The only question was whether he'd accept the invitation. The event can include hundreds of extra rib-jarring swings with the adrenaline of a worldwide television audience and a $1 million prize on the line. For a player who was already balancing the workload of pitching and hitting, it was certainly reasonable to pass on the Derby. Ohtani wanted to give it a shot, though. "I weighed my options and thought about it for a few days," Ohtani said. "I figured it was something I wanted to be a part of." Manager Joe Maddon also wasn't going to stand in the way for the sake of workload management. "It's like every other Home Run Derby. You're going to have these questions about should he do it or not, is he going to get hurt or not, will he get tired or not?" Maddon said. "I just don't function that way. This is an opportunity for him to be showcased even more."

Although the Derby would be a showcase for Ohtani, there was no suggestion that his inclusion was merely for publicity or to draw a television audience from Japan. Ohtani had been blasting balls over fences at a jaw-dropping pace all season. Ohtani and Vladimir Guerrero Jr. of the Toronto Blue Jays had been jockeying for the Major League lead in homers since late April. From May 14 until the All-Star break, Ohtani actually had more homers (23) than singles (14).

The Angels faced the Kansas City Royals and former top prospect Kris Bubic on June 8 at Angel Stadium. In the first inning, the twenty-three-year-old lefthander threw Ohtani a 2-and-2 changeup that ended up over the heart of the plate. Ohtani blasted it 470 feet—the longest homer of his career. The ball landed in the seats just a few feet from the fence alongside the green batter's eye. "That's the farthest ball I think I've seen hit here," said Maddon, who had spent twelve years as a Major League coach or manager with the Angels. "I've never seen one hit there before." The Angels ended up scoring 6 runs in 4 innings against Bubic, and Maddon said the tone was set by Ohtani's blast. "It has an impact on that pitcher, I promise you," he said. "That kid's pretty good, and we roughed him up early. It can take confidence away from the pitcher."

A couple weeks later the Angels were at Tampa Bay's Tropicana Field, where Maddon had managed for nine years. The cavernous indoor home of the Rays has four concentric circular catwalks that hang high above the field. The "A" ring, over the center of the field, is the smallest. The fourth ring, the "D" ring, hugs the outer walls of the ballpark. That's the catwalk that Ohtani hit when he crushed an Andrew Kittridge changeup far over the right field fence. It was registered as a 453-foot homer by StatCast. Maddon wasn't buying it. "There's no way that's 453, I'm sorry," Maddon said. "I've been here many times and I've never seen that in a game or in batting practice."

Ohtani did it again just before the All-Star break, when the Angels were in Seattle on July 9. Ohtani had struggled against lefties at various points throughout his career, but he had no trouble with a fastball that Marco Gonzales left at the top of the strike zone in the fourth inning. Ohtani crushed it 463 feet into the upper deck at T-Mobile Park. He was just the sixth player to hit a ball into that part of the upper deck at the twenty-one-year-old ballpark. Television viewers didn't even see the ball land because the camera operator didn't pan high enough to capture the monster shot. Instead, the frame was filled with fans in the lower deck, many of them looking up and wondering where the ball had gone. Only three people were sitting in that part of the ballpark, including Reggie Pelka, who had gone with two friends to the distant part of the stadium to get away from the crowd and "chill," according to

Sam Blum, the Angels beat writer for *The Athletic*. Blum trekked up to the farthest reaches of T-Mobile Park to get the story on the blast. Pelka and his friends certainly didn't expect a baseball to find them. "It just kept getting closer and closer, and I was like, 'What the fuck?'" Pelka told Blum. "I didn't know what was about to happen."

Pelka was about to become part of a show that gained steam with each homer that Ohtani hit, delighting the fans and his teammates. Ohtani and shortstop José Iglesias developed a tradition of engaging in entertaining and elaborate high fives in the dugout after each of Ohtani's blasts. (Much to the chagrin of the fans, the tradition ended when Iglesias was released in September.)

Ohtani had said in his first interview of Spring Training that he wanted to have more fun, and clearly he was doing that, at the plate and on the mound. In a May start at Angel Stadium against Tampa Bay, outfielder Austin Meadows blistered a comebacker that Ohtani snagged. Ohtani then playfully apologized to Meadows as he was running to first. Ohtani would often joke with opponents while on the field, demonstrating his improving English and Spanish.

Ohtani also became more demonstrative with his celebrations on the mound after a big out, pumping his fist and screaming when he came through in a big moment. Japanese players are often more subdued than their Western counterparts, but Ohtani showed something new in 2021.

Maddon said throughout the year that it wasn't a surprise. He believed Ohtani's performance and his demeanor were connected.

"I don't see the same stress I saw on his face last year," Maddon said. "The core of what I try to do here is to have players feel as though they have the freedom to be themselves. And in return for that I think, without even asking, you get even greater respect and discipline returned to you. He, I think, is enjoying the concept of being free to be Shohei and being more in charge of what he's doing. I think he's really digging on it. With that, I believe you're going to see a greater freedom in his game, that he's not going to be concerned about either getting hurt or disappointing somebody. He is just going to go play."

* * *

There is no stage in the majors like New York.

The Angels opened a series at Yankee Stadium on June 28. It was Shohei Ohtani's chance to show what he could do under the brightest spotlight baseball has to offer in the regular season. Although 2021 was Ohtani's fourth season in the majors, this was just his second time playing at Yankee Stadium. In the pandemic-shortened 2020 season, the Angels were limited to games against the two Western divisions. In 2019, the Angels' only trip to New York came in September, after Ohtani had been shut down for the season because of knee surgery. Ohtani played in New York in May 2018, but he was hitless at the plate and conspicuously absent from the mound.

It was another opportunity for the *New York Daily News*, a tabloid with a reputation for sensationalistic, taunting headlines, to take a shot at Ohtani. In December 2017, after news broke that the Yankees did not make Ohtani's seven-team short list, the *Daily News* called Ohtani "chicken," suggesting he was afraid of pitching in the high-pressure New York market. In 2018, the Angels scratched Ohtani from his scheduled start in New York so they could manage his workload. Again, that didn't sit well with the *Daily News*. The back page: "Say It Ain't Sho! What Are You Afraid Of? Ohtani Won't Take Mound vs. Murderer's Row 2.0." Ohtani still hit in all three games in New York in 2018, but he was 0 for 9.

Given Ohtani's failure in 2018 and absence in 2019 and 2020, New York fans certainly could have been skeptical of Ohtani as he arrived at Yankee Stadium in the summer of 2021. After all those comparisons to Babe Ruth, Ohtani had something to prove in the Bronx, at the twelve-year-old ballpark across the street from the site of the "House that Ruth Built," the original Yankee Stadium.

Manager Joe Maddon didn't bother dousing the narrative with any "just another game" routine. Maddon acknowledged there would be a little more electricity to the Ohtani show in New York, and he promised that Ohtani would deliver. "I know he's going to enjoy it," Maddon said before the start of the series. "He will be ready for it. It's one of those things that he embraces. He definitely likes these kinds of moments. He's got a slow heartbeat, a lot of self-confidence."

Ohtani proved Maddon's point quickly. In the top of the first inning in the first game of the series, Ohtani got a 3-and-2 changeup from righthander Michael King and he crushed it. The ball left the bat at 117.2 mph—one of his hardest-hit homers of the season—and sailed 416 feet, into the seats beyond the right-field fence. "That definitely sent a message," Maddon said. "That was just the right way to start a trip to New York, with him hitting a home run."

The Angels won the game, too, despite pitcher Dylan Bundy becoming so sick from heat exhaustion that he threw up behind the mound in the second inning. Lefty José Suarez pitched well enough over 5⅓ innings of relief for the Angels to come out on top, 5–3. The next night, Ohtani hit two more homers against Yankees righthander Jameson Taillon. They were Ohtani's twenty-seventh and twenty-eighth homers of the season, with the Angels still three games away from the halfway point of the schedule.

The Angels, however, lost the second game of the series, 11–5, making it a fitting summation of the first three months of the season. Ohtani was doing amazing things, but it wasn't enough to make the Angels winners. They were still hovering under .500, at 38–41.

A night later, though, in the third game of the series, the script was flipped. It was Ohtani's turn to pitch at Yankee Stadium for the first time.

Ohtani began the game by walking DJ LeMahieu, even though the 3-and-2 pitch appeared to nick the top of the strike zone. Ohtani then walked Luke Voit and Gary Sánchez, loading the bases. In the first month of the season, Ohtani had suffered control problems, but not since then. He had walked more than two hitters only once in his previous seven games, and on this night in New York he'd just walked the first three hitters of the game.

Ohtani then gave up back-to-back singles to Giancarlo Stanton and Gleyber Torres, each driving in a run. After a strikeout and a run-scoring groundout, Ohtani hit Clint Frazier with a pitch to reload the bases. He walked Brett Gardner to push home the fourth run of the inning.

That was all for Ohtani. His much-anticipated start at Yankee Stadium was a dud, the worst outing of his big league career. The three runners he left on base all came around to score with reliever Aaron Slegers on the mound. Ohtani was charged with seven runs, ballooning his ERA from 2.58 to 3.60 in one inning.

In contrast to much of the season, though, Ohtani's teammates bailed him out. Down 7–2 in the first, the Angels came back to win the game, 11–8. Bundy, who was available in relief because he'd thrown just 43 pitches before getting sick two nights earlier, worked 2 critical scoreless innings to help bridge the gap to the other relievers. The hitters exploded for 7 runs in the ninth, including a grand slam by Jared Walsh against the Yankees dominant closer, Aroldis Chapman. The game ended at 1:08 a.m. local time because of two rain delays totaling 2 hours, 13 minutes, but the late hour did nothing to dampen the Angels' enthusiasm.

"The postgame high-fives were the loudest and most exciting of the year, by far," Ohtani said. "That's for sure. I didn't have the results I wanted, but the team picked me up."

As for his performance, Ohtani said it was simply a "command issue." He was "yanking" his pitches. When he was asked if the pressure of Yankee Stadium had gotten to him, he suggested the 3 homers he had hit in the previous two games proved otherwise.

The spotlight was never an issue for Ohtani, and soon he would show just how much he enjoyed being on one of the game's biggest stages.

CHAPTER 13

Star Among Stars

Shohei Ohtani became the first player ever to be chosen as an All-Star both as a pitcher and a position player. The selection process for the 2021 Midsummer Classic involved two very different groups of voters: the fans chose the starting lineups and Major League players voted to fill out the pitching staff and the rest of the rosters. Among fans, Ohtani was the runaway winner as the American League's starting DH, which was no surprise because his numbers were far superior to any other candidate. Fan voting was open worldwide, so Ohtani certainly earned significant support from Japan. On the pitching front, the players might have been a tougher sell. Statistically, Ohtani was not an obvious choice for one of the five starting pitcher spots, especially after the debacle at Yankee Stadium. Still, players were impressed, and he was announced as one of the top five pitchers when the results were revealed on July 4.

At the All-Star break, Ohtani was hitting .279 with 33 homers, 70 RBIs and 12 stolen bases. He had an OPS of 1.062. He led the majors in homers and was a close second to Vladimir Guerrero Jr. (1.089) of the Toronto Blue Jays in OPS. As a pitcher, he was 4–1 with a 3.49 ERA. He had thrown 67 innings in 13 starts, striking out 87. Ohtani had also been durable, playing in 85 of the Angels' 90 games.

At the July 12 media event, the day before the All-Star Game at Denver's Coors Field, baseball's biggest stars sat at tables in two rows in an outdoor plaza and answered one question after another about Ohtani. The best baseball players in the world freely admitted that Ohtani was in a class by himself.

"That's obviously pretty special to do what he's doing offensively and on the mound," said Los Angeles Dodgers third baseman Justin Turner. "To be elite at both of those things is incredible. I can't really speak from the pitching side of it, but knowing how hard this game is to play offensively, I think it's probably a once-in-a-lifetime guy that we're seeing right now. He's a generational player that people are going to talk about for a long time."

Turner's Dodgers teammate, first baseman Max Muncy, summed up Ohtani's performance: "The guy is hitting balls farther than anyone in the league, throwing it harder than anyone in the league, running faster than anyone in the league. He's a freak of nature. It's really fun to watch."

Atlanta Braves first baseman Freddie Freeman: "It's absolutely incredible what he's doing."

Ohtani had been brilliant with the Angels at the plate and on the mound, but his precise role in the All-Star Game was to be determined by Kevin Cash. The manager of the Tampa Bay Rays, Cash had earned the right to manage the American League All-Star team by virtue of winning the pennant with the Rays the previous year.

With Ohtani, the first question was whether he'd pitch at all. Technically, Cash could have used Ohtani to pitch even if he *hadn't* been selected as a pitcher. That would have been seen as more of a gimmick or publicity stunt, because Ohtani would be taking mound time from someone selected to the All-Star team as a pitcher. But the path had been cleared for Cash and MLB to plan for him to pitch and DH if he was willing. Each year there are a few pitchers selected as All-Stars that don't pitch in the game, opting instead to give their arms much-needed midseason rest. If Ohtani or the Angels would have preferred a break, he could have simply stuck to DH for the All-Star Game. But it seems that no one wanted to keep the game's only two-way star from putting all his talents on display in the game.

"It is very good for the game," Angels manager Joe Maddon said after learning a few days before the All-Stars took the field that Cash planned to use Ohtani as a pitcher, too. "The maximum participation of Shohei, within limits, is the right thing to do. That means hitting and pitching. He's already hitting in the Home Run Derby. What else could you possibly want? We just have to do it in a manner that is not going to in some way be destructive to him."

That meant Ohtani wouldn't merely pitch. He would start. Ohtani was already starting at DH, so if he pitched in relief it would complicate his pitching preparation. Ohtani had been starting games as a pitcher all season, and also hitting in most of them. "It made the most sense to do something that he's already done, rather than ask him to hit and then come in and pitch later in the game," Cash said. "This is something he has done for his team in Anaheim, and we felt most comfortable that that's the right way to treat it."

Ohtani beamed when the official announcement of his starting assignment was made during a nationally televised press conference. Ohtani and Cash sat at the dais with Washington Nationals ace Max Scherzer, who was starting for the National League, and Dodgers manager Dave Roberts, who led the National League team.

"Obviously it's a huge honor," Ohtani said. "I wasn't expecting to be chosen as a pitcher, but I was and Kevin and everyone else has very high expectations of me, so I just want to match those expectations."

Major League Baseball still needed to bend the rules for Ohtani by allowing the American League to have its DH pitch without losing the use of the DH for the rest of the game. "I thank Major League Baseball for tweaking the rules," Cash said, "because if they didn't I know I'd screw it up the rest of the way."

It was a no-brainer for MLB to put the rules aside. From 2003–15, MLB tried to make the All-Star Game a more serious event by linking it to the World Series. The league that won the All-Star Game had home-field advantage in the World Series. Since 2016, though, the game has been purely an exhibition, so relaxing the rules is more palatable.

"This is what the fans want to see," said Cash, who had also penciled Ohtani in as the leadoff hitter. "This is what I want to see. To have the opportunity to do something with a generational talent is special."

Ohtani was fully on board with the plan, too. He had agreed to participate in the Home Run Derby and then start on the mound in the All-Star Game the next day, along with a couple at-bats in the game as the DH. Certainly, he could have used some rest after doing so much for the Angels in the first half, but he wasn't going to pass on this opportunity.

"I'm expecting to be pretty fatigued and exhausted after these two days," Ohtani said during the All-Star Game press conference, "but there's a lot of people that want to watch it. And I want to make those guys happy, so that's what I'm going to do."

* * *

Days before Shohei Ohtani was introduced as the starting pitcher and leadoff hitter for the American League, Major League Baseball released a thirty-second commercial to highlight the two-way star. The spot included clips of Ohtani pitching and hitting, backed by the voices of excited announcers speaking English and Japanese. Words flashed on the screen. *Pitcher. Hitter. All-Star. Phenom. Derby Slugger. Global Superstar. Heartthrob. Speedster. First Two-Way All-Star In History. It's Sho-Time.*

Ohtani's first name lent itself perfectly to the campaign, said Barbara McHugh, MLB senior vice president of marketing.

"It plays off his name and what he's doing—he's putting on a show," McHugh said. "We want to make sure we're capitalizing on that and making it as major as possible. He's been one of the most unique and transformational players in baseball history."

McHugh added: "We've had our eye on Shohei for a while now. It's been a lot of planning and building on his momentum."

MLB had already plastered an enormous picture of Ohtani on the side of the building at its New York headquarters.

MLB's eagerness to jump on the Ohtani bandwagon came just three years after Commissioner Rob Manfred made controversial comments about Ohtani's teammate, Mike Trout, at the All-Star Game. By the time Trout was preparing to play the July spectacle in Washington in 2018, the Angels center fielder had already established himself as the best player in the sport. He had won two MVP Awards, and his career often drew comparisons to Hall of Famers like Mickey Mantle, Willie Mays, and Ken Griffey Jr. While Trout was doing amazing things on the baseball field, though, he was otherwise relatively anonymous. That was something of an indictment of MLB.

"The way the league promotes itself doesn't put enough emphasis on national exposure for their players, unlike the NFL or NBA," said Henry Schafer, the executive vice president of Q Scores, a firm that measures consumer appeal of personalities.

Schafer said they survey Americans to determine what percentage of people recognize the name of a particular figure. The Q Score then represents the percentage of those respondents who say that figure is one of his or her favorite personalities. In 2021, the most recognizable male athlete was Tiger Woods, at 85 percent, Schafer said. The highest Q Score for an athlete belonged to Giannis Antetokounmpo of the NBA's Milwaukee Bucks and Patrick Mahomes of the NFL's Kansas City Chiefs, who both had scores of 29.

Schafer said that in 2018 Trout was known by just 21 percent of Americans, compared with 70 percent for Los Angeles Lakers star LeBron James. James, however, had a Q Score of 20, compared to Trout's 24, Schafer said, which means that more of the people familiar with Trout had a positive image of him than those familiar with James. It demonstrates that there is something to be said for only being known for what you do well, as opposed to being known by more people.

Trout had been asked often in his career about his relatively low profile, and he'd always insisted that it didn't bother him. He had no desire to be more *famous* if it came at the expense of time spent trying to be the best baseball player he could be. With his free time, he preferred to live a quiet life with his family, go fishing, and cheer for his favorite football team, the Philadelphia Eagles.

The question of Trout's public stature was posed to Manfred during the Commissioner's annual meeting with members of the Baseball Writers' Association of America hours before the 2018 All-Star Game. Could MLB do anything to increase Trout's visibility, even though Trout didn't seem interested?

"Player marketing requires one thing, for sure: the player," Manfred said. "You cannot market a player passively. You can't market anything passively. You need people to engage with those to whom they are trying to market in order to have effective marketing." Manfred went on to say this wasn't a criticism of Trout. "Mike is a great, great player, and a really nice person, but he's made certain decisions with what he wants to do and what he doesn't want to do, and how he wants to spend his free time and how he doesn't want to spend his free time," Manfred said. "That's up to him. If he wants to engage and be more active in that area, I think we could help him make his brand really, really big, but he has to make a decision that he's prepared to engage in that area. It takes time and effort."

While many felt Manfred was attacking Trout for choosing his family over doing commercials and talk shows, Trout took no offense at the Commissioner's comments. The next day, with the discussion still going in the media, Trout released a statement to defuse the situation: "I have received lots of questions about Commissioner Manfred's recent statement. I am not a petty guy and would really encourage everyone to just move forward. Everything is cool between the Commissioner and myself. End of story. I am ready to just play some baseball!" The Angels also released a statement on Trout's behalf, praising him for choosing charities and his family over self-promotion.

Three years later, Trout was still a relatively anonymous star. He'd won a third MVP award in 2019. Just before that season, he signed a twelve-year, $426.5-million deal with the Angels, the largest contract in the history of North American team sports. It added ten years to the two remaining on his previous deal, essentially allowing him to play his entire career with the Angels. Approaching his thirtieth birthday in July 2021, Trout was still considered the best player in the majors. He had been elected by the fans to start the All-Star Game, even though he was unable to play because of his strained calf. Because the Angels had been absent from the postseason for much of Trout's career, the All-Star Game had been Trout's best chance every year to be seen by the largest possible audience.

Without Trout on the field, the 2021 All-Star Game was Ohtani's show, and Schafer said it gave him a boost. Ohtani's recognition rose to 15 percent in the summer of 2021, and his Q Score to 23 percent, Schafer said. Both numbers were up from 2018, although perhaps lower than you might expect for a player having such a historic season.

"Even though he is in a major market, the time difference doesn't give him national exposure," Schafer said, referring to the West Coast being three hours behind the East Coast. "On the East Coast they rarely see Angels games. The press coverage he gets on the West Coast is a lot, but it doesn't spill over to the rest of the country. He had a great showing in the Home Run Derby this year, and that contributed a lot to his likability, which is a good case in point. He's a tremendous athlete. Give him national exposure. More people are going to be aware of what he's capable of."

Schafer concedes that one of the issues with Ohtani's exposure is the language barrier, which prevents him from doing much in terms of endorsements in the United States.

Of course, Ohtani is able to sell Japanese products. Overall, his $6 million in earnings from endorsements in 2021 were the most in Major League Baseball, according to *Forbes*. That was double his $3 million salary. It was also double the $3 million that Trout made from advertisements, *Forbes* reported. Tomoya Suzuki, president of Japan-focused sports marketing firm Trans Insight Corporation, said that Ohtani could make much more if he were so inclined. "He is very, very picky in terms of endorsements," Suzuki said. "I've heard he declined a lot of offers." Ohtani's agent, Nez Balelo, said Ohtani wants to make sure that he "is not bogged down and distracted so he can do what is most important to him, which is play and be productive on the baseball field."

The All-Star Game provided the perfect opportunity for Ohtani to raise his public profile without detracting from his focus on playing baseball. Competing in the Home Run Derby and participating as a pitcher and hitter in the All-Star Game would certainly be grueling, but the payoff would go beyond his own interests. "If more people are watching baseball, it makes me happy," Ohtani said. "It's good for the sport."

* * *

More people watched the 2021 Home Run Derby than any other Derby since 2017, thanks in part to Shohei Ohtani. The event drew an average of 7.1 million viewers to ESPN. The audience peaked at 8.7 million viewers when Ohtani and Washington Nationals outfielder Juan Soto were swinging away in their first-round matchup.

The Home Run Derby became a staple of ESPN's broadcast schedule in 1991, and since then it has changed formats a few times. When players were each allowed a certain number of "outs"—any swing that didn't result in a homer—the event sometimes stretched to three hours. In order to speed up the competition, the Derby was changed to a timed event in 2015. Players had a fixed amount of time to swing for the fences. They were also matched in head-to-head duels, with a tournament format. The 2021 Derby had an additional feature, as all the players wore number 44 to honor Hank Aaron. The legendary slugger who had held baseball's all-time home run record for thirty-three years had died earlier in 2021.

Ohtani entered the event as the number one seed by virtue of his big-league-leading 33 homers. He drew a matchup against Soto, a twenty-two-year-old native of the Dominican Republic who was one of the sport's brightest young stars. Soto had reached the big leagues at age nineteen in 2018. While Ohtani was winning the American League Rookie of the Year that year, Soto finished second in the National League. In Soto's second year, he helped the Nationals to the World Series title. In the pandemic-shortened 2020 season, the Nationals struggled but Soto didn't. He won the batting title with a .351 average, and he led the major leagues with an OPS of 1.185. He made the All-Star team for the first time in 2021—just like Ohtani—but his power had not shown up in the first half. Soto had hit 34 homers in his only other full season, in 2019, but in the first half of 2021 he had just 11 homers, one-third of Ohtani's total.

Ohtani and Soto had to wait out the other three first-round matchups before taking their cuts, and once they did Soto got off to a hot start. The lefthanded hitter sprayed homers all over Coors Field. He hit 22 homers in four minutes, which included one minute of "bonus time" he'd earned for hitting at least two homers more than 475 feet.

Ohtani then stepped to the plate with a familiar face nearby. His interpreter, Ippei Mizuhara, was squatting behind the plate as the catcher. The catcher doesn't have much to do in a Home Run Derby, because most of the pitches never get to him, so Mizuhara was happy to be there to support Ohtani. "Having someone that's more nervous than me right behind me makes me less nervous," Ohtani joked, through Mizuhara, in an MLB Network interview before the Derby. Once Ohtani began swinging against his hand-picked pitcher, Angels bullpen catcher Jason Brown, he didn't deliver the show everyone had expected. Ohtani hit a series of low line drives and groundballs to the right side. He didn't hit his first homer for fifty seconds and he had only 5 homers when he called a timeout with 1:19 remaining on the clock. Ohtani was visibly exhausted, but smiling, as he toweled himself off. Just then, teammate and fellow All-Star Jared Walsh came to the plate holding a cell phone that he put to Ohtani's ear. It was Mike Trout calling to give him a quick pep talk. "Relax and be yourself," Trout told him, as Ohtani recalled later that night.

Still needing 17 homers, Ohtani started on a roll after the break. He hit 11 more homers before his time ran out, with the last two sailing more than 500 feet into the upper deck. That earned him the minute of bonus time, which was enough for him to tie Soto with 22 homers, all of them to right field.

Each player then received an extra minute in a tie-breaker round. Soto continued to spray balls to all fields, knocking out another 6. Ohtani then matched him again, this time leaving himself fifteen seconds of swings to win it. Ohtani hit the fence twice after it was tied, sending the match to a second tie-breaker, a three-swing duel. There was no more clock. Soto waited for his pitch, letting a few go by. When he connected, he hit homers to center field, right-center, and right field. One of his homers was a 506-foot shot into the upper deck. By going three-for-three, Soto left Ohtani no room for error. Ohtani's first swing was a groundball to the right side, and the match was over. Ohtani and Soto hugged and laughed.

Although Ohtani lost, many Angels fans were relieved. He was clearly exhausted from one round, and there was no need to keep pushing himself for the sake of a made-for-TV exhibition.

A handful of Angels employees, however, had no idea at the time how much they should have been rooting for Ohtani to keep going. Ohtani had told his agent before the Derby that he was going to divide his winnings from the event among about thirty Angels trainers, clubhouse workers, and media relations staffers. Ohtani would have earned $1 million if he'd won the event. The New York Mets' Pete Alonso won, defending his 2019 title after the pandemic had wiped out the event in 2020. Ohtani settled for the $150,000 that he received simply by competing. He distributed the money after returning to Anaheim a few days later, pleasantly surprising the recipients.

Shortly after Ohtani was eliminated from the Derby, he met with a crowd of reporters in the hallway outside the American League clubhouse. He smiled and said that the event was "fun," but it was also tiring. "The last thirty seconds of both rounds were really exhausting," Ohtani said. "I was gassed."

When reporters asked how Ohtani would manage to recharge enough to pitch the next day, he said: "I'm just going to get as much sleep as I can. That's all I can do."

* * *

Even if Shohei Ohtani hadn't been a participant, the ninety-first All-Star Game in Major League history would have carried a little more electricity than others. Fans packed Denver's Coors Field with no regard for social distancing and few masks. In mid-July, the United States was in one of the high points in the recovery from the coronavirus pandemic that had canceled so much of 2020.

By the time the night was over, there would be 49,184 fans filling the twenty-six-year-old ballpark situated just blocks from the heart of downtown. The All-Star Game had been at Coors Field once before, in 1998. This time the team and city didn't have the normal time to prepare for the event, because they'd only been awarded the game in April. Commissioner Rob Manfred decided to pull the game from Atlanta as a means of protesting Georgia's recently passed Election Integrity Act, which many viewed as a thinly veiled effort to suppress the minority vote.

Baseball instead brought one of its jewel events to the Mile High City, where the thin air created the sport's most offensively charged atmosphere. The Rockies began storing baseballs in a humidor at Coors Field in 2002 in an effort to keep the balls from drying out, which helped blunt the impact of the high altitude on homers. Still, pitching in Colorado is a special kind of challenge, and the All-Star Game would pit baseball's best hitters and pitchers together in this atmosphere.

Shohei Ohtani, of course, was going to be the only one to experience both sides of the equation.

The novelty of it all was highlighted when broadcaster Joe Buck introduced the starting lineups to the crowd and the television audience. "Leading off, the designated hitter, *and the pitcher*, Shohei Ohtani!" At that moment, Ohtani was throwing in the outfield, preparing to begin warming up in the bullpen. He continued his warmups while all the other starters jogged out to the first- and third-base lines to wave to the cameras and show their respect for the National Anthems of the United States and Canada. Ohtani then had to do something no other pitcher does: walk from the bullpen to the dugout, grab a bat and step into the batter's box to start the game. Aside from the fact that he was wearing dark blue pants and a dark blue jersey—special All-Star Game uniforms that were generally loathed by fans on social media—he seemed to be just as comfortable as if he were preparing to pitch for the Angels on a Tuesday night in Kansas City. He even bent over to pick up a scrap of paper while he walked through the outfield, continuing a habit he'd maintained ever since a high school coach in Japan told his team that good luck came to those who picked up trash.

A few minutes later, Ohtani stepped into the box against Max Scherzer. Ohtani took a hack at Scherzer's first pitch, a 95.5-mph fastball over the middle, and he fouled it off. The next pitch was a cutter and Ohtani yanked it into the shift. Second baseman Adam Frazier backhanded it and had to make a quick throw to nail Ohtani, who hustled down the line at twenty-nine-feet per second, nearly his maximum speed. His legs showed no fatigue from the previous night's Derby, and he'd soon get to test his arm.

San Diego Padres shortstop Fernando Tatís Jr. led off for the National League All-Stars in the bottom of the first. Ohtani threw him a couple fastballs and then got him swinging through a slider, moving the count to 1-and-2 and setting him up for the splitter. Tatís fouled it off. Ohtani came back with a slider and Tatís hit a routine flyball to left field. "I thought he was going to throw me all fastballs," Tatís said later in an interview room. "Come on man, you throw 100! But he threw sliders and a split finger. He got lucky this time." Tatís chuckled.

Max Muncy, the Dodgers' first baseman, was next. Ohtani took care of him on three pitches, getting him on an easy groundball to second baseman Marcus Semien.

Nolan Arenado then stepped to the plate, and the crowd erupted. The third baseman had starred with the Rockies for the first eight years of his career, winning eight Gold Gloves and making five All-Star teams. The rebuilding Rockies had traded Arenado to the St. Louis Cardinals prior to the 2021 season, though. He had already come back to Colorado earlier in the season, and the Coors Field crowd greeted him warmly then. This time a full ballpark gave him a loud ovation as he stepped to the plate. He tipped his helmet to thank the fans.

The atmosphere may have juiced up Ohtani, too. He hadn't exceeded 97.4 mph with any of his pitches to Tatís or Muncy, but he started Arenado off with a 99.5-mph fastball in the dirt. The two fought through a six-pitch duel, with Arenado fouling off a 100.2-mph fastball on a 1-and-2 pitch. It was the first time since Ohtani's first start of the season, on April 4, that he'd cracked 100 mph. "Of course he did," Arenado said with a laugh. Ohtani said later that he had no need to save his energy, like he would in a normal game, because he knew he was just pitching one inning. "Just let it rip," he said. Ohtani then missed with a 99.7-mph fastball before giving Arenado a vintage splitter. Arenado dropped the barrel of the bat to tap it to shortstop, as Ohtani finished off a 1-2-3 inning on 14 pitches. "He's as good as advertised," Arenado said. "He's incredible."

Although Ohtani was done as a pitcher, he remained in the game for one more plate appearance as the DH because of the special rules tweak from MLB. Ohtani faced Milwaukee Brewers righthander Corbin Burnes—who would go on to win the Cy Young Award—and he pulled a first-pitch cutter for a routine groundout to first base. With that, Ohtani's All-Star performance was done. He ended up as the winning pitcher because the American League never relinquished the lead it took on Rafael Devers's RBI double in the top of the second, on the way to a 5–2 victory. Vladimir Guerrero Jr. won the MVP award after hitting a 468-foot homer.

The box score didn't show that Ohtani did anything special, besides the fact that he had hit *and* pitched. Also, he'd done it a day after competing in the Home Run Derby, which made the performance all the more impressive. Muncy, a former Derby participant and a frequent visitor to Colorado as a National League West rival, had a special appreciation for what Ohtani had done by competing in the Derby and pitching the next day, all in the thin air.

"It's incredible," Muncy said. "This is a tough place to play. It's hard to breathe here. You get tired really quickly. You could see last night they got gassed pretty quickly. For him to be able to come back and pitch today, it's pretty incredible."

Muncy and the other National League All-Stars were getting a rare look at Ohtani. But Jared Walsh, Ohtani's teammate with the Angels and fellow All-Star, was used to seeing Ohtani perform as a two-way player. Walsh, who had also been used as a two-way player briefly before he had a breakout as a hitter, tried to put Ohtani in perspective afterward.

"I haven't normalized what he's doing," Walsh said. "It's not normal. Years from now I'll look back and understand what's going on. Right now he's a teammate and friend and it seems like he hits a home run every night."

CHAPTER

14

Brilliance Amid Disappointment

The 2021 All-Star Game extravaganza amounted to a two-day celebration of Shohei Ohtani. For those forty-eight hours, Ohtani was in the spotlight as the number one star in Major League Baseball. Immediately afterward, though, the harsh reality surrounding him could not be ignored. When Ohtani exchanged his navy blue All-Star uniform for an Angels uniform, everyone was reminded that Ohtani's sensational season was happening against the backdrop of a disappointing Angels season.

The Angels returned to action after the break on July 16, and the trading deadline loomed on July 30. The deadline is one of the most significant dates on the calendar during the regular season because it's often when teams decide whether they are going to push to make the playoffs or give up and focus on the future. The contending teams—the buyers—will give up prospects and other young players to acquire established players to bolster their rosters for the final two months. The teams on the other side of those transactions—the sellers—are typically giving up hope for the current season. Most general managers choose not to view it in such black-and-white terms. Sometimes they make moves that can't be so neatly categorized as "buying" or "selling."

Still, when the deadline passes, leaving teams unable to significantly change their rosters for the rest of the season, it's usually clear which teams are going in which direction.

Ohtani's historic, once-in-a-lifetime season should rightly have been lifting the Angels toward the playoffs. Instead, at the All-Star break they were a middling 45–44, which put them in fourth place in the American League West, 9 games behind the first-place Houston Astros. They were also 5½ games behind the Oakland A's, who sat in the second wild card spot. The July schedule offered the Angels an opportunity to make up some ground before the deadline. They played the Seattle Mariners—also ahead of them in the division and wild-card races—six times. They also had three games against Oakland before the deadline, sandwiched around seven games against the Minnesota Twins and Colorado Rockies, who were both having terrible seasons.

When the Angels hit this critical portion of the schedule, they were still playing shorthanded. Mike Trout, who had suffered a strained right calf on May 17, was supposed to be back sometime in early to mid-July. Although he was already a little behind schedule at the All-Star break, there were encouraging signs early in the second half. Trout was on the road for a trip to Oakland and Minnesota, the first time he'd traveled with the team since he got hurt. On July 19 and 20, Trout was on the field running the bases at the Oakland Coliseum. He said he would be ready to begin a rehab assignment any day. That would mean three or four games in the minors and then a return to the Angels lineup. Trout worked out on the field again in Minnesota, but then he was conspicuously absent. Manager Joe Maddon said that Trout "felt something" in his calf as he accelerated his workouts, so his rehab was on hold. A week before the trade deadline, the Angels suddenly had no idea when Trout would return.

Anthony Rendon, who was supposed to join Trout and Ohtani among arguably the best trio of hitters in the majors, was also out, also with an uncertain timeline for return. In the second year of a seven-year, $245-million deal, Rendon was enduring a frustrating season. The third baseman had suffered a groin injury in April, costing him two weeks. In May, he had fouled a ball off his knee and missed another eleven days. Just when he began to show signs that he would be healthy and productive, he went down with a hamstring injury in early July. At nearly the same time as Trout's rehab stalled in late July, Maddon said that Rendon still wasn't doing any baseball activities.

The Angels pitching staff was also in shambles. Righthander Dylan Bundy, their Opening Day starter, had pitched so poorly that he lost his spot in the rotation. Lefthander José Quintana, who had signed a one-year, $8-million deal over the winter, was sent to the bullpen in June. Righthander Alex Cobb, who was enjoying a bounceback season, was on the injured list for the second time with a blister issue, and had also developed a wrist injury while he was out. Lefthander Andrew Heaney had continued his typical rollercoaster performance, at times looking solid and other times terrible.

That the Angels were able to hang around the .500 mark with so much going wrong was partly a testament to Shohei Ohtani, who was still carrying the team as both its best hitter and its best pitcher. He hit 4 homers in his first thirteen games after the break, to go with a .298 average and a 1.069 OPS. Ohtani pitched twice between the All-Star break and the trade deadline, allowing 1 run in 13 innings. He struck out 13 and walked 1. After Ohtani tossed 7 innings against the Rockies on July 26, Maddon said Ohtani's value was so evident that he was clearly the league's MVP. "I know there are other guys having good years, but you have to stop and analyze what's going on here," Maddon said. "There's nobody who comes close to what he's doing. It's way imbalanced. To me, it's not even close. When people talk about it being close, it's not. What he's doing is so unique, so different. To compare him to anyone else, you just can't." At that point, Ohtani had a 3.04 ERA, along with a Major League–leading 35 homers.

During that victory over the Rockies, though, the Angels lost first baseman Jared Walsh to an abdominal injury. Just weeks after his appearance at the All-Star Game, Walsh joined Trout and Rendon on the injured list. Ohtani was suddenly even more isolated in the Angels lineup.

On the morning of the trade deadline, the Angels had a skeleton lineup and a patchwork rotation. They had not made the necessary push in those games against the teams they were chasing, the Mariners and A's. The Angels were 51–51, trailing the Astros by 11½ games in the division. They were 6 games behind Oakland in the race for the second wild card spot. The Mariners, New York Yankees, Toronto Blue Jays, and Cleveland Indians were also ahead of them in the wild card race. Although General Manager Perry Minasian said later that he was "very aggressive" in trying to add players to help, he acquired no major leaguers and traded away two. He shipped Heaney to the Yankees for two Minor League pitchers, and he sent lefthanded reliever Tony Watson to the San Francisco Giants for three Minor League pitchers. The Angels held on to their most valuable trade chip, closer Raisel Iglesias. Minasian said he didn't dismantle the team because "this group has earned the opportunity to continue to compete with how they've played and the circumstances they've played under."

That's what Minasian said, but within days his actions sent the message that the team was, in fact, shifting its focus away from 2021 and to the future. Lefthander Reid Detmers, the Angels' first-round pick in the 2020 draft, was summoned to replace Heaney in the big league rotation. Detmers had just turned twenty-two and he'd pitched just thirteen professional games, all but one at Double-A. The Angels recalled righthander Chris Rodriguez and put him in the rotation. Rodriguez had just turned twenty-three. He had barely pitched in the previous three seasons, after a serious back injury and the pandemic-related loss of the 2020 Minor League season cost him development time. An impressive spring won him a job, and then he pitched well in relief in the big leagues for a couple months. The Angels sent him back to the minors to get stretched out as a starter, and days after the trade deadline they were ready to give him another shot. The Angels also brought outfielder Jo Adell back to the majors and said he would play every day. Adell was the team's top prospect going into the 2020 season, but he had been a disappointment in the shortened season and returned to the minors in 2021. After three months at Triple-A, Adell had shown the progress the front office wanted to see.

The opportunities for Detmers, Rodriguez, and Adell came just as the Angels announced that Rendon would miss the rest of the season to undergo hip surgery. Trout was still out with no scheduled return. Amid all of that, the Angels seemed ready to play out the final two months as mere extras in the background of The Shohei Ohtani Show.

• • •

Shohei Ohtani demonstrated how far he'd come as a pitcher with his performance against the Texas Rangers on August 4. In sharp contrast to the start of the season, when Ohtani had exceptional stuff but poor command, Ohtani took the mound against the Rangers without the normal electricity on his fastball or bite on his breaking balls. He was pitching with a few extra days of rest because of a fluke injury. A foul ball had shot into the Angels dugout on July 28 and pegged Ohtani in the thumb. Working on eight days' rest against the Rangers, Ohtani had to grind his way through 6 innings without his best stuff, but he nonetheless held the Rangers to one run on his way to his fifth straight victory. "He's got a great feel for everything that he does," Manager Joe Maddon said. "Maybe not his most dynamic performance, but highly effective because he knows what he's doing up there."

After his August 12 start against the Blue Jays, one in which he allowed 2 runs in 6 innings, Ohtani said he again had to work around substandard stuff. "Honestly I haven't been feeling that great," Ohtani said, "but when I don't have my best stuff I found ways to get outs and get through innings. But I'm not feeling that good on the mound right now. Physically I feel really good. I feel like I'm getting better each outing. I still haven't hit my potential. I still have room to get better going forward."

At this point Ohtani had started 17 times and pitched 92 innings, after throwing just 1⅔ innings in the previous two seasons combined. Anytime there was mention of declining stuff, there were certain to be questions about fatigue. Ohtani briefly quieted that talk with an outstanding game on August 18 at Detroit. He pitched 8 innings for the first time in his career, allowing 1 run. He struck out 8 and didn't walk a hitter. He also hit his fortieth homer.

In late August Ohtani was still doing what Maddon had described as "Little League stuff" earlier in the summer. "You're the best player on the team," Maddon said. "You hit and you pitch and you're the first in line for the ice cream cone." Appropriately, Ohtani got a chance to bring his game to the Mecca of Little League baseball in late August. The Angels faced the Cleveland Indians in Williamsport, Pennsylvania, home of the Little League World Series. Each year Major League Baseball has a game in a Minor League ballpark in Williamsport, allowing the big league stars to mingle with the best teams of eleven- and twelve-year-olds in the world. It's the perfect opportunity for MLB to connect its next generation to its current stars. Ohtani and the rest of players from the Angels and Indians signed autographs and talked to the kids, turning a rainy day into an unforgettable one for dozens of young players. As Mike Trout spoke in a press conference about what kind of player he was as a twelve-year-old, he echoed Maddon's point about Ohtani. "I played shortstop. I pitched," Trout said. "Kind of what Ohtani's doing right now in The Show. . . . It's special. Shohei's a different cat."

For all the awe that Ohtani inspired, his season was beginning to show some cracks. On August 25 in Baltimore, against an Orioles team that had lost nineteen games in a row, Ohtani gave up 4 runs in 5 innings. The bigger issue was his performance at the plate, though. Ohtani hit .174 from August 16 to September 15. He had hit only 5 homers in that span, losing the big league lead. Although some suggested that Ohtani's swing had been altered by the Home Run Derby, no one around the team was buying that. Ohtani had been fine offensively in the weeks immediately after the Derby. Plus, two of the hottest hitters in the majors in the second half were the Washington Nationals' Juan Soto and Kansas City Royals' Salvador Pérez, who had also participated in the Derby.

The more likely scenario was that Ohtani was finally feeling the effects of the skeleton lineup around him. Without Trout or Rendon, Ohtani often hit with journeyman Phil Gosselin behind him. No pitcher was going to give Ohtani anything to hit with Gosselin on deck. Rather than simply taking his walks, Ohtani was swinging at pitches out of the zone. "The last month, I haven't really been seeing pitches over the plate where I could make good contact," Ohtani said. "When I do, I need to make sure I put a good swing on it and drive the ball. Otherwise, it's simple. I just need to lay off pitches that are close or are balls and swing at strikes."

Hitting coach Jeremy Reed had another explanation for Ohtani's slump. It was something that both Ohtani and Maddon had been reluctant to admit.

"Fatigue matters," Reed said. "This guy has gone wire-to-wire pitching and hitting, and it's September."

From the first day of Spring Training, the Angels had been open about their new plan for using Ohtani without so many restrictions. All of those built-in days off that the Angels had for Ohtani in 2018 were gone, because they trusted Ohtani would speak up when he needed a rest. It could not have worked better for four months. Ohtani was performing at a high level at the plate and on the mound. He clearly enjoyed the chance to play so much, and the Angels believed he actually performed better because of the freedom. By early September, Maddon was not showing any inclination to give Ohtani more rest, and Ohtani certainly wasn't going to request it.

On September 3, Maddon left Ohtani on the mound against the Texas Rangers for 117 pitches. His previous high in 2021 was 105 pitches, and his high before surgery, in 2018, had been 110. Ohtani was pitching for the first time since he had been hit in the wrist by a pitch. Maddon said the extra days he had off after getting hit actually allowed him to give Ohtani a longer leash. Also, Maddon said he saw no signs of fatigue during the game. In fact, in that game Ohtani threw two fastballs at 100 mph, something he had not done in a regular season game since April 4. Ohtani retired all six hitters in the fifth and sixth, and Maddon sent him back to the mound for the seventh with his pitch-count at 92. Ohtani worked around a single and a walk and he finished the inning, later saying he was grateful that Maddon had stuck with him. "I thought there was a good chance I'd be taken out there but Joe had faith in me and I'm glad I was able to come out on top," Ohtani said. "I think it'll definitely help in the future, especially not giving up that last run. That looks really good and I think Joe will have faith to keep putting me out there when I'm past 100 pitches."

Maddon repeated an idea he'd mentioned when he pushed Ohtani back in April. He said those games would pay dividends in the long run. "I like when guys go more deeply into the game like that," Maddon said. "The mind once stretched has a difficult time going back to its original form, so does a pitcher. When he goes that deep and gets out of a jam late and has his 'A stuff' late, it does something for him down the road. . . . This was absolutely a growth moment for him."

Maddon reiterated his faith in Ohtani by writing his name in the lineup at DH the next day. A meaningless game in September, the day after reaching a career-high pitch count, seemed like an obvious day for a break. Maddon said Ohtani assured him that he was fine. "I just don't know how he does it, where he comes from," Maddon said. "It's just so unusual to be able to pitch like that, throw that many pitches, throw that hard, and then be able to even DH the next day, but I've not heard from him or anybody else anything negative about that."

The game was amid Ohtani's offensive slump, though, and the next time he took the mound, there were signs that fatigue might be affecting his pitching, too.

On September 10 in Houston, the night started well enough for Ohtani, who blasted his forty-fourth homer in the first inning. In the bottom of the first, Ohtani worked around 2 singles and didn't allow a run, and he worked a perfect second. In the third, Ohtani gave up 3 runs on 4 hits. Ohtani threw 30 pitches in the inning, and the Astros made contact on every one of their swings. In the fourth, he retired only one of the first four hitters he faced before getting pulled. All three of the baserunners he allowed ended up scoring, and Ohtani allowed 6 runs in 3⅓ innings. "He just didn't have his best stuff," Maddon said. "There was no swing-and-miss tonight." The Astros whiffed on just 7.1 percent of their swings against Ohtani, compared with his average of 28.9 percent for the season. "I thought he battled, but in my mind's eye, there was no reason to push it," Maddon said. "When he's not having his day I don't want to extend him."

Afterward, Ohtani said something that sent up red flags. Asked if his 117 pitches in the previous game had any impact, Ohtani said: "I would say there's a little bit of soreness left from my last outing."

Interpreter Ippei Mizuhara used the word "soreness" as a translation for *hari*, but other Japanese reporters suggested it may have been an imprecise word choice, and that "tightness" might have been better. The next day, Maddon said there was no indication from Ohtani or Mizuhara that there was any issue that would require medical intervention. Four days later, the story changed. Ohtani was doing his normal between-starts throwing routine in Chicago on September 15, preparing to start at home against the Oakland A's on September 17. Ohtani didn't feel right, so the Angels scratched him from the start.

This time, Maddon used the word "soreness," while insisting that it was just "from a long year," and not any kind of injury. Maddon said there was no plan for Ohtani to see a doctor or undergo any tests. Considering that the Angels were out of the playoff race and the season would be finished in just over two weeks, the Angels considered simply shutting down Ohtani as a pitcher. While being careful to leave the option open if Ohtani felt better, Maddon said the Angels would be careful with their prized player. "If there's any kind of lingering soreness, you may not see him pitch," Maddon said. "I just don't know that answer yet."

* * *

Just when it seemed that Shohei Ohtani's historic season was going to end with a whimper, he changed the narrative.

At the plate, Ohtani had been in a slump for a month, perhaps because he was fatigued, perhaps because he was pressing to carry an injury-ravaged lineup, perhaps because pitchers weren't throwing him strikes. It was certainly a combination of everything, and it had dragged his average down to .254 and his OPS to .956 on September 15. Ohtani was in the middle of a nine-game drought without a homer. Just as the Angels were discussing the idea of shelving him as a pitcher for the rest of the season, Manager Joe Maddon was asked if they might also just have him stop hitting. "I've actually broached the subject with him and he feels he's still good and he still wants to get after it," Maddon said. "We'll look at it. If he needs it, he's gonna get it. Absolutely."

Back in Anaheim the next day, Ohtani resumed throwing and reported to Maddon that he felt much better, so much so that the Angels slated him to start on the mound on September 19, just two days later than the original schedule. "It's consistent with the whole attitude we've had all year where we're not going to baby him, just let him go out and play baseball," Maddon said. "Had he come back and said, 'Listen I'm still a bit tender,' we probably would've gone in a different direction." Ohtani said he did not want to finish the season having been shut down prematurely, not after the way his other three seasons in the big leagues had ended. "I need to keep on throwing," Ohtani said. "Every time I throw I learn something and get better. I'm going to pitch next year and beyond. The whole experience from this year is going to help me down the road." Ohtani emphatically demonstrated that he was healthy in that start against Oakland. He allowed 2 runs, equaling his career high with 8 innings. He threw 108 pitches, inducing the A's to whiff on 43 percent of their swings. They came up empty on 18 of their 38 swings (47 percent) against his splitter. He threw 55 splitters, using the pitch to strike out the side in the seventh.

Over the next week Ohtani also showed an improved approach at the plate. Pitchers had been working around him for most of the second half, but since the middle of August his discipline had waned. He was increasingly swinging at bad pitches. Around the middle of September, Ohtani started taking more walks. Over a four-game span from September 22–25, Ohtani walked 13 times, including 4 intentional walks. The Seattle Mariners walked him in the seventh and ninth innings on September 24, both times when he represented the tying run. He became the first player since Barry Bonds in 2003 to draw at least 3 walks in three straight games. That was when Bonds was in the midst of one of the sport's most historic offensive binges. Although Ohtani wasn't hitting at the level that Bonds had in 2003, he was hitting in the middle of a lineup that provided him no protection. "I love that he's taking the walks," Maddon said. "It's much better than swinging at bad pitches, striking out, making bad outs. He can contribute in other ways, just by scoring runs, getting on base, stealing bases. He needs to do that."

The walks helped Ohtani post a 1.128 OPS over the last eleven games of the season, including a .540 on-base percentage. The lack of strikes prevented Ohtani from a real shot at either the Angels' single-season home run record—Troy Glaus hit 47 in 2000—or the 2021 Major League home run title. Ohtani hit two homers in his last twenty-one games, finishing with 46. Vladimir Guerrero Jr. of the Toronto Blue Jays and Salvador Pérez of the Kansas City Royals each hit 48 homers.

Ohtani did pick up a few other statistical milestones in his final weeks, scoring his hundredth run and notching his hundredth RBI in the final week. He also stole 25 bases.

As for pitching milestones, Ohtani certainly would have liked to have reached 10 victories. Double-figures in victories is a precious achievement in Japanese baseball, more so than in the major leagues. Ohtani improved to 9–1 on September 3, then took a loss and a no-decision in his next two starts. Facing the Mariners at Angel Stadium on September 26, Ohtani gave up 1 run in 7 innings, striking out 10 and walking none. Just like his previous outing against the A's, Ohtani pitched well enough to get a victory. He didn't win either time. The Angels bullpen allowed the go-ahead runs in both games.

After a second straight hard-luck no-decision, and with a week in between of getting walked because he was alone in the lineup, Ohtani let his disappointment show in a postgame interview. The Angels had just lost their eighty-second game, ensuring a sixth straight losing season, four of them with Ohtani.

"It's very frustrating," Ohtani said. "It's very disappointing. I always look forward to being in the playoff race at the end."

Later, Ohtani was asked about how that disappointment would impact the decisions he would face about his career. Set to be a free agent after the 2023 season, the star was asked flatly if he wanted to stay with the Angels.

"I really like the team," Ohtani said. "I love the fans. I love the atmosphere of the team, but more than that I want to win. That's the biggest thing for me. So I'll leave it at that."

His answer was dissected for days, with fans parsing the words interpreter Ippei Mizuhara used in English as well as the actual words that Ohtani had spoken in Japanese. His comments came on the heels of statements from Mike Trout and Maddon, who both expressed frustration with losing and a desire to see the franchise make the necessary upgrades to win.

A couple days later, the Angels were beginning their final trip of the season, in Arlington, Texas. General Manager Perry Minasian stood on the field and faced questions from American and Japanese reporters about his take on the recent comments from Ohtani, Trout, and Maddon. Minasian said he didn't interpret them as a challenge to management. He said he already knew the Angels needed changes to win, and nothing he'd heard or read from anyone altered the direction he planned for the winter. "Nobody wants to play on a losing team," Minasian said. "That's something that I would expect everybody to say. Not shocking at all. As far as the winter goes, that doesn't change anything."

A few days after that, before the Angels played their final game of the season, Ohtani clarified his earlier words. Despite his disappointment with losing, he was still prepared to talk about a contract extension. "Of course I'll be very open to negotiation," Ohtani said. "The team's supported me for this whole four years and I'm really appreciative of that. Whether or not there's any long contract extension, I just want to be ready to perform next season."

There was one last piece of business for Ohtani and the Angels in 2021. They beat the Mariners on the final day of the season, and Ohtani hit his forty-sixth homer. The Angels ended up with a 77–85 record that was certainly unsatisfying, but could have been much worse if not for Ohtani. They mostly played without Mike Trout and Anthony Rendon. Ohtani was the only starting pitcher who lasted the entire year in the rotation.

Ohtani actually proved to be the most durable player on the team. The only position players who were active every day of the season were second baseman David Fletcher, catcher Kurt Suzuki, and Ohtani, who didn't merely stay healthy, but barely needed any days off. After having forced days off before and after he pitched when he was a two-way player in 2018, Ohtani made it through an entire season without any of those restrictions in 2021. He played in 155 of the Angels' 162 games.

"It was definitely challenging, but at the same time I had a lot of fun with it," Ohtani said after unanimously winning the MVP award in November. "I felt like the expectations from the team were very high and I wanted to do my best to try to answer those expectations."

He surpassed them.

"I've always dealt with a lot of doubters, especially from my days in Japan," Ohtani said. "I tried to not let that pressure get to me. I just wanted to have fun and see what kind of numbers I could put up, and what kind of performance I could put up."

CHAPTER 15

"Unicorn"

Rick Ankiel was the best high school baseball player in the country in the spring of 1997. A lefthanded pitcher at Port St. Lucie High School in Florida, Ankiel was 11–1 with an 0.47 ERA and 162 strikeouts in 74 innings. At the plate, he hit .359 with 7 homers. Scouts believed Ankiel had the talent to be taken among the first ten picks of the draft, but he slipped out of the first round due to money-related questions: how much would it take for him to sign a pro contract and forgo a scholarship to the University of Miami?

The St. Louis Cardinals finally grabbed him in the second round, and they signed him for $2.5 million. Although Ankiel immediately became one of the top pitching prospects in baseball and flew through the minor leagues, he still thought about hitting. When he occasionally suggested to coaches or members of the Cardinals' front office that he could be a true two-way player, not merely a *pitcher who can hit*, they dismissed the idea. "You always think about it, but they didn't allow it," Ankiel said in 2021. "You mention it and they said 'haha, sounds good, beat it.'"

Ankiel reached the majors in 1999, weeks after his twentieth birthday. He was the runner-up for the National League Rookie of the

Year Award in 2000, posting an 11–7 record with a 3.50 ERA. In the 2000 playoffs, Ankiel mysteriously lost control of his pitches, though. He pitched 4 innings in 3 games, walking 11 and throwing 9 wild pitches. Ankiel was never the same after that October, cursed with an inability to consistently throw strikes. He had a mental block—known in sports circles as *the yips*—that was still with him even after years of rehabbing two elbow injuries. He finally gave up on his pitching career, but not on his baseball career.

Ankiel started over in the minors, this time as an outfielder. Then, he played 536 games as a big league outfielder from 2007–13. He hit .240 with 76 homers and a .724 OPS in 2,115 at-bats. In the first phase of his career, as a pitcher, he was 13–10 with a 3.90 ERA.

Aside from being an example of perseverance, Ankiel holds the distinction of being one of just three players to have 10 victories and 70 homers in the big leagues. The other two are Babe Ruth and Shohei Ohtani.

As Ohtani was tearing up the majors in 2021, Ruth had been gone for seventy-three years. Ankiel, though, was alive and well, and he was happy to provide his unique perspective on what Ohtani had accomplished.

"I think it's amazing," Ankiel said after the season. "You look at him as a pitcher and the stuff is absolutely incredible. I don't think we've seen the best. . . . Watching what he can do, it blows me away. I think that you're looking at someone that could win the batting title and the home run title and the Cy Young. In the same year. That's what's so incredible."

Ankiel also believes that Ohtani can be a groundbreaker. Ankiel never got the chance to try to be a two-way player. Thanks to Ohtani, the story might be different for the next generation.

"I think he's going to start a trend," Ankiel said. "I don't see why he wouldn't. When I look at him, I think *what an awesome role model for kids.*"

Farhan Zaidi, the San Francisco Giants president of baseball operations, agreed that the potential two-way players in amateur baseball ought to have a new perspective after watching Ohtani. That's only part of the equation, though. Big league front offices also need to have the faith to give those players a chance.

"[Ohtani] kind of changed the way two-way players think about themselves. Now they're all *I could do that*," Zaidi said with a chuckle. "In all seriousness, it's sort of aspirational for a lot of guys. Seeing him execute at a high level provides a little bit of proof of concept.

"Does it change the way we view those potential guys? It's hard to say. I think people probably bandy around the term *unicorn* with him as much as anyone. He's really such a rare, rare talent that I don't think you want to make the mistake of thinking you can replicate it."

While it may be accurate to say that Ohtani's performance increases the chances of another two-way player, it's akin to saying that buying a second lottery ticket doubles your chances at becoming a millionaire.

Dave Dombrowski, who spent two decades at the top of baseball operations departments and won the World Series with the Florida Marlins and Boston Red Sox, said Ohtani might only make a small difference in the perception of two-way players.

"I guess he would probably have changed some minds, but I wouldn't make too many decisions based upon Shohei Ohtani, with his skills," said Dombrowski, now the Philadelphia Phillies president of baseball operations. "I think he is a very unusual case. There haven't been many people in baseball history who have done that."

• • •

The list of those who at some point showed the talent to be professional two-way players is short, but it is nonetheless a list.

Dave Winfield was exclusively a pitcher for his first three seasons at the University of Minnesota. In a college summer league in Alaska in 1972, he opened the eyes of scouts by hitting 15 homers. In 1973, Winfield hit and pitched for Minnesota, leading the team to the College World Series. Winfield was voted the Most Outstanding Player in the Series, hitting .467 and striking out 14 in a shutout in the opening game. The San Diego Padres picked Winfield fourth overall in the draft that summer. Winfield was such a good athlete that he was also drafted by the NFL's Minnesota Vikings and two professional basketball teams, the NBA's Atlanta Hawks and ABA's Utah Stars. While Winfield had plenty of career options, he stuck with baseball and with the outfield. The Padres sent him straight to the major leagues. He played 22 seasons in the big leagues, on his way to the Hall of Fame. He never threw a single pitch in the majors.

Winfield was clearly the best of a small group of players who were talented enough to be considered for the first round of the baseball draft as pitchers or hitters, according to draft expert Jim Callis of MLB.com. The draft dates back to 1965, and Callis wrote in 2020 that there had been only eleven players that the industry considered first-round talents in either role.

The list includes former MVP outfielder Josh Hamilton, first baseman John Olerud, outfielder Nick Markakis, and outfielder Aaron Hicks. Like Winfield, they all pitched as amateurs but were successful enough as everyday players that they never pitched in the majors.

Most of the other players on the list, including Ankiel, eventually switched from one role to the other because of injuries or performance issues. The Baltimore Orioles selected Adam Loewen in the first round in 2003. He appeared in the majors as a pitcher from 2006–08, got hurt, and came back as an outfielder in 2011. He returned as a pitcher in 2015–16. All told, Loewen pitched 63 big league games and played eight in the outfield in an unspectacular career.

Ken Brett, the older brother of Hall of Famer George Brett, never played a position other than pitcher in the majors. He was a good enough hitter that his teams forfeited the use of the DH a couple times to have him hit, and they also used him to pinch-hit. He was not so much a two-way player as an early version of Madison Bumgarner or Brandon Woodruff, modern day *pitchers who can hit.*

Baseball history is also littered with players who switched roles before reaching the majors. Four of the best closers in Major League history—Trevor Hoffman, Troy Percival, Kenley Jansen, and Joe Nathan—were position players when they began their Minor League careers. Hoffman and Nathan were shortstops, and Percival and Jansen were catchers. Tim Wakefield went on to win 200 games in the majors, mostly as a knuckleball pitcher, after an unsuccessful Minor League start as an infielder. Their organizations all saw early in their careers that their arms were far better than their bats.

The switch occurred earlier for players like Mark McGwire and Jacob deGrom. McGwire pitched and played first base at USC, but he was exclusively a hitter during a Major League career that saw him belt 583 homers. DeGrom was the shortstop at Stetson University in Florida before moving to the mound, and he became a two-time Cy Young winner.

While all of those players had demonstrated a high level of talent as pitchers and hitters at some point as amateurs or minor leaguers, none were two-way players.

The list of players who pitched and even semi-regularly played another role—either a DH or a position—during the same season is much shorter. Most of the players who did it played in the first half of the twentieth century. The only players who even came close in the twenty-first century were Brooks Kieschnick and Michael Lorenzen, and each did so just barely.

Kieschnick was a star two-way player at the University of Texas before the Chicago Cubs took him with the tenth pick in the 1993 draft. Kieschnick was exclusively an outfielder from 1996–2001. With his career floundering, Kieschnick joined the Chicago White Sox and pitched and hit at Triple-A in 2002. The following season, the Milwaukee Brewers gave him a shot as a two-way player. In 2003, Kieschnick pitched 53 innings and also had 70 at-bats, including 50 as a pinch-hitter, DH, or outfielder. In 2004, the final year of his career, he pitched 43 innings and had 63 at-bats, including 44 as a pinch-hitter. He did not start a game as a position player.

Lorenzen was a pitcher and outfielder at Cal State Fullerton, and in 2012 was a finalist for the John Olerud Two-Way Player of the Year Award. The Cincinnati Reds selected Lorenzen with the thirty-eighth pick in the 2013 draft, and two years later he was in the big league starting rotation. From 2015–18, Lorenzen was exclusively a pitcher for the Reds, aside from a few pinch-hitting appearances. In 2019, Lorenzen also played twenty-nine games in the outfield, including six starts. On September 4, 2019, Lorenzen earned the win, hit a homer, and played in the field, making him the first player to accomplish that trifecta in the same game since Babe Ruth in 1921. In 2020–21, Lorenzen was essentially back to being a full-time pitcher. He appeared in four games, totaling 6 innings, in the outfield in those two seasons. Coincidentally, the Angels signed Lorenzen in November 2021 with a plan to put him in the rotation with Ohtani.

* * *

Although Brooks Kieschnick and Michael Lorenzen haven't amounted to much as two-way players, they nonetheless broke out of traditional specialized roles. Kieschnick did so before Shohei Ohtani, and Lorenzen after. Even if there are no more players like Ohtani, his success could prompt teams to at least look for more players like Kieschnick or Lorenzen. Rick Ankiel suggested that baseball's trend toward using more relief pitchers could lead to increased value for a player who can pitch out of the bullpen and play a position, adding roster flexibility.

"If anything, [Ohtani] will cause clubs to at least think twice about allowing the player to do both," New York Mets president of baseball operations Sandy Alderson said. "And that's a good thing. We need to be more openminded."

The most well-known two-way player still working his way up in baseball is Brendan McKay of the Tampa Bay Rays, although his career has been derailed by injuries. The Rays selected McKay out of the University of Louisville with the fourth overall pick in the 2017 draft, after

Ohtani had succeeded as a two-way player in Japan but a year before he did in the majors. The Rays gave McKay a full workload doing both roles in the minors for three seasons. He was more advanced as a pitcher, though. He had an impressive 2.19 ERA but a disappointing .679 OPS in the minors. When he reached the majors in 2019, McKay pitched thirteen games and had just one start at DH. He also pinch-hit three times. He wasn't in the majors at all in 2020 or 2021, missing time because of shoulder surgery and COVID-19. He underwent thoracic outlet surgery in November 2021, further putting his career on hold.

Hunter Greene was hyped as a potential two-way player at Notre Dame High School in suburban Los Angeles before the Reds took him with the second overall pick in the 2017 draft, two spots ahead of McKay. Greene had 30 at-bats in his first summer of professional baseball, posting a .600 OPS. He didn't hit at all in his first full season, in 2018, and then he underwent Tommy John surgery. When he returned to action in 2021, he was a full-time pitcher.

While the two-way dream seems unrealistic for McKay and Greene, there are two-way hopefuls from the 2020 and 2021 drafts who are just beginning their careers.

Masyn Wynn was rated by Baseball America as the number eight prospect in the Cardinals' system heading into the 2022 season. Wynn impressed as a shortstop and a pitcher before the Cardinals took him in the second round of the 2020 draft. Early in his Minor League career, the Cardinals had him focus on hitting and playing shortstop. He posted a .680 OPS in his first Minor League season in 2021, but his 98-mph fastball is waiting for the Cardinals when they are ready to begin developing it.

"Before I got drafted, I wanted to be a two-way player," Wynn said. "I still do. But it's so hard to do that in pro baseball. Shohei Ohtani, what he does is amazing. People don't realize how hard that is to do."

The Pittsburgh Pirates used their third-round pick in 2021 on Bubba Chandler, who is getting the opportunity to play shortstop and pitch. Chandler barely played at the lowest level of the Pirates' farm system in 2021, and he has not yet pitched professionally. John Baker, the Pirates director of playing and coaching development, said the early returns were encouraging.

"With every hit he gets, with every home run he hits, our pitching coordinator sheds one more tear," Baker said. "Bubba is a special, special talent. How this kid can control his body and move on the field, it's exceptional; it stands out in an environment of standouts. We will explore the multi-positional thing until the game tells us otherwise."

Players like Wynn and Chandler still have a long way to go before they can follow Ohtani's footsteps—or even Lorenzen's. One of the significant problems is that a player doesn't simply need the raw talent to perform in the big leagues in both roles. That talent has to be developed at the same time.

"It's one thing to have the ability and the potential to have success on both sides," Rays president of baseball operations Erik Neander said. "It's another thing for each side developmentally to be in sync with one another, where one is not pulling ahead of the other in a way that would in turn increase the pressure to focus on one side, because there's just no precedent for doing both."

Case in point: Ankiel said that his hitting never got a chance to develop in his first time in the minors because his pitching was so advanced. He was in the big leagues as a pitcher just two years after he was drafted. "Let's say you're an unbelievable pitcher, and the hitting needs time in the minor leagues," Ankiel said. "Most organizations probably aren't going to wait for you to mature [as a hitter]. If you can help us in the big leagues now as a pitcher, you're coming."

The opposite happened to Jared Walsh, Ohtani's teammate. Walsh played first base and outfield in the minors, and eventually the Angels added pitching to his repertoire. It was a way to provide one more tool for a player whose Minor League career had stalled. When Walsh got to the big leagues in 2019, the Angels used him to hit and to pitch, although his mound time was limited to five games as a mop-up reliever. Walsh hurt his arm in the spring of 2020 and couldn't pitch that season. In September 2020, Walsh had a sensational month at the plate, positioning him to be the Angels everyday first baseman in 2021. At that point he became too valuable as a hitter for the Angels to spend any more time trying to see what he could be as a pitcher. Walsh joined Ohtani as an All-Star in 2021. He also spent much of the year speaking from his unique perspective—a former two-way player who was Ohtani's teammate—about how impressive it all was.

"Getting big league hitters out is extremely difficult and getting hits off of big league pitching is extremely difficult," Walsh said. "Bringing that focus every day is a serious, serious grind. Physically, it's an extreme toll on your body, especially when you're creating as much force to hit balls 115 mph and throw balls 100 mph like he does. . . . He's absolutely a unicorn. That's the only way to sum him up."

＊　＊　＊

As Texas Rangers general manager and former big league pitcher Chris Young considered the future of two-way players in the majors, he suddenly found himself in need of a fact check.

"If you can do both, I certainly think teams will be open to that," Young said. "It gives you flexibility. I don't think teams will put any limits on guys that have that ability to do both. But I think Ohtani is one in . . . what's the population of earth?"

About 7.75 billion.

Young was standing alongside a golf course at the General Managers' Meetings in Carlsbad, California, in November 2021. All of the top executives from the thirty big league teams had converged for the annual event, and they were spread throughout a courtyard next to a practice green, answering questions from dozens of reporters on just about any topic facing the game. As they described what they had just seen from Shohei Ohtani and opined on whether it would have any impact on the future of the sport, they agreed he was too much of an outlier to start a trend.

"To call him an outlier is an understatement for what he's done," Washington Nationals GM Mike Rizzo said. "If other people have that skillset, obviously we would be open to it. But that skillset is so rare. I've been doing this for forty years and he's the first. They're not falling off trees."

Jerry Dipoto, the Seattle Mariners president of baseball operations, had pursued Ohtani heavily before the Japanese star picked the Angels in 2017. Dipoto said he thought Ohtani was "Elvis" when he was scouting him, but what he did in the majors in 2021 exceeded his expectations.

"He's an awesome player," Dipoto said. "To do what he does on both sides, and to be so consistent doing it, if I didn't get a ticket for free, I'd pay for it."

Dipoto then referenced the traditional 20-to-80 system that scouts use to grade a player's specific skills. Legendary Dodgers executive Branch Rickey created the scale in the first half of the twentieth century. It goes from 20 to 80, rather than 0 to 100, because a normal standard deviation results in so few players at the extremes that the grades aren't necessary. A player whose skill is average in the major leagues would be graded as a 50. Position players are graded on their raw tools: hitting, hitting for power, defense, running speed, and arm strength. Pitchers are graded on each pitch they throw (fastball, curveball, slider, etc.) with an overall grade for control. The vast majority of major leaguers have no skills that grade as 80s and probably no 70s. Even an All-Star or MVP caliber player may have just one 80-grade skill, with a couple 60s or 70s if he's truly elite. Most big leaguers, even everyday players, are a mix of 40s, 50s and 60s.

That's why Ohtani made such an impression on Dipoto.

"It's such a unique skillset," Dipoto said. "Do you have 80 power, an 80 fastball, and an 80 run tool? It's a super small class."

How small?

"There's one in the world."

CHAPTER

16

Encore

In 2021, Shohei Ohtani put together the type of season that exceeded even the lofty expectations the baseball world had for him when he left Japan in 2017. It took him four years in the majors, but the "Babe Ruth of Japan" lived up to the billing on his way to a unanimous MVP award. As he received the Commissioner's Historic Achievement Award during the 2021 World Series, Ohtani had a message for anyone who thought it was a once-in-a-lifetime season. "I feel pretty confident that I could repeat what I did this year," Ohtani said. "I just need to go out there and play every day and put up good numbers, and I think I'll be able to at least have a similar season as this year."

Ohtani's personal history suggested those weren't empty words. In 2016 in Japan, he had a 1.86 ERA and a 1.022 OPS. Before he was injured in 2018, his rookie season with the Angels, Ohtani had a 3.10 ERA and a .907 OPS. Both of those seasons were in line with his 3.18 ERA and .965 OPS in 2021. Those sensational seasons were interspersed with others in which injuries or slumps left him short of expectations, so he still had something to prove heading into 2022.

The first clues of Ohtani's brilliance in 2021 emerged in Spring Training, but in 2022 there wasn't much of a spring to evaluate him.

Baseball's collective bargaining agreement, which set the financial parameters between the players and teams, expired in December 2021. Owners locked out the players until a new agreement could be reached. For more than three months, no players were signed and none were traded. Players and teams could not have any contact with each other. In fact, the Angels had to formally "fire" Ippei Mizuhara, Ohtani's interpreter, because he was officially part of the staff, and would have been prohibited from talking to Ohtani. They rehired him as soon as the lockout ended.

During Spring Training, Ohtani and the Angels received some good news with the creation of what came to be known as The Ohtani Rule. Previously, a team had to forfeit the use of the designated hitter if it wanted its pitcher to hit. The new rule permitted a player to be the pitcher *and* the designated hitter. When Ohtani the pitcher came out of the game, Ohtani the DH remained. "It's wonderful news for us," Manager Joe Maddon said in Spring Training. "He might be the only guy who can utilize it with any sort of consistency. From our perspective, it's deserved based on what he can do." Even though the rule only benefited Ohtani and the Angels, it was created because Major League Baseball wanted to showcase its premier star.

As the season got underway, Ohtani soon demonstrated he was even better on the mound than he'd been in 2021. Ohtani was another year removed from his 2018 Tommy John surgery, and he had another winter of uninterrupted workouts. He also had another year of experience to learn when and how to push himself. The average velocity of his four-seam fastball in 2022 increased from 95.6 mph to 97.3 mph. He had hit 100 mph eleven times in 2021, but he did it forty times in 2022.

His first 100 mph pitch of the season was during his May 5 start at Boston's Fenway Park. Pitching for the first time in the ballpark Babe Ruth called home, Ohtani worked 7 scoreless innings, striking out 11 and walking none. He threw 82 percent of his 99 pitches for strikes, a career high. The Red Sox swung and missed at 29 pitches, also a career high for Ohtani. In the fifth inning, Ohtani gave up a leadoff double to Jackie Bradley Jr. He escaped the inning with a fly ball and then strikeouts of Trevor Story and Rafael Devers, including a 100 mph fastball to Devers. "I was trying to get a strikeout every time someone was on base," Ohtani said. Catcher Max Stassi added: "I've caught some really good pitchers, some Cy Young Award winners, and they have the same thing. When guys get in scoring position, they elevate it to another gear. They know the impact of the situation and they rise above it. That's what Shohei did today."

Ohtani's season on the mound was a steady stream of consistent, often dominant, performances. He took a perfect game into the sixth inning on April 20 against the Astros in Houston. He finished by allowing 1 hit with 12 strikeouts. He struck out a career-high 13 in 8 scoreless innings against the Kansas City Royals on June 22. That game was particularly notable because the day before he hit a pair of homers and drove in 8 runs, the best offensive day of his career. Ohtani made his longest run at a no-hitter on September 29 against the Oakland A's, coming up just four outs short. Oakland's Conner Capel poked a single off the glove of shortstop Livan Soto, attempting a backhand stop.

In that game, Ohtani also demonstrated the adaptability that was at the heart of his improvement. Ohtani's first two fastballs of the game that night were 94.1 mph and 93.7 mph, well below his average. He scrapped the fastball and used the pitch that had become a larger and larger part of his repertoire since the end of 2021.

The word "sweeper" entered the baseball lexicon in 2023 to describe a pitch that is between a slider and a curve. It is a slider with less velocity and more downward movement. Ohtani had been throwing the pitch since his days in Japan, but he started throwing it more at the end of the 2021 season. It continued to become an increasing part of his repertoire through 2022 and into 2023. In 2022, sweepers accounted for 37 percent of his pitches, including a couple games when he threw it more than half the time. By the end of the season,

Ohtani had thrown 983 sweepers, which was 267 more than runner-up Jordan Lyles of the Baltimore Orioles. No one threw it better, either. Most pitchers sacrifice velocity to make the pitch move more, but Ohtani was still able to throw the pitch at an average of 85.3 mph, fifth hardest of any pitcher who threw at least fifty sweepers. "He's maintaining shape, but adding velocity, and that's a special gift," pitching coach Matt Wise said. Opponents hit .165 against Ohtani's sweeper in 2022.

Ohtani also broke out a new two-seam fastball during the 2022 season. Ohtani's arsenal included a fairly straight four-seamer and a variety of other pitches—sweeper, slider, splitter, cutter, and curve—that all broke down and/or away from a right-handed hitter. In June 2022, Ohtani was at the plate against New York Yankees right-handed reliever Clay Holmes, who threw him two 100 mph two-seam fastballs. Two-seamers break to the throwing arm side. Ohtani had nothing in his arsenal with that movement. Seeing Holmes's two-seamer inspired him to begin experimenting with the pitch in July. Gradually, he began working it into games. By September, the pitch was already "elite," Stassi said. By the end of the season, Ohtani was one of eleven pitchers in the majors who threw at least fifty two-seamers and four-seamers each to average 97 mph or harder on both. He was one of ten pitchers who averaged 97 mph with at least 16 inches of run on his two-seamer. And this was a pitch he had never thrown before July. "Guys spend years trying to figure out how to throw a pitch," Stassi said. "His hand placement and awareness of how to spin the ball is out of this world, literally."

The additional pitches helped Ohtani fashion a season which improved his 2021 performance in just about every metric. He cut his ERA from 3.18 to 2.33. He increased his strikeout rate from 10.8 to 11.9 per 9 innings and reduced his walks from 3.0 to 2.4. Ohtani went 15-9, an improvement of 6 victories from 2021. He became the first American League or National League player since Babe Ruth in 1918 to reach double-digits in victories and homers. (It had happened twice in the Negro Leagues after Ruth, by Ed Rile with the 1927 Detroit Stars and Bullet Rogan with the 1922 Kansas City Monarchs.) Ohtani pitched 166 innings, which was 35 2/3 more than in 2021.

By pitching more than 162 innings, Ohtani qualified for the ERA title. He was the first player in Major League history to qualify as a pitcher while also having enough plate appearances to qualify for the batting title.

As Ohtani was putting the finishing touches on his season, Angels manager Phil Nevin was not reserved in his description of the star. "He's the best baseball player I think anybody has ever seen, to be honest," Nevin said. "I really believe that. All around, I don't think there's any argument you can make that he's not the best baseball player that's played the game."

* * *

No one had ever made the All-Star team as both a pitcher and a hitter until Shohei Ohtani did it in 2021, and then he did it again in 2022. As the teams were working out before the All-Star Game at Dodger Stadium, longtime big league pitcher CC Sabathia marveled at how much Ohtani had improved on the mound, while still performing as one of the best hitters in the game. "It's gonna be hard not to give him the MVP every year," Sabathia said. "It's down to (Aaron) Judge and Ohtani, but for me, I'll give it to Ohtani."

Judge was in the midst of a historic season himself. The outfielder finished with 62 homers, which broke the American League record set by Roger Maris in 1961. Many fans still believed that Maris held the "legitimate" Major League home run record because all of the National League players who subsequently hit more than 61 homers—Barry Bonds, Mark McGwire, Sammy Sosa—did so under the cloud of steroids. Besides the homers, Judge hit .311 with an OPS of 1.111. Judge also led the league with 131 RBIs. Minnesota Twins infielder Luis Arráez hit .316, barely preventing Judge from winning the Triple Crown.

Ohtani's offensive numbers were nowhere near Judge's, and not even at the level Ohtani reached in 2021. Ohtani hit .273 with 34 homers and an .875 OPS in 2022. His homers declined from 46 and his OPS from .963. On the plus side, his batting average improved from .257, and he cut his strikeout rate from 30 percent to 24 percent.

The peripheral statistics underlying Ohtani's offensive performance were still elite, and similar to what he had done in 2021. His average exit velocity was in the 97th percentile and hard-hit percentage was in the 92nd percentile.

The memorable moments and tape measure homers were sparse, though. The lasting snapshot of Ohtani's 2022 season at the plate was the game-tying 3-run homer in the bottom of the ninth of his 2-homer game against the Royals in June. The Angels lost in extra innings that night, and the game served as another reminder that Ohtani's greatness was cast against the backdrop of a team struggling to be relevant in the pennant race.

As MVP voters weighed Ohtani's two-way performance against what Judge did for a first-place team, it was increasingly clear that they were going to side with Judge. When the results were announced in November, Judge earned twenty-eight of thirty first-place votes, cast by two writers representing each AL city. "I went back and forth until about late September," explained Dan Connolly, an MVP voter who covers the Baltimore Orioles for *The Athletic*. "Ohtani is something we haven't seen before in my lifetime. But neither is 62 homers in the AL. Once it seemed likely Judge would hit that number and be close to a Triple Crown, I figured I'd be selecting Judge and then Ohtani. So, it was always close for me, but when Judge picked up the record, I felt a little more confident in my choice." Marc Topkin, an MVP voter who covers the Tampa Bay Rays for the *Tampa Bay Times*, had a similar sentiment: "What Ohtani did was remarkable again, another amazing season like we've never seen before. In any other year, I would think he would be the clear winner. But what Judge did this year was truly historic, and carried a team that needed his help to the postseason."

* * *

Although the Angels didn't give Ohtani a chance to play for a championship, Japan did.

In 2006, Ohtani was eleven years old when he watched Ichiro Suzuki, one of his early idols, lead Japan to a championship in the inaugural World Baseball Classic. Since then, the WBC has been a nationwide obsession in Japan. The tournament allowed the best baseball players in the world to represent their countries. The event returned in 2009—Japan won again—and in 2013 and 2017. Ohtani wanted to participate in 2017, following his fourth season in Nippon Professional Baseball, but an ankle injury suffered during the 2016 Japan Series prevented him from playing. The 2021 WBC was postponed because of COVID-19. When it was a go for 2023, there was never any doubt that Ohtani would play. Mike Trout announced he would play for Team USA at the 2022 All-Star Game and immediately there was friendly trash-talking between Trout and Ohtani about a possible USA-Japan matchup in the WBC. It continued as both players began Spring Training with the Angels before they split to opposite sides of the globe for the start of the tournament.

Ohtani returned to Japan for the first portion of the WBC amid historic fanfare. Ever since he played his final game for the Hokkaido Nippon-Ham Fighters in 2017, his fans in Japan could only watch him on middle-of-the-night TV broadcasts from the USA, or else travel across the Pacific to see him in person. "There was a great deal of excitement" about Ohtani playing again in Japan, said Naoyuki Yanagihara of Sports Nippon. "There were hundreds of people lining up at 3 or 4 in the morning to buy WBC merchandise." All seven of Japan's WBC games drew Japanese television ratings similar to the Super Bowl in the United States, according to the Sports Business Journal. Ohtani went from about 1.7 million Instagram followers to more than 4 million by the WBC final. Ohtani was eager to perform for his fans. Typically, he takes batting practice in the indoor cages instead of on the field, but he regularly hit on the field during the WBC. "He wanted to show (the people of) Japan his skills," said Masaya Kotani, a writer from Full-Count. "He grew up watching Ichiro and I think there were thoughts within him that he wanted to give back whatever he can."

Ohtani took the mound for Japan in its first game of the tournament, against China. The crowd at the Tokyo Dome roared for Ohtani but went eerily silent as he prepared to unleash his first pitch of the game, exploding again after the ball was released. "How quiet the stadium was, even though it was a full stadium, that kind of gave me chills," Ohtani said. "It was a weird feeling." Even some of Ohtani's Japan teammates were awed by being on the same field with a player they had watched on TV. "We never get to see him play so I was extremely nervous in the first inning because it was so emotional," second baseman Shugo Maki said. "It was just so exciting."

Ohtani pitched 4 scoreless innings and had 2 hits in the victory over China. He was 6 for 12 with a homer as Japan won all four games in pool play. His most memorable at-bats were a homer and a strikeout. He blasted a 448-foot 3-run homer to start the scoring against Australia. Fans sitting near where the ball landed passed the souvenir around to take selfies with it. Ohtani also struck out against Czech Republic lefthander Ondřej Satoria, who whiffed Ohtani on a curveball. It sparked a celebration in a Czech dugout filled with men who played baseball during breaks from their full-time jobs, in contrast to the professional athletes on the other WBC teams. Satoria was an electrician. Afterward, Ohtani received a Czech jersey signed by the entire team.

Ohtani took the mound again in Tokyo in a quarterfinal game against Italy. Ohtani gave up 2 runs in 4 2/3 innings in another victory, sending the team to Miami for the semifinals. Japan won a dramatic semifinal against Mexico, scoring 2 runs in the bottom of the ninth. Ohtani began the winning rally with a double. Team USA beat

Cuba in the other semifinal, setting the stage for the Japan-USA final that everyone wanted to see.

It was uncertain if Ohtani would be able to pitch to Trout because it had only been four days since he started against Italy, not the normal five he has between starts. Throughout the WBC, Major League teams were in contact with the international teams to make sure their pitchers were used in a manner consistent with their preparation for the season. There was some question whether the Angels would balk at Ohtani disrupting his normal schedule to pitch in the championship game, but Ohtani was not about to miss this opportunity. The Angels didn't stand in the way. Angels Manager Phil Nevin said from Spring Training in Arizona that Ohtani had the team's blessing to pitch in relief if the situation arose. "I trust him in the way he'd prepare for that," Nevin said. "I know this is a really big night for baseball. I'm excited to watch it." Nevin, and everyone else, was especially intrigued by the possibility of Ohtani facing Trout. "Who wouldn't want to see the two best players in the world go at it, right? Then we'd have a lot of fun talking about it the rest of the year."

Before the game, a video was posted on Twitter of Ohtani delivering an inspirational speech in the Japan clubhouse. "Let's stop admiring them," Ohtani said, according to a *Los Angeles Times* translation. "If you admire them, you can't surpass them. We came here to surpass them, to reach the top. For one day, let's throw away our admiration for them and just think about winning."

Japan took an early 2-1 lead on a 2-run homer by Munetaka Murakami. A conga line of Japanese hurlers then emerged from the bullpen, each working 1 or 2 innings to move Japan closer to a title. The anticipation built when Ohtani jogged down to the bullpen a couple of times to start throwing, returning to the dugout before his at-bats. Yu Darvish, a fellow Major Leaguer who had been one of Ohtani's idols when he was young, took the mound in the eighth with a 3-1 lead. He gave up a homer to Kyle Schwarber to cut the margin in half. Trea Turner then singled, which moved the lineup just enough. No. 7 hitter J.T. Realmuto hit a popup and then Cedric Mullins hit a flyout, ensuring that Trout, the No. 2 hitter, would get a chance in the ninth inning. As Japan batted in the bottom of the eighth, Ohtani quickly fired a few pitches in the bullpen. The gate in the outfield fence then swung open and Ohtani jogged out to take the mound in the ninth, with a 1-run lead and Trout looming.

Ohtani, who had not pitched in relief since the Japan Series in 2016, was clearly amped. His second pitch to Jeff McNeil was a 101.5-mph fastball in the dirt. Ohtani eventually walked McNeil on a 99.4-mph fastball just below the knees. Team USA had three straight MVPs lined up to face Ohtani: Mookie Betts, Trout, and Paul Goldschmidt. Ohtani defused the situation by getting Betts to pound the ball into the ground, and Japan turned a double play, bringing Trout up with the bases empty.

Mark DeRosa, the manager of Team USA, was taken by Ohtani's calm as Trout came to the plate. "I saw him take a big deep breath to try to control his emotions," DeRosa said. "I can't even imagine being in that moment, the two best players on the planet locking horns as teammates in that spot."

At that moment, observers surely marveled at the sheer improbability of it all. Ohtani and Trout began the tournament two weeks earlier, playing on opposite sides of the globe. Each team had played six games to get this point, and somehow, the precise matchup that everyone wanted to see had arrived in the precise situation that everyone wanted it.

Championship game.

Ninth inning.

Two outs.

One-run game.

Ohtani vs. Trout.

The first five pitches alternated balls and strikes. Trout swung through two fastballs, one at 100.0 mph and one at 99.8 mph. Both pitches were right through the heart of the plate. On the 3-and-2 pitch, would Ohtani challenge him with a fastball, or would he throw his devastating sweeper?

Ohtani paused and blew on his fingers as he stood on the mound. He then stepped on the rubber, set himself and unleashed a sweeper. Trout swung but the ball darted away from his bat, smacking into the catcher's mitt.

"That was pretty much the perfect pitch," Trout said months later. "That's the first time I ever stepped into the box against him, not even in Spring Training. I got to see what other guys are seeing across the league. It's pretty nasty."

The metrics on the pitch—87.4 mph with 18.9 inches of horizontal movement—made it objectively one of the best pitches Ohtani had thrown since coming to the Major Leagues. Only four of his 1,660 sweepers in the big leagues had as much velocity and horizontal break. "There's not a hitter alive that's going to hit that pitch," said Nevin.

Ohtani screamed, raised his arms, and hurled his glove and his cap into the air as his teammates bolted out of the dugout to celebrate. "This is the best moment of my life," said Ohtani, who was named the tournament MVP.

Ohtani flashed back to how he felt when he was a boy watching Ichiro lead Japan to titles in 2006 and 2009. "I've seen Japan winning and I just wanted to be part of it," Ohtani said. "I really appreciate that I was able to have a great experience. As I say, the next generation, the kids who are playing baseball, I was hoping that those people would like to play baseball. That would make me happy."

A few days after Ohtani experienced the exhilaration of a WBC championship, he was back in Tempe, Arizona, wearing an Angels uniform and pitching on a back field against minor leaguers. He was tuning up for the season with a team that had never provided Ohtani the opportunity to feel what he did in the WBC. Seeing Ohtani compete in the high-pressure atmosphere of the WBC only served to reinforce the notion that the baseball world would be better if Ohtani (and Trout) could get to the playoffs. It gave new life to questions about whether Ohtani would rather play somewhere else when his Angels contract was up at the end of the 2023 season. Ohtani responded to a question about his looming free agency by saying the WBC had stoked his fire to win . . . with the Angels.

"After experiencing those games, win or go home, I definitely felt like I want to experience that here too."

* * *

The Angels did not post a winning record in Ohtani's first four seasons, but 2022 looked like it might end the drought. In late May, the Angels were 27-17, which was a pace for 99 victories. Ohtani and Trout were both off to good starts. Rookie lefthander Reid Detmers threw a no-hitter. The Angels won series on the road against the Houston Astros and Boston Red Sox, both times with Ohtani delivering dominating pitching performances. Manager Joe Maddon was living such a charmed life that even when he made the inexplicable decision in April to issue an intentional walk with the bases loaded in the fourth inning of a game the Angels were losing, it worked out. The Angels came back from a 4-run deficit to win.

It was all a mirage, though. Third baseman Anthony Rendon and outfielder Taylor Ward both suffered injuries in May. The Angels bullpen, which had perhaps been overused to protect so many leads early in the season, imploded. The Angels lost fourteen games in a row. Twelve games into that streak Maddon was fired and replaced by the third base coach, Phil Nevin. The cushion provided by the hot start meant the Angels were still in striking distance of the playoffs when the streak ended. They played better for a couple weeks to maintain some hope. In late June, though, the Angels had a bench-clearing brawl in a game with the Seattle Mariners, resulting in a 10-game suspension for Nevin. Three active players and three coaches were also suspended. It came a couple weeks after Rendon was shut down for wrist surgery and a couple weeks before Trout suffered a back injury that cost him five weeks. It was the beginning of the end, sending the Angels tumbling toward a 73-89 finish, their seventh straight losing season.

Because the collapse happened in the weeks leading up to the August 2 trading deadline, discussion about the Angels trading Ohtani circulated throughout the baseball world. Ohtani was in the middle of a second straight historic season, and he still was under Angels control for another season beyond 2022, so the Angels could realistically get a significant haul of young talent if they traded him. That made all the sense in the world to everyone outside of the Angels offices.

But the Angels were never going to trade Ohtani. First, owner Arte Moreno wouldn't allow it. Moreno, who bought the team in 2003, was pondering a sale of the team, although that news wasn't common knowledge until the Angels announced it a few weeks after the trading deadline. Ohtani's presence made the Angels a more valuable asset. The next owner could decide if he or she wanted to trade Ohtani or try to sign him to an extension. There were also baseball reasons to hold on to Ohtani. Any trade would have netted the Angels a handful of minor leaguers, but they weren't likely to get MLB-ready players, especially not in the middle of the season. Even if the Angels might have improved the long-term outlook of the franchise, they would be doing so at the expense of the short-term. They would definitely be worse in 2023 without Ohtani. That meant sacrificing another year of Trout's prime, while also missing out on prime years for improving young players like Ward and pitchers Patrick Sandoval and Detmers. Despite the disaster of 2022, General Manager Perry Minasian and his staff still believed they had a strong enough core that they could make a run in 2023 with Ohtani on the roster. In November at the general managers' meetings—the first roster-building event of the offseason— Minasian went on the record and said decisively that the Angels were not going to trade Ohtani over the winter. "Ohtani is not getting moved," Minasian said. "He's going to be here. He'll be with us to start the season. I know there's been rumors and all types of things, but he will be here. He'll be part of the club. I said this before and I'll say it again: We love the player. I think our goal is for him to be here for a long time."

Keeping Ohtani for 2023 and keeping him "for a long time," of course, were two different things. At that time, Ohtani had one year left before reaching the six years of service time required for free agency. Between three and six years, the player has no control over his team, but he does have some leverage for his salary because of the arbitration process. A neutral panel of arbitrators settles disputes between the player and team over the salary, using players of similar service time and accomplishment for comparison. Ohtani had just completed his fifth season in 2022. For his final year under Angels control, the team agreed to pay him a record salary of $30 million. The previous record for an arbitration-eligible player was $27 million for outfielder Mookie Betts when he was signed by the Boston Red Sox. The Angels and Ohtani's agent, Nez Balelo, agreed to the figure a few days before the 2022 season ended, which set aside a piece of business that normally would have happened in January or February 2023. That deal was just the appetizer for what comes next.

The record for the largest single contract in baseball history is Trout's 12-year, $426.5 million contract, signed just before the 2019 season. Nothing since has even cracked $400 million. The first question for the Angels was whether they would be able to agree on a new contract with Ohtani before he reached free agency at the end of the 2023 season. There was a surprising turn in that drama in January 2023 when Moreno suddenly announced he was not going to sell the team after all. Moreno insisted in subsequent interviews that he had met with buyers willing to pay well above $2.5 billion, but he simply decided he wanted to remain in the baseball business because he loved it. He also loved having Ohtani. "I'd like to keep Ohtani," Moreno said. "He's one of a kind. He's a great person. He's obviously one of the most popular baseball players in the world, and he's an international star. He's a great teammate. He works hard. He's a funny guy, and he has a really good rapport with fans." Moreno also knew that he'd get back a portion of whatever he paid Ohtani in sponsorship dollars from Japanese companies, ticket sales to Japanese fans, and merchandise.

The Angels had been able to pay Ohtani far below his market value for his first six years, but as he approached free agency, that was going to end. Assessing his market value was difficult because there were no comparable players to use for determining a fair salary. On the mound, Ohtani had performed in 2021-22 like a No. 1 starter, the kind of player who typically gets $25 million to $35 million a year. Offensively, there are fewer comps because Ohtani is strictly a DH. JD Martinez, who was also primarily a DH, signed six years earlier for $22 million a year. Given those parameters, and adjusting for inflation, Ohtani would appear to be worth at least $50 million a year. That doesn't even include his value to a team off the field, in terms of selling tickets and sponsorships. At the start of 2023, the highest single-season salary for a player was the $43.3 million the New York Mets were paying pitcher Max Scherzer. It seems a lock that Ohtani will surpass that annual salary, but it remains to be seen how high he will go and for how many years. Ohtani celebrated his twenty-ninth birthday during the 2023 season. Projecting how long he could be a two-way player is impossible because no one else has done it. Babe Ruth only did it for two years, abandoning the mound when he was twenty-five.

Predictions of Ohtani's next contract made for popular fodder among writers before the 2023 season even began, continuing throughout the year. Stories routinely cited unnamed Major League executives predicting that Ohtani would sign for $500 million or even $600 million, shattering the record.

Wherever Ohtani's next contract lands, and whichever team pays him, it is going to be a historic deal, fitting for a once-in-a-lifetime player.

ACKNOWLEDGMENTS

Late in Spring Training 2018, Shohei Ohtani looked overmatched, seemingly not ready for the major leagues. A couple months later, when he was in the midst of one of the most incredible big league debuts anyone had seen, I began writing a book.

I was four chapters into the story in June that year when Ohtani's ulnar collateral ligament put his dream and my book on hold. Nearly three years later, Ohtani was again throwing 101-mph fastballs and hitting balls over the fence. The story came back to life.

Ohtani's performance in 2021 was nothing short of incredible, obviously worthy of a book. My goal was to go beyond a surface-level description of what he did in that amazing season, providing the context that explained it. From his successful start in 2018 to the low points in 2019 and 2020, to the crescendo in 2021, Ohtani's journey has been a rollercoaster.

I hope that you've enjoyed the ride, which I could not have navigated without plenty of help.

Every baseball writer leans heavily on the assistance of a team's media relations staff, and the Angels had their hands full with the throng of media that followed Ohtani for the first four years of his career. In 2021, the group included Adam Chodzko, Matt Birch, and Grace McNamee, who deserves special recognition as the Japanese-speaking liaison between Ohtani and the media from both sides of the Pacific.

For those of us in the American media, interpreter Ippei Mizuhara provided an invaluable service. Mizuhara has done his job well ever since Ohtani joined the Angels. Almost all of the quotes in this book attributed to Ohtani are via Mizuhara's translations.

The rest of the Angels have also been patient with four years' worth of seemingly endless questions about Ohtani, helping all of us better understand the extent of his talent. Jared Walsh was especially helpful because he had the perspective of a former two-way player. Walsh probably talked about Ohtani more than himself in interviews in 2021. Normally a former thirty-ninth-round pick becoming an All-Star would be a team's best story, but Walsh was a good sport as the media cast him in the role of Ohtani's sidekick. Among Angels' past and current players, Mike Trout, Alex Cobb, David Fletcher, Andrew Heaney, Martín Maldonado, Kurt Suzuki, and Max Stassi stood out with the insight they shared about Ohtani. Hitting coach Jeremy Reed and pitching coach Matt Wise were also generous with their time.

No one in an Angels uniform talked about Ohtani as much as the three managers he had in four years: Mike Scioscia, Brad Ausmus, and Joe Maddon. Maddon, who spoke to the media twice a day throughout the 2021 season, was the daily narrator for Ohtani's sensational campaign. As such, he was the perfect choice to write the foreword for this book, so I thank him for his contribution.

Former Angels general manager Billy Eppler and his successor, Perry Minasian, each provided essential information about what was going on behind the scenes with Ohtani.

I would also like to thank agent Nez Balelo of Creative Artists Agency for the time he spent discussing Ohtani.

My media colleagues from Japan have also been helpful throughout the past four years, most notably Yuichi Matsushita, Sam Onoda, Nobuhiro Saito, and Tomohiko Yasuoka. I want to thank Tomoya Shimura for helping me connect with a Japanese audience on social media.

As a first-time author, I am also grateful for the guidance provided by some of my friends who had previously written baseball books, including Tim Brown, Andrew Baggarly, John Shea, Josh Suchon, and Jason Turbow.

Jason helped to connect me with his agent, Jud Laghi. Without Jud, this project never would have happened. I had little experience in the publishing world, so Jud was instrumental in helping me find the right publisher.

The staff at Diversion Books, led by Executive Editor and Editor in Chief Keith Wallman, helped mold my manuscript into a book. Copyeditor Leigh Grossman of Swordsmith Productions polished my writing with the eye of an editor who is also a baseball fan.

I also owe thanks to some of the mentors who helped a kid achieve his dream of becoming a baseball writer. Jim Street, Justice Hill, Bill Plaschke, Lowell Cohn, and Kevin Bronson each taught me important lessons at various points in my journey, from my time at Ohio University to the present. Todd Harmonson, Tom Moore, and Todd Bailey—my editors at the Southern California News Group—made this book possible by entrusting me with the responsibility of covering the Angels since 2012.

While my career as a baseball writer sent me flying around the country chronicling the exploits of Barry Bonds or Mike Trout or Shohei Ohtani, my family had to get by without me. I am grateful to Lori for keeping things running smoothly in my absence, and for making sure that Lindsey and Justin grew up to be the amazing young adults they are.

Lindsey had already set the bar for me by publishing a book as an eleven-year-old. (*Captain Cookie* is still available. Google it.) Justin is a baseball fan who was with me on a trip to the Hall of Fame in Cooperstown when this project was revived. I hope when Justin reads this book, he learns something about his dad, as well as Ohtani.

As I was completing the writing, I was thankful for the support and encouragement of Anita, whose affinity for proper grammar led to our first connection.

Of course, the person most responsible for this book's existence is Shohei Ohtani himself. For years I had seen so many of my colleagues write books, but I had not found the right story for me. I was lucky enough to be in the right place to have a front-row seat as Ohtani fashioned a season like no other.

NOTES

CHAPTER 1

1 **"He was a child who would try anything":** "Father of baseball star Ohtani Coached Son with Life Tips in 'Very Ordinary' Upbringing," *The Mainchi*, December 11, 2017.

2 **"I was always anxiously waiting for the weekend so I could play.":** Arden Zwelling, "The Next Babe Ruth," Sportsnet.ca.

3 **"I assumed there must be many players better than me":** Arden Zwelling, "The Next Babe Ruth."

3 **"You can't run. You can't throw.":** Dylan Hernandez, "Japanese Baseball Star Shohei Ohtani Could Be Double Threat in Big Leagues," *Los Angeles Times*, September 29, 2017.

5 **"Shohei never complained."** Dylan Hernandez, "Japanese Baseball Star Shohei Ohtani Could Be Double Threat in Big Leagues."

6 **"I don't want to lose to those players.":** Ken Belson, "Hoping to Skip Japan League for U.S." *The New York Times*, October 24, 2012.

6 **"I knew for certain he'd be our number one draft pick":** Tomoya Shimura, "Shohei Ohtani: Who Is the Angels New Guy?" *Orange County Register*, February 9, 2008.

7 **"I felt like I was negotiating with an adult":** Tomoya Shimura, "Shohei Ohtani: Who Is the Angels New Guy?"

8 **"Ohtani is the player who changed my way of thinking.":** Scott Miller, "Shohei Ohtani: The 'Best Baseball Player in the World' Isn't in MLB . . . Yet," Bleacher Report, March 6, 2017.

CHAPTER 2

11 **"you have to get along with fans as well as sponsors as a professional player"**: Jason Coskrey, "Otani Ready for New Challenges with Fighters," *Japan Times*, January 30, 2013.

12 **"I'd be the laughingstock of baseball"**: Robert Creamer, *Babe: The Legend Comes to Life* (1974).

13 **"joked right then that he would give Frazee $150,000 for Ruth"**: "Frazee States Col. Ruppert Offered $150,000 For Ruth," *Boston Herald and Journal*, May 29, 1918.

14 **"there is nothing I like better than to get in there and take a hard swing"**: Leigh Montville, *The Big Bam: The Life and Times of Babe Ruth* (2006).

14 **"for I am young and strong and don't mind the work"**: F. C. Lane, "The Season's Sensation," *Baseball Magazine*, October 1918.

17 **"I've learned a lot about the kinds of food I eat"**: Arden Zwelling, "The Next Babe Ruth," Sportsnet.ca.

18 **"By the end of the game there were about three left."**: Jim Allen, "Otani Turns Heads with Bat During Fighters' Trip to U.S.," *Japan Times*, February 15, 2016.

20 **"the best baseball player in the world"**: Scott Miller, "Shohei Ohtani: The 'Best Baseball Player in the World' Isn't in MLB . . . Yet," Bleacher Report, March 6, 2017.

21 **"When the time comes, I'll know I'm ready."**: Arden Zwelling, "Fans Will Lose if Injury Keeps 'Japanese Babe Ruth' off WBC Mound," Sportsnet.ca.

21 **"I'll put my soul into it."**: "Otani Eyes MLB Move After Next Season," *Japan Times*, December 5, 2016.

21 **"Originally I thought I was going to get better"**: Daniel Kramer, "Injury Forces Japan's Ohtani Out of World Baseball Classic," MLB.com, February 3, 2017.

22 **"I don't really think I've been especially good"**: Jason Coskrey, "Otani Heating Up in a Hurry," *Japan Times*, August 26, 2017.

23   **"I just want to do my best through the end of the season":**
Dylan Hernandez, "Japanese Baseball Star Shohei Ohtani
Could Be Double Threat in Big Leagues," *Los Angeles Times*,
September 29, 2017.

CHAPTER 3

25   **"I'm going to be the first guy under the new system and
new rules to go over there":** Arden Zwelling, "The Next Babe
Ruth," Sportsnet.ca.

25   **"The key is if he lives up to the hype.":** Phil Rogers, "Mass
Appeal: Off-field Opportunities Await Ohtani," MLB.com,
December 4, 2017.

36   **"It's a lot easier to do what he's doing as a DH":** Andy Bag-
garly, "As Giants Arrive in Anaheim, Madison Bumgarner
Reconsiders Shohei Ohtani: 'I Didn't Think It Would Work,'"
The Athletic, April 20, 2018.

36   **"It really just seemed like it was predetermined that he
wanted to DH.":** Andy McCullough, "Inside the Dodgers'
Failed, Frustrating Bid for Two-way Sensation Shohei Ohtani,"
Los Angeles Times, March 7, 2018.

36   **"We appreciated that it was an uphill battle, but it was well
worth the effort.":** Andy McCullough, "Inside the Dodgers'
Failed, Frustrating Bid for Two-way Sensation Shohei Ohtani,"
Los Angeles Times, March 7, 2018.

41   **"Eppler made this happen.":** Ken Rosenthal, @Ken_Rosen-
thal, Twitter. December 8, 2017. "Agent (not from CAA) on
Ohtani signing: 'Eppler made this happen. 100% all him. He
has been on Ohtani since he was in HS and I will bet he absolutely crushed the presentation. This is a credit to him.' Eppler
visited Japan while with NYY and after becoming LAA GM in
Oct. 2015."

CHAPTER 6

68 **"We watched this go on for about thirty minutes":** Mike Digiovanna, "Dodgers Snapshot: Nomomania Grips L.A. and Japan When Hideo Nomo Dominates in 1995." *Los Angeles Times*, March 28, 2020.

72 **"Our following has just grown.":** Dave Sheinin, "'Every Day Is the Craziest': Japanese Press Tailing Shohei Ohtani Is Already Worn Out," *The Washington Post*, April 12, 2018.

75 **"I didn't think it would work":** Andy Baggarly, "As Giants Arrive in Anaheim, Madison Bumgarner Reconsiders Shohei Ohtani: 'I Didn't Think It Would Work,'" *The Athletic*, April 20, 2018.

CHAPTER 8

99 **"I know he's here today":** J. P. Hoornstra, "Angels No-hit Mariners on a Night of Remembrance for Tyler Skaggs," *Orange County Register*, July 13, 2019.

104 **"When our movement was restricted, I was still able to practice":** Yuichi Matsushita, "Baseball: Angels' Shohei Ohtani Opens Up on Most Difficult Season," *Kyodo News*, November 20, 2020.

108 **"I was frustrated I couldn't get it done, and that was the hardest":** Yuichi Matsushita, "Baseball: Angels' Shohei Ohtani Opens Up on Most Difficult Season," *Kyodo News*, November 20, 2020.

109 **"I'd pretty much never experienced the feeling of wanting to do something but being completely unable to do it.":** Yuichi Matsushita, "Baseball: Angels' Shohei Ohtani Opens Up on Most Difficult Season," November 20, 2020.

CHAPTER 9

114 **"his life choices had led to a disappointing performance":**
Joe Winkworth, "I Have Been the Babe and a Boob," *Collier's*,
October 31, 1925.

115 **"He gets his hands on shots he had no business making.":**
Leigh Montville, *The Big Bam*.

CHAPTER 10

137 **"I'm glad the blister peeled off today before the games actually matter.":** J.P. Hoornstra, "Angels' Shohei Ohtani Develops Blister, Loses to Dodgers in Final Spring Training Start," *Orange County Register*, March 29, 2021.

CHAPTER 12

161 **"a boost in visitation to games because of Shohei Ohtani":**
Bill Shaikin, "Angels' Shohei Ohtani brings in dollars as he bangs out hits," *Los Angeles Times*, July 26, 2019.

161 **"Ohtani was a source of pride for everyone from Japan":**
Gabriel San Roman, "For Japanese Americans in Orange County, Shohei Ohtani Is Already Their MVP," *Los Angeles Times*, September 30, 2021.

161 **"to support him":** Gabriel San Roman, "For Japanese Americans in Orange County, Shohei Ohtani is already their MVP," *Los Angeles Times*, September 30, 2021.

163 **"Did he really grow up here?":** Matt Monaghan, "Ohtani's hometown pulls out all the stops," MLB.com, August 16, 2021.

166 **"It just kept getting closer and closer":** Sam Blum, "'It Just Kept Getting Closer and Closer': Shohei Ohtani Hits Memorable, if Not Meaningful, Home Run," *The Athletic*, July 10, 2021.

CHAPTER 14

174   **"on his momentum":** Jabari Young, "MLB has big plans for Shohei Ohtani, a 'once in a century' player," CNBC.com, July 13, 2021.

177   **"declined a lot of offers":** Justin Birnbaum, "How MLB Superstar Shohei Ohtani Made $6 Million In Endorsements Without Even Trying," Forbes, July 8, 2021.

177   **"productive on the baseball field":** Justin Birnbaum, "How MLB Superstar Shohei Ohtani Made $6 Million In Endorsements Without Even Trying," Forbes, July 8, 2021.

CHAPTER 15

203   **"People don't realize how hard that is to do.":** Dave Eminian, "The St. Louis Cardinals have a 19-year-old two-way prospect. He's playing in Peoria," *Peoria Journal Star*, August 2, 2021.

204   **"We will explore the multi-positional thing until the game tells us otherwise.":** Jason Mackey, "'Special talent' Bubba Chandler may be start of something for Pirates," *Pittsburgh Post-Gazette*, September 7, 2021.

204   **"because there's just no precedent for doing both":** Ken Rosenthal, "Rosenthal: Shohei Ohtani keeps pushing MLB's boundaries. Whatever his future holds, let's enjoy his remarkable present," *The Athletic*, July 8, 2021.

CHAPTER 16

214   **"We never get to see him play":** Jim Allen, "Baseball: Shohei Ohtani makes most of his Japan WBC debut," *Kyodo News*, March 10, 2023.

220   **"I'd like to keep Ohtani":** Jon Heyman, "Angels owner Arte Moreno hopes to keep Shohei Ohtani with 'impossible' task looming," *New York Post*, February 8, 2023.

SOURCES

ARTICLES

Allen, Jim. "Amateur Tazawa Bypassing Japan Leagues for MLB," ESPN.com, September 12, 2008.

Arthur, Robert. "Shohei Ohtani is paying for his own contract," *Baseball Prospectus*, July 21, 2021.

Anderson, R.J. "MLB Prospect Watch: Six who could follow in Shohei Ohtani's footsteps as baseball's next two-way player," CBSSports .com, May 28, 2021.

Baxter, Kevin. "Best comparisons to Shohei Ohtani's two-way exploits came in the Negro Leagues," *Los Angeles Times*, July 12, 2021.

Blum, Ronald. "Ohtani agent asks MLB teams for written answers," Associated Press, November 25, 2017.

Boston Herald and Journal. "Frazee States Col. Ruppert Offered $150,000 For Ruth," May 29, 1918.

Callis, Jim. "The top two-way players in Draft history," MLB.com, May 20, 2020.

Caple, Jim. "Long before Shohei Ohtani and Ichiro, pitcher Masanori Murakami blazed a trail for Japanese major leaguers," *The Athletic*, May 9, 2018.

Castrovince, Anthony. "Negro Leagues had their own two-way stars," MLB.com, April 26, 2021.

Coskrey, Jason. "Bar set high for rookie stars Sugano, Otani," *Japan Times*, April 2, 2013.

Coskrey, Jason. "Fighters rookie Otani makes solid impression in mound debut," *Japan Times*, May 24, 2013.

Hammond, Rich. "Shohei Ohtani's batting-practice blast at Angel Stadium measured 513 feet," *Orange County Register*, May 19, 2018.

Haring, Bruce. "Major League Baseball All-Star Game Ratings Up Slightly, But Home Run Derby A Big Hit," Deadline, July 14, 2021.

Hoornstra, J.P. "Shohei Ohtani's elbow injury will force Angels to scramble at two positions," *Orange County Register*, June 8, 2018.

Jennings, L.A. "Boxing The Great Bambino." Vice, July 14, 2016.

Kaufman, Joey. "Angels pitchers Garrett Richards, Andrew Heaney hoping stem-cell treatment helps them avoid Tommy John surgery," *Orange County Register*, June 26, 2016.

Keown, Tim. "The one baseball's been waiting for," *ESPN The Magazine*, April 6, 2018.

Kepner, Tyler and David Waldstein. "Shohei Ohtani Spurns the Yankees, Seeking a Smaller Market," *New York Times*, December 3, 2017.

Kuty, Brendan. "Masahiro Tanaka injury: Yankees doctor explains crucial step in elbow rehab." NJ.com, July 13, 2014.

Kyodo News Service. "Fighters rookie Otani throws first bullpen," *Japan Times*, February 4, 2013.

Kleinschmidt, Jessica. "Shohei Ohtani wrote out his life goals in high school, and they'll leave you feeling underachieved," MLB.com, December 6, 2017.

Kurosawa, Jun. "L.A. Angels' Shohei Ohtani Holds American Baseball Fans in Awe," *Japan Forward*, April 21, 2018.

Lindbergh, Ben. "Ten Stats That Sum Up Shohei Ohtani's Historic 2021 Season," The Ringer, October 5, 2021.

Mains, Rob. "The Greatest Two-Way Players of All Time," Baseball Prospectus, July 20, 2021.

Monaghan, Matt. "100 years ago, Babe Ruth became Babe Ruth with a 500-foot homer into an Alligator Farm," MLB.com, March 16, 2018.

Mooney, Patrick. "Virtual reality: Kyle Hendricks takes you inside the Cubs' meeting with Shohei Ohtani," *The Athletic*, January 17, 2018.

O'Connell, Robert. "A game of speech—But also for baseball interpreters, so much more," SI.com, June 21, 2021.

Ortiz, Jorge. "The quest for a 100-mph fastball: Can MLB prospects safely develop velocity?" *USA Today*, June 7, 2016.

Passan, Jeff. "Recent physical shows Angels' Shohei Ohtani has a damaged elbow ligament," Yahoo!, December 12, 2017.

Passan, Jeff. "The verdict is in on Shohei Ohtani's bat and it's not good," Yahoo!, March 9, 2018.

Teaford, Elliott. "Angels rookie Shohei Ohtani nearly perfect in Big A mound debut," *Orange County Register*, April 8, 2018.

Witz, Billy. "The Shohei Ohtani Rules: Handling a Two-Way Experiment With Care," *New York Times*, April 27, 2018.

BOOKS

Whiting, Robert. *You Gotta Have Wa!* 1989, 2009.

Wood, Allan. *Babe Ruth and the 1918 Red Sox.* 2001.

VIDEO

Morosi, Jon. Interview with Shohei Ohtani, MLB Network, February 2017.

WEBSITES

Baseball-reference, FanGraphs, SeamHeads, Wikipedia.

INDEX

ABOUT THE AUTHOR

Jeff Fletcher is an award-winning sports reporter who has been writing about Major League Baseball since 1997, including thousands of regular season games and dozens of World Series games and All-Star Games. He has worked in the press boxes of more than forty Major League ballparks.

Fletcher has covered the Los Angeles Angels for the Southern California News Group since 2012, reporting on the careers of Mike Trout and Shohei Ohtani more than any other American reporter. He previously covered the Oakland A's and San Francisco Giants, chronicling the *Moneyball* era for the A's and the greatest years of Barry Bonds's career with the Giants. He covered Bonds's 500th, 600th, and 700th homers, as well as his record-breaking 756th homer.

Fletcher also worked as a national baseball writer for FanHouse, allowing him to travel the country in search of the most interesting stories from around the big leagues.

He has served for several years as the chairman of the Los Angeles chapter of the Baseball Writers' Association of America and secretary-treasurer of the San Francisco–Oakland chapter. Fletcher has been a Hall of Fame voter since 2006.

Fletcher grew up in Ohio and attended Ohio University's prestigious Scripps School of Journalism. Since graduation, he has been a regular mentor to journalism students. Fletcher had internships at the *Knoxville News Sentinel, Baltimore Sun*, and *Los Angeles Times*.

In his free time, Fletcher enjoys spending time with his two college-aged children, traveling, and playing poker. He regularly competes at the World Series of Poker. He tends to take multiyear breaks in his golf game but hopes to return to the course again.